Rod Farley

THE
WORKING
COOK

THE COOKBOOK OF THE

 AMERICAN VOCATIONAL ASSOCIATION

Acknowledgements

The American Vocational Association wishes to thank everyone who has worked so diligently to make this cookbook a success. Without two special people, this project would never have become a reality. Paul Lentz, Chair of the AVA Building Fund Committee, came into his position with the idea, and laid the groundwork for its inception. Charles Buzzell, AVA's Executive Director, provided the insightful leadership that paved the way for the national release and marketing of a book that's destined to become a household favorite.

The Cookbook Committee extends its appreciation to the American Vocational Association Board of Directors for their vision and their encouragement in the adoption of this project.

Don Bright, President, 1989–1990
Kermeta (Kay) Clayton, President Elect
Niel Edmunds, Past President
Charles H. Buzzell, Executive Director
Paul O. Lentz, Building Fund Chairman

COOKBOOK COMMITTEE
Roberta Looper, Chairman
Jane King, AVA Board of Directors Liaison
Rosemary Kolde, Director of Convention Sales
Kristin Robinson, Director of Marketing
Region I – **Charleyne Gilbert**
Region II – **Suanne Knopf**
Region III – **Nancy Clem**
Region IV –**Marilyn Butler**
Region V – **Jane Stein**

Special thanks to the following groups

★ the AVA members, friends, and family who have enriched us all by sharing their favorite recipes through this cookbook.
★ the Commercial Arts students and teachers whose hard work and creativity have brightened the pages of our book.
★ all AVA staff members who have donated their time to help develop the book.

This book is a collection of our favorite recipes which are not necessarily original recipes.

Published by Favorite Recipes Press
P.O. Box 305142, Nashville, TN 37230

First Printing: 1989, 15,000
Manufactured in the United States of America
Copyright© The American Vocational Association
1410 King St., Alexandria, Virginia 22314
Library of Congress Number: 89-11688
ISBN: 0-87197-252-2

America Works Thanks To Vocational Education

For the users of **The Working Cook** who are unfamiliar with vocational education, here is some food for thought:

Vocational education encompasses a tremendous variety of school programs designed to equip students with work and life skills. It prepares students for more than 400 occupations that require specialized training below the baccalaureate level. Almost 14 million students (both youth and adults) were enrolled in vocational programs in more than 26,000 institutions across the country last year.

Vocational education has been shown to prevent many young people from "dropping out" of school because it takes learning out of the abstract and, with practical "hands-on" techniques, shows students the relationship between learning and their "real life" needs.

The majority of high school vocational graduates enter some form of post-secondary program, and half of those high school graduates go to four-year colleges and universities.

Vocational training increases students' chances for job placement, and employers find that new employees who have had relevant vocational education are more productive and require less on-the-job training than those who have not had vocational education.

Vocational education not only capitalizes on the students' natural talents and interests in academic areas such as math, language, sciences and the arts but also helps students to apply that knowledge and those skills to occupational areas such as agriculture, business, home economics, health and industrial trades and technologies—in preparation for rewarding, high-paying jobs and careers.

All across America, people are working in careers they love, enriching themselves and others, thanks to vocational education.

Introduction

Sharing good food is one of the true pleasures of life. Families have many of their happiest moments lingering around the dinner table, conversing over a midnight snack and catching up around a groaning buffet table at a family reunion.

As members of the American Vocational Association, we are all an extended family. Over the years, because of our affiliation with AVA, we have come to know vocational educators from all parts of the country. Through the annual convention and through state and local meetings, workshops and seminars, we share information about our programs, educational trends, innovative techniques and strategies that work. Much of this exchange goes on through formal meetings, but quite a bit takes place in informal settings, usually while sharing a meal, a quick snack or hors d'oeuvres at a reception.

That is why the idea for an American Vocational Association cookbook was so logical. **The Working Cook** has been more than a year in the making. We have requested favorite recipes from members in every state. Response has been overwhelming—and delicious.

Vocational educators are creative people as is demonstrated over and over by the diversity of our programs and originality of our approaches to problem-solving. It is, therefore, not surprising that so many of our members express their creativity in the kitchen as well as in the classroom. **The Working Cook** makes this point decisively. Some of our members might be considered professionals when it comes to recipe creation because they teach in food service programs. However, it is obvious that the good cooks in vocational education go far beyond this special group, as you will see when you delve into this volume.

We have pulled together recipes with regional flavor to reflect AVA's five regions. We encourage you to try these menus and experience the delights of all the sectional differences that make our country and our programs so unique. By doing so you will reap the benefits of another dimension of our common knowledge and skills.

You will find from notes provided by the contributors that many of the recipes in this book have already been shared at AVA meetings or gatherings. The tradition is there. This book simply brings rewards that many members have already been reaping to all the AVA family.

I am especially pleased to write the introduction for **The Working Cook** because cooking has been my lifetime hobby. When I began my term on the AVA Board of Directors in 1983, I made it a practice to bring one or more treats from my kitchen to each meeting. Over time the chocolate-mint fudge I frequently brought became the favorite. It has also been popular at other vocational education meetings with my business education colleagues or with members of the Ohio Vocational Association in my home state. Now I'm pleased to share it with all vocational educators.

DON BRIGHT'S MINT FUDGE

5 cups sugar
1   12-ounce can evaporated
*   milk*
8 ounces margarine
1/4 teaspoon salt

1/4 teaspoon mint extract
1   18-ounce package
*   chocolate chips*
1   10-ounce package
*   miniature marshmallows*

Heat sugar, milk and margarine in saucepan until mixture comes to a boil. Boil for 7 minutes. Add salt and mint flavoring. Boil for 1 minute longer. Combine chocolate chips and miniature marshmallows in large bowl. Pour cooked mixture over chips and marshmallows; stir until smooth and creamy. Pour into large greased container. Cool overnight. Cut and serve. May add nuts with chips and marshmallows if desired. Yield: 5 pounds.

Enjoy this recipe and all the others in **The Working Cook**. All profits from the sale of this book will be donated to the AVA Headquarters Building Fund. This building will help us strengthen the image of vocational education in the nation's capital. Thank you for your support—and enjoy.

Don Bright

AVA President

The Building Fund

AMERICAN VOCATIONAL
ASSOCIATION

The American Vocational Association's Building Fund was established in 1984 to finance the construction of a home for The American Vocational Association. The headquarters building is now fully operational in Alexandria, Virginia, just minutes away from the nation's capital. It serves as a working and meeting place for vocational educators, and makes a statement to policymakers that voc ed is strong, and a permanent part of our nation's educational system.

Through the fundraising efforts of individual members, state associations, and divisional groups, we hope to raise $2.7 million to meet the mortgage of our building. The more we can reduce our indebtedness on the loan, the more resources we can devote to programs and services that meet the needs of vocational education.

The building is both a commitment and a legacy to the future of our profession, and one in which all vocational educators have an investment. Your support of the AVA Building Fund will make the difference to generations of vocational educators and students to come.

Contents

Illustrations 10

Appetizers and Beverages 11
    Region 1 Menu — Northeastern Fall Tailgate Party . . . 12

Soups and Salads 37
    Region 2 Menu — Southeastern Seafood Feast 38

Main Dishes 55
    Region 3 Menu — Hearty Midwestern Supper 56
    Meats 57
    Poultry 79
    Seafood 92

Vegetables and Side Dishes 105
    Region 4 Menu — Deep South Chicken and Fish Fry . . 106

Breakfasts and Brunches 123
    Region 5 Menu — Big West Breakfast 124

Breads 141
    Wine and Cheese Reception for Twenty-Five 142

Desserts 159
    All-American Dessert Buffet 160
    Cakes 174
    Candies 183
    Cookies 187
    Pies 192

Nutritional Guidelines 198

Charts 199
    Substitution Chart 199
    Equivalent Chart 200
    Quantities to Serve 100 202

Index 203

Order Information 208

★ Asterisk by contributor's name on recipes indicates the office held.

Illustrations

Carey Hardin—Area Vo-Tech High School; Mary Chambers, Teacher;
Jonesboro, Arkansas . . . . Cover

Eric Cratty—Lawrence County AVTS; Gerald Zona, Teacher;
New Castle, Pennsylvania 1

Rod Farley—Putnam County Vo-Tech; Lynne McNiel, Teacher;
Eleanor,West Virginia 2

Lisa Marie Timblin—Lawrence County AVTS; Gerald Zona, Teacher;
Ellwood, Pennsylvania 11

Jenny Rasey—Lawrence County AVTS; Gerald Zona, Teacher;
New Bedford, Pennsylvania 37

M. Carolyn Edwards—Bessemer State Tech College; Tom Immler, Teacher;
Birmingham, Alabama 37

Rod Farley—Putnam County Vo-Tech; Lynne McNiel, Teacher;
Eleanor, West Virginia 55

Shannon Allison—Lawrence County AVTS; Gerald Zona, Teacher;
New Castle, Pennsylvania 55

Jeff Goughler—Lawrence County AVTS; Gerald Zona, Teacher;
Pittsburgh, Pennsylvania 64

Jeff Goughler—Lawrence County AVTS; Gerald Zona, Teacher;
Pittsburgh, Pennsylvania 69

Marjorie A. Adcock—Palomar College; Neil Bruington, Teacher;
Carlsbad, California 92

Daniel R. Johnson—Olympus High School; Dick Powell, Teacher;
Salt Lake City, Utah 105

Noah Tietze—Warwick Area Vo-Tech Center; Mr. Corrigan, Teacher;
Warwick, Rhode Island 105

Amanda Godfrey—Area Vo-Tech High School; Mary Chambers, Teacher;
Jonesboro, Arkansas 117

Ava Buck—Putnam County Vo-Tech; Lynne McNiel, Teacher;
Leon, West Virginia 123

Adrienne A. Fulkerson—Lawrence County AVTS; Gerald Zona, Teacher;
New Castle, Pennsylvania 131

Jody Tomski—Lawrence County AVTS; Gerald Zona, Teacher;
New Castle, Pennslyvania 141

Daniel R. Johnson—Olympus High School; Dick Powell, Teacher;
Salt Lake City, Utah 141

Lisa Marie Timblin—Lawrence County AVTS; Gerald Zona, Teacher;
Ellwood, Pennsylvania 159

Todd Arrington—Putnam County Vo-Tech; Lynne McNiel, Teacher;
Eleanor, West Virginia 159

Artist: *Lisa Marie Timblin*—Lawrence County AVTS; Gerald Zona, Teacher;
Ellwood, Pennsylvania

APPETIZERS
&
BEVERAGES

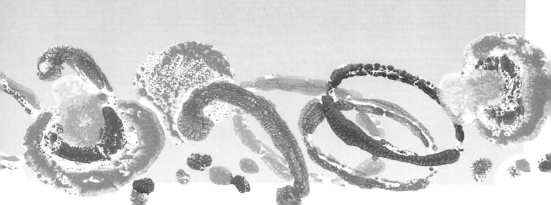

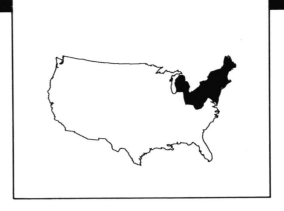

Northeastern
Fall Tailgate Party
Region I

Beef Steak Tartar
page 14

Lisa's Favorite Fruit Soup
page 39

Broccoli and Cauliflower Salad
page 51

Chicken Breasts Piquant
page 84

Zucchini Bread
page 149

Marinated Peaches
page 171

Coconut Macaroons
page 189

Holiday Punch
page 35

BACON WATER CHESTNUTS

Yields: 60 servings   *Pan Size: broiler pan*   *Preheat: 350 degrees*

1 12-ounce bottle of chili sauce
1 pound dark brown sugar
1 pound sliced bacon

2 8-ounce cans whole water
   chestnuts, drained

Combine chili sauce and brown sugar in saucepan. Cook over low heat for 1 hour. Set aside. Cut bacon strips into thirds. Wrap bacon piece around each water chestnut; secure with toothpick. Place on rack in broiler pan. Bake for 45 minutes or until bacon is crisp. Drain well. Place in hot sauce; turn and stir to coat well. Remove from sauce; arrange on serving tray. May prepare ahead and reheat before serving.

Approx Per Serving: Cal 86; Prot 2.6 g; T Fat 3.7 g; Chol 6.4 mg;
    Carbo 10.5 g; Sod 201.0 mg; Potas 128.0 mg.
    Nutritional information includes entire amount of sauce.

Carol W. Stevenson, President
Virginia Home Economics Teachers Assn.
Ashland, Virginia

BARBECUED WATER CHESTNUTS

Yields: 40 servings   *Pan Size: 9x13 inch*   *Preheat: 325 degrees*

1 pound sliced lean bacon
2 8-ounce cans whole water
   chestnuts, drained

²/₃ cup catsup
1 cup sugar

Cut bacon strips into halves. Wrap bacon piece around each water chestnut; secure with round toothpick half. Place in baking pan. Bake for 1 hour. Remove to clean foil-lined pan. Mix catsup and sugar in bowl. Pour over water chestnuts. Bake for 45 minutes to 1 hour. Serve hot.

Approx Per Serving: Cal 101; Prot 3.7 g; T Fat 5.6 g; Chol 9.6 mg;
    Carbo 8.9 g; Sod 230.0 mg; Potas 138.0 mg.

Don Bright, AVA President 1989-1990
AVA Building Fund Committee
Bowling Green, Ohio

BEEF STEAK TARTAR

Yields: 4 servings

8 ounces top round	Chopped onion
1 egg yolk	Chopped chives
Black caviar	Chopped dill pickles
Chopped anchovies	Salt and pepper to taste
Capers	4 slices rye or black bread

Grind beef finely. Shape into mound on serving plate or bread board. Make well in center. Place egg yolk in well. Arrange small mounds of caviar, anchovies, capers, onion, chives and pickles around beef. Mix desired amounts of beef, egg yolk, caviar, anchovies, capers, onion, chives, pickles and salt and pepper. Spread on bread as for open-faced sandwiches.

Nutritional information not available.

Ralph Gilgenast
Talleyville, Delaware

BEER BALLS

Yields: 24 meatballs   *Pan Size: large saucepan*

1 pound ground beef	2 tablespoons Worcestershire
1/2 cup catsup	sauce
1/2 cup beer	2 tablespoons wine-garlic
2 tablespoons sugar	vinegar

Shape ground beef into small meatballs; sprinkle with salt and pepper to taste. Brown on all sides in skillet; drain. Combine catsup, beer, sugar, Worcestershire sauce and vinegar in large saucepan. Cook for 30 minutes or until thick. Add meatballs to sauce. Simmer for 15 minutes or longer. Serve warm from chafing dish.

Approx Per Meatball: Cal 68; Prot 4.6 g; T Fat 4.0 g; Chol 16.9 mg;
    Carbo 3.0 g; Sod 87.4 mg; Potas 88.3 mg.

Pat Stanley
FSCS Dept., Cal State
Los Angeles, California

CHEDDAR CRACKERS

Yields: 48 crackers   *Pan Size: baking sheet*   *Preheat: 375 degrees*

1/2 cup margarine
8 ounces Cheddar cheese
1/2 envelope dry onion soup
   mix

1/2 teaspoon salt
1 teaspoon red pepper
1 teaspoon oregano
1 cup flour

Let margarine and cheese stand at room temperature in bowl until softened. Mix well. Add soup mix, seasonings and flour; mix well. Shape into two or three 1-inch diameter rolls; wrap in foil. Chill until firm or store in freezer. Slice into 1/4-inch slices; arrange on baking sheet. Bake for 12 minutes or until light brown.

Approx Per Serving: Cal 46; Prot 1.5 g; T Fat 3.5 g; Chol 5.0 mg;
   Carbo 2.1 g; Sod 83.6 mg; Potas 9.8 mg.

Nadine F. Marcum
Little Rock, Arkansas

PARMESAN CHEESE CUBES

Yields: 48 servings   *Pan Size: baking sheet*   *Preheat: 350 degrees*

1 1-pound loaf white
   sandwich bread
2 eggs, beaten

1/2 cup milk
1 cup melted butter

Cut crusts from bread. Beat eggs with milk. Dip 1 slice bread into egg mixture; place between 2 slices bread as for sandwich. Cut into 9 cubes. Dip each cube into melted butter; sprinkle generously on all sides with cheese. Place on baking sheet. Repeat with remaining bread. Chill in refrigerator overnight. Bake for 12 to 15 minutes or until golden brown.

Approx Per Serving: Cal 65; Prot 1.2 g; T Fat 4.5 g; Chol 22.1 mg;
   Carbo 4.9 g; Sod 84.9 mg; Potas 17.9 mg.

Carol Whitney Darling
Millersport, Ohio

SUPER CHEESE TWISTS

Yields: 48 servings   *Pan Size: baking sheet*   *Preheat: 375 degrees*

1 cup grated Swiss cheese
3 tablespoons shredded
  Cheddar cheese
3 tablespoons shredded
  Parmesan cheese
2 cups flour
1/2 teaspoon salt

14 tablespoons butter
1 egg, well beaten
2 1/2 tablespoons milk
1 egg, well beaten
1 tablespoon poppy seed
1 teaspoon salt

Combine cheeses in small bowl; mix until mixture resembles cornmeal. Sift flour and 1/2 teaspoon salt into medium bowl. Add half the cheese mixture and butter; mix until crumbly. Add 1 egg and milk; mix well. Chill for 1 hour. Roll 1/4 inch thick on lightly floured surface. Cut into 1/2x3-inch strips. Twist 2 strips together; place on baking sheet. Brush with beaten egg. Sprinkle with mixture of remaining cheese mixture, poppy seed and 1 teaspoon salt. Bake for 15 minutes or until golden brown. Cool on wire rack. Twists may be frozen before or after baking.

Approx Per Serving: Cal 66; Prot 1.8 g; T Fat 4.6 g; Chol 23.4 mg;
    Carbo 4.2 g; Sod 113.0 mg; Potas 14.5 mg.

Dana Q. Markam
Roanoke, Virginia

SURPRISE CHEESE PUFFS

Yields: 24 servings   *Pan Size: baking sheet*   *Preheat: 425 degrees*

1 cup shredded Cheddar
  cheese
1/4 cup margarine, softened
1/2 cup flour

1/2 teaspoon paprika
1/4 teaspoon salt
24 small pimento-stuffed
  olives

Combine cheese and margarine in bowl; mix with fork until well blended. Add flour, paprika and salt; mix well. Pat olives dry with paper towels. Shape 1 teaspoon cheese mixture around each olive, covering completely; arrange on baking sheet. Freeze until firm. Store in freezer containers or plastic bags. Place frozen olive balls on baking sheet. Bake for 15 to 20 minutes or until light brown. If olive balls are not frozen before baking reduce baking time to 8 to 10 minutes.

Approx Per Serving: Cal 50; Prot 1.5 g; T Fat 4.1 g; Chol 5.0 mg;
    Carbo 2.1 g; Sod 170.0 mg; Potas 11.2 mg.

Martha Crisp
Owensboro, Kentucky

MICROWAVE STUFFED CLAMS

Yields: 10 servings   *Pan Size: clam shells*   ≈*M*≈

1/3 cup finely minced onion
2²/3 tablespoons butter
1 8-ounce can clams
Fine crumbs of 5 or 6 slices
  white bread

Finely chopped parsley to
  taste
Finely chopped green bell
  pepper to taste

Microwave onion and butter in large covered bowl on High for 1¹/2 to 2 minutes or until transparent. Drain clams reserving juice. Mince clams. Add clams, crumbs and enough clam juice to moisten onion mixture. Mix in parsley and green pepper. Spoon into clam shells or custard cups. Arrange in circle in microwave. Microwave on High for 2 minutes. Rearrange clam shells. Microwave for 2 minutes longer. May broil for 2 minutes or until brown on top. May prepare and freeze for future use or refrigerate for 1 to 2 days before microwaving.

Approx Per Serving: Cal 95; Prot 6.9 g; T Fat 4.0 g; Chol 23.4 mg;
    Carbo 7.6 g; Sod 113.0 mg; Potas 165.0 mg.

Barbara Hansen
Pomona, California

CLAMS CASINO

Yields: 12 servings   *Pan Size: clam shells*   *Preheat: Broiler*

12 cherrystone clams
Juice of 1 lemon
1 small onion, chopped
1 clove of garlic, chopped
1/4 cup chopped green bell
  pepper

1/4 cup chopped celery
2 tablespoons oil
1/2 cup chopped ham
1/4 cup toasted bread crumbs
3 slices bacon

Parboil or steam clams or leave uncooked. Prepare clams on a half shell in baking pan. Sprinkle with lemon juice. Sauté onion, garlic, bell pepper and celery in oil in skillet. Add salt and pepper to taste. Stir in ham. Heat for several minutes. Add bread crumbs; mix well. Spoon crumb mixture over clams. Cut bacon strips into fourths; place one piece on each clam. Broil until bacon is crisp. Garnish with lemon wedges.

Approx Per Serving: Cal 70; Prot 3.6 g; T Fat 5.1 g; Chol 9.2 mg;
    Carbo 2.9 g; Sod 177.0 mg; Potas 93.1 mg.

Dolores Palladino
Sarasota, Florida

HAM APPETIZERS

Yields: 24 servings   *Pan Size: foil pan*   *Preheat: 400 degrees*

1/2 cup butter, softened
1 tablespoon poppy seed
1 teaspoon prepared mustard
1 teaspoon Worcestershire
   sauce

1 small onion, finely chopped
1 24-count package dinner
   rolls
1 6-ounce can chunk ham
6 ounces Swiss cheese, sliced

Mix butter with poppy seed, mustard, Worcestershire sauce and onion in bowl. Slice rolls in half horizontally; spread bottom and top layer with butter mixture. Layer ham and cheese over bottom layer. Replace top layer and place rolls in original foil baking pan. Bake for 10 minutes. Cover with foil. Bake for 10 minutes longer. May prepare and refrigerate until baking time or bake and reheat in microwave. May be frozen.

Approx Per Serving: Cal 159; Prot 5.4 g; T Fat 8.5 g; Chol 19.5 mg;
   Carbo 14.5 g; Sod 301.0 mg; Potas 75.8 mg.

Lynette Miller
Tupelo, Mississippi

HAM ROLLS

Yield: 24 servings   *Pan Size: baking pan*   *Preheat: 350 degrees*

2 24-count packages dinner
   rolls
8 ounces (or more) sliced ham
2 6-ounce packages Swiss
   cheese
1/2 cup melted margarine
1 1/2 tablespoons poppy seed

1 1/2 teaspoons Worcestershire
   sauce
1 1/2 tablespoons prepared
   mustard
1 teaspoon onion flakes
2 tablespoons sesame seed

Slice dinner rolls in half. Layer ham and cheese on bottom portion of rolls. Place top of rolls on ham and cheese to form large sandwich. Place in baking pan. Pour mixture of melted margarine, poppy seed, Worcestershire sauce, mustard and onion flakes over rolls. Chill, overnight, or until margarine is firm. Sprinkle with sesame seed. Bake, covered with foil, for 20 minutes or until heated through. Cut into individual sandwiches.

Approx Per Serving: Cal 345; Prot 10.1 g; T Fat 20.4 g; Chol 16.6 mg;
   Carbo 28.8 g; Sod 617.0 mg; Potas 133.0 mg.

Jackie Permenter, Consultant, Special Projects
Department of Education
Nashville, Tennessee

HAM AND SAUERKRAUT BALLS

Yields: 10 servings   *Pan Size: deep fryer*   *Preheat: 350 degrees*

2 cups sauerkraut
1 cup chopped ham
1 cup chopped mozzarella
  cheese
1/4 cup chopped onion
1/4 cup chopped green bell
  pepper
1 egg

2 teaspoons prepared mustard
1 teaspoon celery seed
1/4 cup Parmesan cheese
Oil for deep frying
1/4 cup flour
1 egg
2 tablespoons milk
1 cup dry bread crumbs

Drain sauerkraut; squeeze dry. Combine with ham, mozzarella cheese, onion, green pepper, 1 egg, mustard, celery seed and Parmesan cheese in bowl; mix well. Shape into 1 1/2-inch balls. Roll in flour, dip into mixture of 1 egg beaten with milk and roll in crumbs to coat. Deep-fry until dark golden brown; drain on paper towels. May substitute Swiss or Cheddar cheese for mozzarella cheese.

Approx Per Serving: Cal 115; Prot 7.9 g; T Fat 7.9 g; Chol 48.6 mg;
     Carbo 3.1 g; Sod 723.0 mg; Potas 177.0 mg.
     Nutritional information does not include oil for deep frying.

Mary Klaurens
Former AVA Vice President, Marketing Education Div.
Minneapolis, Minnesota

COUNTRY HAM BALLS

Yields: 10 servings   *Pan Size: 9x13 inch*   *Preheat: 350 degrees*

1 pound country ham, ground
8 ounces mild or hot pork
  sausage
1 cup bread crumbs
1 cup milk

1/2 cup vinegar
1/2 cup packed brown sugar
1/4 cup water
1/2 teaspoon prepared mustard

Combine ham and sausage in bowl; mix well. Add crumbs and milk; mix well. Shape into balls; place in baking dish. Mix vinegar, brown sugar, water and mustard in saucepan. Bring to a boil. Pour over ham balls. Bake, covered, for 45 minutes. Bake, uncovered, for 15 minutes. Meatballs may be frozen before baking.

Approx Per Serving: Cal 230; Prot 12.0 g; T Fat 13.5 g; Chol 36.0 mg;
     Carbo 14.9 g; Sod 772.0 mg; Potas 286.0 mg.

Nora V. Sweat
Elizabethtown, Kentucky

OYSTER CRACKER SNACK MIX

Yields: 24 servings   *Pan Size: large container*

24 ounces oyster crackers	2 teaspoons dillweed
1 cup oil	2 teaspoons lemon pepper
1 envelope dry ranch salad dressing mix	2 teaspoons garlic powder

Place crackers in large container. Mix oil and remaining ingredients in small bowl. Pour oil mixture over crackers; mix gently. Let stand until mixture is completely absorbed, stirring occasionally. Store in tightly covered container for 5 to 7 days before serving.

Approx Per Serving: Cal 201; Prot 2.7 g; T Fat 12.4 g; Chol 0.0 mg;
    Carbo 20.1 g; Sod 355.0 mg; Potas 36.7 mg.
    Nutritional information does not include salad dressing mix.

Frances Bishop, Home Economics Teacher
Sr. High School, Denton, Texas

PEPPER JELLY

Yields: 48 ounces   *Pan Size: 6 quart*

1/2 cup jalapeño peppers	6 cups sugar
3/4 cup coarsely chopped green bell peppers	1/4 teaspoon salt
1 1/2 cups apple cider vinegar	6 ounces Certo
	Red or green food coloring

Seed peppers; chop, grind or pureé in food processor or blender container. Combine peppers with any juices, vinegar, sugar and salt in saucepan. Bring to a full rolling boil. Boil for 1 minute. Remove from heat. Let stand for 10 minutes. Add Certo and desired amount of food coloring. Bring to a full rolling boil. Boil for 1 minute. Let stand for several minutes. Skim. Pour into six 8-ounce jelly glasses. Seal with 2-piece lids. Serve over cream cheese with assorted crackers or as accompaniment to ham or roast pork. Note: Wear rubber gloves when handling jalapeño peppers to protect hands. Peppers may be chopped and frozen in recipe-sized portions until ready for use.

Approx Per Ounce: Cal 197; Prot 0.1 g; T Fat 0.1 g; Chol 0.0 mg;
    Carbo 51.3 g; Sod 107.0 mg; Potas 47.3 mg.
    Nutritional information does not include Certo.

Dot Trusty
Tylertown, Mississippi

PARTY PIZZA

Yields: 40 servings   *Pan Size: baking sheet*   *Preheat: 350 degrees*

1 pound mild pork sausage
1/8 teaspoon garlic salt
3/8 teaspoon oregano

1 loaf party rye bread
1 1/2 cups shredded mozzarella cheese

Combine sausage, garlic salt and oregano in bowl; mix well. Spread 1 tablespoon mixture on each bread slice. Top with a small amount of cheese; place on baking sheet. Bake for 20 to 25 minutes or until cheese is bubbly.

Approx Per Serving: Cal 89; Prot 3.1 g; T Fat 5.9 g; Chol 11.1 mg;
    Carbo 5.7 g; Sod 178.0 mg; Potas 49.1 mg.

Carol Whitney Darling
Millersport, Ohio

POLISH PIZZA

Yields: 50 servings   *Pan Size: baking sheet*   *Preheat: 425 degrees*

1 pound ground beef
1 pound pork sausage
1 teaspoon garlic salt
1 teaspoon Worcestershire sauce

2 teaspoons minced onion
1 pound Velveeta cheese
1 loaf thinly sliced party rye bread

Brown ground beef and sausage in skillet, stirring until crumbly; drain well. Stir in garlic salt, Worcestershire sauce, onion and cheese. Cook until cheese melts, stirring constantly. Shape into 2 rolls about 10 inches long and 2 inches in diameter. Wrap each in plastic wrap. Freeze cheese mixture and bread until firm. Slice cheese rolls about 1/4 inch thick. Place each slice on bread slice. Arrange on baking sheet. Bake for 10 to 12 minutes or until bubbly. Serve hot.

Approx Per Serving: Cal 122; Prot 6.0 g; T Fat 8.7 g; Chol 22.9 mg;
    Carbo 4.6 g; Sod 305.0 mg; Potas 79.1 mg.

Nancy Clem
Princeton, Indiana

SAUSAGE BALLS

Yields: 36 appetizers   *Pan Size: baking sheet*   *Preheat: 350 degrees*

1 pound mild sausage
4 ounces Cheddar cheese,
shredded

3 cups buttermilk baking
mix

Let sausage and cheese stand at room temperature until softened. Combine with baking mix in large bowl; mix until consistency of dough. Shape into small balls; place on baking sheet. Bake until cooked through; drain well. May freeze sausage balls before baking.

Approx Per Appetizer: Cal 111; Prot 3.0 g; T Fat 7.6 g; Chol 11.9 mg;
    Carbo 7.2 g; Sod 236.0 mg; Potas 43.9 mg.

Martha Crisp
Owensboro, Kentucky

SHERRIED WALNUTS

Yields: 3 cups   *Pan Size: 3 quart*

1¹/₂ cups sugar
¹/₂ cup Sherry

¹/₂ teaspoon cinnamon
3 cups walnut halves

Dissolve sugar in Sherry in saucepan. Bring to a boil. Boil until mixture reaches 245 degrees on candy thermometer; remove from heat. Add cinnamon and walnuts; stir until walnuts are completely coated. Pour onto buttered tray; separate walnuts. Let stand until cool. Store in airtight container. May freeze for 3 to 4 weeks.

Approx Per Cup: Cal 1075; Prot 14.4 g; T Fat 61.9 g; Chol 0.0 mg;
    Carbo 119.0 g; Sod 16.3 mg; Potas 537.0 mg.

Dana Q. Markham
Roanoke, Virginia

CARAMEL APPLE DIP

Yields: 32 tablespoons   *Pan Size: bowl*

8 ounces cream cheese, softened	**1 cup packed brown sugar**
	1 teaspoon vanilla extract

Combine cream cheese, brown sugar and vanilla in small bowl; blend well. Store in refrigerator. Serve with crisp apple slices.

Approx Per Serving: Cal 50; Prot 0.5 g; T Fat 2.5 g; Chol 7.7 mg; Carbo 6.8 g; Sod 24.0 mg; Potas 32.1 mg.

Jan Bowers
Emporia, Kansas

BRIE EN CROUTE AU POIRE

Yields: 12 servings   *Pan Size: baking sheet*   *Preheat: 375 degrees*

1 10-count package refrigerator biscuit dough	**½ teaspoon water**
1 8-ounce round Brie	**¼ teaspoon coarsely ground pepper**
1 egg yolk, beaten	

Separate biscuits; arrange on bread board and pat into 8-inch circle. Position Brie in center of circle. Moisten dough edge with a small amount of water; fold over Brie to enclose completely and seal. Place seam side down on ungreased baking sheet. Brush with mixture of egg yolk and water; sprinkle with pepper. Bake for 10 to 15 minutes or until golden brown. Let stand for 30 minutes before cutting. Place on serving plate. Arrange grapes and slices of kiwifruit, apples and pears around Brie.

Approx Per Serving: Cal 74; Prot 4.3 g; T Fat 5.9 g; Chol 41.4 mg; Carbo 0.9 g; Sod 140.0 mg; Potas 31.9 mg.

Rosemary L. Hedlund
Des Moines Area Community College, Ankeny, Iowa

BRIE IN PHYLLO

Yields: 24 servings   *Pan Size: 12x15 inch*   *Preheat: 425 degrees*

1 2-pound round Brie
¼ cup apricot preserves
½ to 1 cup melted butter

12 18x24-inch sheets phyllo
dough (8 ounces)

Cut rind from top of Brie. Spread preserves over top. Brush butter over 1 sheet phyllo; place Brie in center and fold phyllo over Brie. Repeat with remaining butter and phyllo, turning Brie over each time. Place phyllo-wrapped Brie on baking sheet; brush with butter. Wrap in plastic wrap and foil. Refrigerate for up to 2 days. Bake for 8 to 12 minutes or until golden brown. Let stand for 10 minutes. Garnish with fresh fruit. Serve with plain unsalted crackers.

Approx Per Serving: Cal 202; Prot 7.9 g; T Fat 18.1 g; Chol 58.0 mg;
    Carbo 2.3 g; Sod 302.0 mg; Potas 62.4 mg.
    Nutritional information does not include phyllo.

Susan Rogers
Palos Verdes Estates, California

CHEESE BALL

Yields: 50 servings   *Pan Size: medium bowl*

16 ounces cream cheese,
  softened
2 cups shredded sharp
  Cheddar cheese
2 ounces blue cheese,
  crumbled
1 teaspoon lemon juice
¼ teaspoon garlic powder
Cayenne pepper to taste

1 teaspoon chopped pimento
1 teaspoon chopped green bell
  pepper
1 teaspoon chopped onion
1 teaspoon Worcestershire
  sauce
1 cup (about) finely chopped
  pecans

Combine cheeses in bowl; mix well. Add lemon juice, seasonings, pimento, green pepper, onion and Worcestershire sauce; mix well. Shape into ball. Roll in pecans to coat.

Approx Per Serving: Cal 70; Prot 2.2 g; T Fat 6.6 g; Chol 15.5 mg;
    Carbo 0.8 g; Sod 71.7 mg; Potas 28.8 mg.

Beverly Payne
Owensboro, Kentucky

CHEESE FONDUE

Yields: 50 servings   *Pan Size: medium saucepan*

2 pounds Velveeta cheese,
  chopped
3/4 cup hot water
1/4 cup Sherry

1/4 cup Worcestershire sauce
3 dashes of Tabasco sauce
1 loaf French bread
1/2 cup garlic butter, softened

Combine cheese, hot water, Sherry, Worcestershire sauce and Tabasco sauce in saucepan. Heat over low heat until cheese melts and mixture is well blended, stirring constantly. Pour into fondue pot. Slice bread as desired; spread slices with garlic butter. Cut slices into cubes; place on baking sheet. Broil until toasted golden brown. Serve toasted bread cubes for dunking in hot fondue.

Approx Per Serving: Cal 112; Prot 4.9 g; T Fat 7.9 g; Chol 22.2 mg;
    Carbo 5.1 g; Sod 339.0 mg; Potas 48.8 mg.

Stephanie Corbey
Minnetonka, Minnesota

HOT CHEESE DIP

Yields: 12 servings   *Pan Size: Crock•Pot*

1 pound hot pork sausage
2 pounds Velveeta cheese,
  chopped

1 can Ro-Tel tomatoes

Cook sausage in skillet until brown and crumbly; drain well. Combine cheese and tomatoes in Crock•Pot. Heat until cheese melts, stirring occasionally. Serve with bite-sized fresh vegetables and chips for dipping. Leftover dip is delicious over baked potatoes or broccoli.

Approx Per Serving: Cal 445; Prot 21.4 g; T Fat 38.9 g; Chol 97.7 mg;
    Carbo 2.6 g; Sod 1371.0 mg; Potas 251.0 mg.

*Francis and Vivian Tuttle
*AVA President 1987-1988
Stillwater, Oklahoma

PINEAPPLE CHEESE SCULPTURE

Yields: 50 servings

24 ounces sharp Cheddar
cheese, shredded
8 ounces Swiss cheese,
shredded
3 ounces cream cheese,
softened
4 ounces blue cheese,
crumbled
1/2 cup butter, softened

1/2 cup apple juice
2 tablespoons lemon juice
1 tablespoon Worcestershire
sauce
Whole cloves
Paprika to taste
Leafy crown of 1 large
pineapple

Combine cheeses and butter in large mixer bowl. Add juices and Worcestershire sauce gradually, beating constantly. Beat for 5 minutes or until well blended. Chill, covered, for several hours. Shape cheese mixture to shape of standing pineapple on plate. Smooth top flat. Chill, covered with foil, for several hours. Mark cheese with toothpick to resemble pineapple by scoring crisscross lines into diamond shapes; center each diamond with clove. Sprinkle with paprika. Transfer cheese pineapple to serving plate carefully with spatula. Place pineapple crown on top. Arrange wheat thins and other crackers around pineapple.

Approx Per Serving: Cal 99; Prot 4.7 g; T Fat 8.2 g; Chol 24.9 mg;
    Carbo 1.7 g; Sod 146.0 mg; Potas 40.5 mg.

Faye Wilkinson
Hinds Community College, Vicksburg, Mississippi

OREGON CHEESE BALL

Yields: 10 servings   *Pan Size: food processor*

8 ounces cream cheese,
softened
4 ounces Oregon Cheddar
cheese
1/4 cup mayonnaise

1 tablespoon grated onion
1 clove of garlic, crushed
2 teaspoons Worcestershire
sauce
1 cup (about) chopped filberts

Process cheese in food processor container until well mixed. Add mayonnaise, onion, garlic and Worcestershire sauce; mix well. Shape into 2 balls; roll in filberts to coat. Chill until almost serving time. Place on serving plate. Let stand until cheese ball comes to room temperature.

Approx Per Serving: Cal 239; Prot 6.1 g; T Fat 23.2 g; Chol 40.0 mg;
    Carbo 3.2 g; Sod 179.0 mg; Potas 106.0 mg.

Thelma Clemons
Eugene, Oregon

CRAB AND ARTICHOKE DIP

Yields: 20 servings *Pan Size: 1 quart* *Preheat: 350 degrees*

**1 cup chopped canned
   artichoke hearts
1 cup mayonnaise**

**1 cup chopped crab meat
1 cup Parmesan cheese**

Combine artichoke hearts, mayonnaise, crab meat and Parmesan cheese in casserole; mix well. Bake for 25 minutes or until heated through. Serve with assorted crackers.

Approx Per Serving: Cal 108; Prot 3.4 g; T Fat 10.1 g; Chol 15.6 mg;
     Carbo 1.3 g; Sod 166.0 mg; Potas 55.5 mg.

Ed Radford, Building Fund Committee
Town and Country, Missouri

FRUIT DIP

Yield: 20 tablespoons *Pan Size: blender*

**3/4 cup packed brown sugar
1 tablespoon vanilla extract
1 tablespoon cream
1/2 cup confectioners' sugar**

**2 tablespoons Amaretto
8 ounces cream cheese,
   softened**

Combine brown sugar, vanilla, cream, confectioners' sugar and Amaretto in blender container; process until well blended. Add cream cheese gradually, blending constantly. Chill until serving time. Serve with banana slices and whole fresh strawberries.

Approx Per Tablespoon: Cal 89; Prot 0.9 g; T Fat 4.2 g; Chol 13.4 mg;
     Carbo 11.4 g; Sod 37.6 mg; Potas 42.6 mg.

*Niel and Carol Edmunds
*AVA President 1988-1989
Columbia, Missouri

GUACAMOLE DIP

Yields: 8 servings   *Pan Size: medium bowl*

1 small tomato
1 cup mashed avocado
1/4 cup mayonnaise
1 tablespoon lemon juice

1/4 cup finely chopped onion
2 tablespoons finely chopped
  green chilies
1/2 teaspoon salt

Chop tomato finely; drain well. Blend avocado, mayonnaise and lemon juice in bowl. Stir in tomato, onion, green chilies and salt. Chill, covered, for 1 hour. Serve with sliced fresh vegetables and corn chips for dipping.

Approx Per Serving: Cal 102; Prot 0.9 g; T Fat 9.9 g; Chol 4.1 mg;
    Carbo 3.7 g; Sod 177.0 mg; Potas 225.0 mg.

Francie Soliday, President
Oklahoma Vocational Association
Shawnee, Oklahoma

GUATAMALAN GUACAMOLE DIP

Yields: 8 servings   *Pan Size: shallow bowl*

3 ripe avocados
3 green onions, minced
3 tablespoons oil

1/4 teaspoon (rounded)
  oregano leaves, crushed
4 1/2 tablespoons lemon juice

Cut avocados into halves; remove seed and scoop avocado pulp into bowl. Add green onions; mash with fork. Add oil, oregano, lemon juice and salt and pepper to taste; mix well. Serve immediately with tortilla chips.

Approx Per Serving: Cal 140; Prot 1.6 g; T Fat 13.3 g; Chol 0.0 mg;
    Carbo 6.6 g; Sod 8.1 mg; Potas 472.0 mg.

Julia Jenkins
Little Rock, Arkansas

HOLIDAY PÂTÉ

Yields: 8 servings   *Pan Size: 3-cup mold*

8 ounces cream cheese, softened	2 tablespoons finely chopped onion
1 12-ounce can Spam, finely chopped	2 teaspoons Worcestershire sauce
1/4 cup chopped pimento-stuffed olives	2 teaspoons lemon juice
	1/4 teaspoon powdered thyme

Combine cream cheese and Spam in bowl; mix well. Add remaining ingredients; mix well. Press into ring mold. Chill for several hours to 1 week. Unmold onto serving platter. Garnish with chopped parsley and bow made of thin strips of pimento to resemble wreath. Serve with crackers.

Approx Per Serving: Cal 251; Prot 7.6 g; T Fat 23.9 g; Chol 57.3 mg; Carbo 2.2 g; Sod 815.0 mg; Potas 144.0 mg.

Mrs. Joseph L. Davis
Columbus, Ohio

MICROWAVE PARTY APPETIZER PIE

Yields: 8 servings   *Pan Size: pie plate*   ≈M≈

8 ounces cream cheese, softened	2 teaspoons finely chopped green bell pepper
2 tablespoons milk	2 tablespoons instant minced onion
1 2 1/2-ounce jar dried beef, finely chopped	1/2 cup sour cream
1/8 teaspoon pepper	1/4 cup chopped walnuts

Blend cream cheese and milk in 1-quart bowl. Add dried beef, pepper, green pepper and onion; mix well. Stir in sour cream. Spread evenly in pie plate. Microwave, covered with waxed paper, on High for 2 minutes and 38 seconds or until heated through. Let stand for 2 minutes. Sprinkle with walnuts. Serve with assorted crackers.

Approx Per Serving: Cal 174; Prot 5.9 g; T Fat 15.7 g; Chol 52.2 mg; Carbo 3.1 g; Sod 401.0 mg; Potas 133.0 mg.

Anne Larson Schatz
Hemet, California

NOBODY KNOWS RELISH DIP

Yields: 12 servings   *Pan Size: medium bowl*

2 4-ounce cans chopped green
 chilies
4 ounces green salad olives,
 chopped
3 or 4 green onions, chopped

3 or 4 tomatoes, chopped
2 tablespoons wine vinegar
1 tablespoon oil
2 jalapeño peppers, chopped

Combine green chilies, olives, green onions, tomatoes, vinegar, oil and jalapeño peppers in bowl; mix well. Add salt and pepper to taste. Serve with tortilla chips.

Approx Per Serving: Cal 33; Prot 0.7 g; T Fat 2.7 g; Chol 0.0 mg;
 Carbo 2.9 g; Sod 240.0 mg; Potas 110.0 mg.

Diane Dunn-Sluyter
Jefferson City, Missouri

TACO DIP

Yields: 20 servings   *Pan Size: platter*

16 ounces cream cheese,
 softened
1 cup sour cream
1 envelope dry taco seasoning
 mix
1 10-ounce can medium-hot
 picante sauce
1/2 head lettuce, shredded

2 medium tomatoes, chopped
4 green onions, chopped
1/2 cup chopped black olives
1/2 cup chopped pimentos
1 cup shredded Cheddar
 cheese
1 cup shredded Monterey Jack
 cheese

Combine cream cheese, sour cream and taco seasoning mix in bowl; blend well. Spread evenly in platter. Add layers of picante sauce, lettuce, tomatoes, green onions, olives, pimentos and mixture of cheeses. Chill until serving time. Serve with tortilla chips.

Approx Per Serving: Cal 188; Prot 5.8 g; T Fat 15.5 g; Chol 41.2 mg;
 Carbo 7.6 g; Sod 682.0 mg; Potas 154.0 mg.

Catherine Lyons
Owensboro, Kentucky

TUNA DIP

Yields: 8 servings   *Pan Size: medium bowl*

8 ounces cream cheese, softened

2 6-ounce cans water-pack light tuna

1 6-ounce jar tartar sauce

1/4 teaspoon celery salt

Lemon pepper to taste

Combine cream cheese, tuna and tartar sauce in bowl; mix well. Add celery salt and lemon pepper to taste. Serve with assorted crackers.

Approx Per Serving: Cal 267; Prot 15.0 g; T Fat 22.4 g; Chol 61.0 mg; Carbo 1.7 g; Sod 578.0 mg; Potas 184.0 mg.

Nadine F. Marcum
Little Rock, Arkansas

ZESTY TUNA DIP

Yields: 8 servings   *Pan Size: medium bowl*

1 6-ounce can water-pack light tuna

1/4 cup finely chopped dill pickles

1/4 cup Parmesan cheese

1/4 to 1/2 cup horseradish

2 tablespoons A-1 sauce

2/3 cup mayonnaise

1 tablespoon lemon juice

Combine tuna, pickles, cheese, A-1 sauce, mayonnaise and lemon juice in bowl; mix well. Add desired amount of horseradish. Chill until serving time. Serve with assorted crackers.

Approx Per Serving: Cal 180; Prot 7.9 g; T Fat 15.4 g; Chol 24.7 mg; Carbo 3.0 g; Sod 321.0 mg; Potas 136.0 mg.

Charles H. Buzzell
AVA Executive Director
Alexandria, Virginia

SALMON BALL

Yields: 15 servings   *Pan Size: medium bowl*

1   15-ounce can red salmon
2 tablespoons lemon juice
8 ounces cream cheese,
   softened

1 onion, chopped
Parsley flakes
1/2 cup chopped pecans

Combine salmon, lemon juice, cream cheese and onion in bowl; mix well. Chill, covered with plastic wrap, in refrigerator for 2 hours for easier handling. Sprinkle parsley on serving plate. Shape salmon mixture into ball on plate. Top with pecans. Serve with assorted crackers.

Approx Per Serving: Cal 121; Prot 7.1 g; T Fat 9.7 g; Chol 30.9 mg;
   Carbo 1.7 g; Sod 202.0 mg; Potas 137.0 mg.

Sonia Parmer
NCLA President Elect
Largo, Florida

SHRIMP DIP

Yields: 50 servings   *Pan Size: large bowl*

8 ounces cream cheese,
   softened
1 cup Kraft sandwich spread
1/2 cup mayonnaise
1 medium onion, grated
1   4-ounce jar chopped
   pimentos

1/4 cup chopped green onions
2 tablespoons Tabasco sauce
1 tablespoon seasoned salt
1 tablespoon horseradish
2 1/2 pounds cooked shrimp,
   chopped

Combine cream cheese, sandwich spread and mayonnaise in bowl; mix well. Add onion, pimentos, green onions, Tabasco sauce, seasoned salt and horseradish; mix well. Stir in shrimp. Chill in refrigerator for 2 hours or longer to develop flavor. Serve with assorted chips and crackers.

Approx Per Serving: Cal 84; Prot 5.7 g; T Fat 6.4 g; Chol 46.9 mg;
   Carbo 0.8 g; Sod 253.0 mg; Potas 60.8 mg.

Joyce L. Comfort
North Pole, Alaska

MOLDED SHRIMP SPREAD FOR A CROWD

Yields: 24 servings   *Pan Size: 4-cup bowl*

2 4-ounce cans tiny shrimp
8 ounces cream cheese,
  softened
1/2 cup mayonnaise
2 tablespoons minced onion

1 teaspoon (or more)
  Worcestershire sauce
1 cup catsup
2 tablespoons horseradish
2 teaspoons lemon juice

Rinse shrimp with cold water; drain well. Mash shrimp in bowl. Add cream cheese, mayonnaise, onion and Worcestershire sauce to taste; mix well. Spoon into bowl or mold of desired shape. Chill, covered, overnight. Unmold shrimp mixture onto serving plate. Mix catsup, horseradish and lemon juice in small bowl. Pour over mold. Serve with assorted crackers.

Approx Per Serving: Cal 90; Prot 3.2 g; T Fat 7.2 g; Chol 29.4 mg;
  Carbo 3.6 g; Sod 192.0 mg; Potas 81.2 mg.

Joan M. Gehee
Emily Griffith Opportunity School
Denver, Colorado

CELEBRATION PUNCH

Yields: 20 servings   *Pan Size: punch bowl*

4 cups cranberry juice
4 cups pineapple juice
2 tablespoons almond extract

1 cup sugar
2 liters ginger ale

Combine cranberry juice, pineapple juice, almond extract and sugar in large freezer container; mix until sugar dissolves. Freeze until slushy. Spoon into punch bowl. Add ginger ale gradually, stirring gently.

Approx Per Serving: Cal 128; Prot 0.2 g; T Fat 0.0 g; Chol 0.0 mg;
  Carbo 32.5 g; Sod 8.9 mg; Potas 78.8 mg.

Kayleen Long
Huron High School
Huron, South Dakota

CHAMPAGNE PUNCH

Yields: 20 servings   *Pan Size: punch bowl*

3 4/5-quart bottles of
   Champagne
1 1-liter bottle of sparkling
   water

1 12-ounce bottle of peach
   nectar
Decorative ice ring

Chill first 3 ingredients. Combine Champagne, sparkling water and peach nectar in punch bowl; mix gently. Add decorative ice ring. Ladle into punch cups and serve immediately.

Approx Per Serving: Cal 123; Prot 0.3 g; T Fat 0.0 g; Chol 0.0 mg;
     Carbo 5.5 g; Sod 9.8 mg; Potas 126.0 mg.

Nancy Raynor
AVA Vice President, Health Occupation Education Division
Raleigh, North Carolina

MINT SPARKLE

Yields: 12 servings   *Pan Size: large container*

1 10-ounce jar mint jelly
1 cup water
2 12-ounce cans unsweetened
   pineapple juice

1 cup water
1/2 cup lemon juice
1 28-ounce bottle of ginger
   ale, chilled

Combine mint jelly and 1 cup water in small saucepan. Heat over low heat, stirring until jelly melts. Cool. Combine with pineapple juice, remaining 1 cup water and lemon juice in large container. Chill thoroughly. Place ice cubes in tall chilled glasses; fill half full with juice mixture. Tip each glass; pour ginger ale down side to fill. Garnish with lemon slices and fresh mint.

Approx Per Serving: Cal 121; Prot 0.3 g; T Fat 0.1 g; Chol 0.0 mg;
     Carbo 31.1 g; Sod 10.5 mg; Potas 111.0 mg.

Becky Hedrick, Educational Consultant
Home Economics Education
State Advisor, Future Homemakers of America
Nashville, Tennessee

HOLIDAY PUNCH

Yields: 50 servings   *Pan Size: punch bowl*

2 cups sugar
2 cups water
3 cups orange juice
3 cups unsweetened
  pineapple juice

1/3 cup lemon juice
4 12-ounce bottles of red
  cream soda
2 quarts ginger ale

Mix sugar and water in saucepan. Heat until sugar dissolves, stirring occasionally. Add juices. Chill in refrigerator for several hours to overnight. Combine juice mixture with cream soda and ginger ale in punch bowl. May use cream-colored cream soda for yellow punch.

Approx Per Serving: Cal 74; Prot 0.2 g; T Fat 0.0 g; Chol 0.0 mg;
    Carbo 18.7 g; Sod 6.3 mg; Potas 53.0 mg.

Jane King
AVA Vice President, Region I
Cookbook Committee
Newark, Ohio

SANGRIA

Yields: 50 servings   *Pan Size: punch bowl*

1 gallon Burgundy, chilled
1 46-ounce can unsweetened
  pineapple juice, chilled
1 18-ounce can grapefruit
  juice, chilled

1 6-ounce can frozen grape
  juice concentrate, thawed
4 cups Brandy
3 oranges, peeled, sectioned
3 apples, cut into thin wedges

Combine Burgundy, pineapple juice, grapefruit juice, grape juice concentrate and Brandy in punch bowl. Add oranges, apples and desired amount of ice. Serve immediately. Note: This is the punch served at the New Mexico reception at the AVA national conference.

Approx Per Serving: Cal 142; Prot 0.5 g; T Fat 0.1 g; Chol 0.0 mg;
    Carbo 18.9 g; Sod 5.6 mg; Potas 195.0 mg.

Cathy Blue Avis
Albuquerque, New Mexico

MEXICAN CHOCOLATE

Yields: 6 servings   *Pan Size: double boiler*

2 1-ounce squares
   unsweetened chocolate
2 tablespoons hot water
²/₃ cup sugar
¹/₂ teaspoon salt

2 teaspoons cinnamon
2 cups coffee
3 cups hot milk
1 teaspoon vanilla extract

Melt chocolate in water in double boiler. Add mixture of sugar, salt and cinnamon; mix well. Stir in coffee. Heat for 5 minutes. Add mixture of hot milk and vanilla. Heat over low heat for 30 minutes. Beat until frothy; pour into cups. Garnish with whipped cream. The flavor actually improves if instant coffee and powdered milk are used.

Approx Per Serving: Cal 209; Prot 4.7 g; T Fat 7.4 g; Chol 16.5 mg;
    Carbo 33.8 g; Sod 232.0 mg; Potas 254.0 mg.

Joan M. Gehee
Emily Griffith Opportunity School
Denver, Colorado

PERCOLATOR BREW

Yields: 16 servings   *Pan Size: 24 cup*

2 quarts apple cider
1 quart orange juice
1 quart cranberry juice
1¹/₂ cups packed brown sugar

6 whole cinnamon sticks
2 tablespoons whole allspice
2 tablespoons whole cloves

Place cider and juices in percolator. Place brown sugar and spices in percolator basket. Plug in percolator about 45 minutes before serving time. Perk through cycle. Garnish each serving with whipped cream and add 1 ounce Tuaca if desired.

Approx Per Serving: Cal 201; Prot 0.6 g; T Fat 0.4 g; Chol 0.0 mg;
    Carbo 50.4 g; Sod 15.0 mg; Potas 362.0 mg.

Joyce M. Leimbach
Sandusky, Ohio

Artist: *Jenny Rasey*—Lawrence County AVTS; Gerald Zona, Teacher;
                New Bedford, Pennsylvania
Artist: *M. Carolyn Edwards*—Bessemer State Tech College;
                Tom Immler, Teacher; Birmingham, Alabama

SOUPS
&
SALADS

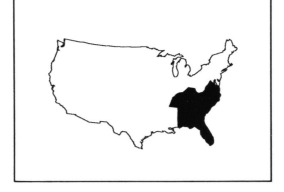

Southeastern Seafood Feast
Region II

Salmon Ball
page 32

Clams Casino
page 17

Charleston She-Crab Soup
page 43

Marinated Vegetable Salad
page 53

Shrimp Salad
page 50

Norfolk Crab Cakes
page 98

Poached Salmon with Raspberry Beurre Blanc
page 95

Pea and Broccoli Casserole
page 113

Yeast Rolls
page 157

Southern Cheesecake
page 164

South Carolina Pecan Pie
page 195

GAZPACHO

Yields: 10 servings   *Pan Size: large bowl*

1 clove of garlic, crushed
2 teaspoons salt
1 cup finely chopped
  cucumber
1 cup finely chopped onion
1 cup finely chopped celery
1 tablespoon chopped parsley

1¼ cups finely chopped green
  bell pepper
1 teaspoon pepper
¼ cup wine vinegar
2 cups finely chopped
  tomatoes
3 cups tomato juice

Mix garlic with salt in stainless steel or glass bowl. Add cucumber, onion, celery, parsley, green pepper, pepper, vinegar, tomatoes and tomato juice; mix well. Chill, covered, for 3 hours before serving.

Approx Per Serving: Cal 35; Prot 1.4 g; T Fat 0.3 g; Chol 0.0 mg;
    Carbo 8.2 g; Sod 706.0 mg; Potas 364.0 mg.

Shirley W. Wells
Richmond, Virginia

LISA'S FAVORITE FRUIT SOUP

Yields: 4 servings   *Pan Size: 2 quart*

2 pounds seasonal fruit
5 cups water
Juice and grated rind of 1
  lemon

½ to 1 cup sugar or honey
1 whole clove
1 cinnamon stick
Pinch of salt

Peel and chop fruit. Combine with water, lemon juice and rind, sugar and seasonings in saucepan. Bring to a boil; reduce heat. Simmer, covered, for 10 to 15 minutes. Discard clove and cinnamon stick. Pureé fruit mixture in blender container. Chill for several hours before serving. May use several fruits in combination such as pears, apples, bananas, peaches, strawberries and blueberries.

Nutritional information not available.

Tricia Boucher-Wallace
Leominster Trade High School
Fitchburg, Massachusetts

BEEF AND BARLEY SOUP

Yields: 12 servings   *Pan Size: 4 quart*

1 pound beef stew meat	1/2 cup barley
1 tablespoon oil	1/2 cup sliced carrots
1/2 cup chopped onion	1/2 cup sliced celery
1 clove of garlic, minced	4 beef bouillon cubes
7 cups water	1/2 teaspoon basil leaves
1 16-ounce can whole tomatoes	1 bay leaf

Cut stew meat into 1/2-inch cubes. Brown in oil in saucepan. Add onion and garlic. Cook until onion is tender; drain. Add water, undrained tomatoes, barley, carrots, celery, bouillon cubes, basil and bay leaf. Bring to a boil; reduce heat. Simmer, covered, for 50 minutes or until barley and beef are tender, stirring occasionally and adding a small amount of additional water if necessary. Remove bay leaf. Serve with warm rolls and tossed salad.

Approx Per Serving: Cal 178; Prot 10.6 g; T Fat 12.9 g; Chol 38.7 mg;
    Carbo 4.9 g; Sod 378.0 mg; Potas 206.0 mg.

Peggy Arnott
Billings, Montana

MICROWAVE CREAM OF BROCCOLI SOUP

Yields: 4 servings   *Pan Size: 3 quart*   ≈M≈

1 1/2 pounds broccoli	1/4 teaspoon instant minced
1/2 cup chopped onion	garlic
2 cups water	1/4 cup butter
4 teaspoons instant chicken	1/4 cup flour
bouillon	1/4 teaspoon white pepper
1/2 teaspoon dry thyme	2 cups half and half
leaves, crushed	

Peel broccoli stems if necessary; slice thinly. Combine with onion, water, bouillon, thyme and garlic in glass casserole. Microwave, covered with plastic wrap, on High for 15 minutes or until very tender. Cool slightly. Pureé half the mixture at a time in blender container until smooth. Microwave butter in 2-quart bowl on High for 45 seconds or until melted. Blend in flour. Microwave for 30 seconds. Stir in pepper and half and half. Microwave for 5 minutes or until smooth and thickened, stirring every minute. Stir in broccoli pureé. Microwave on Medium-High for 3 minutes or until heated through; do not boil. Garnish with dollop of sour cream and sprinkle of chopped chives.

Approx Per Serving: Cal 317; Prot 9.3 g; T Fat 26.1 g; Chol 75.6 mg;
    Carbo 16.3 g; Sod 481.0 mg; Potas 796.0 mg.

Marylyn Mitchell
Pomona, California

ELEGANT SWISS BROCCOLI SOUP

Yields: 4 servings   *Pan Size: 2 quart*

5½ cups milk
1 10-ounce package frozen
  chopped broccoli
2 tablespoons chopped onion

2 tablespoons butter
1 tablespoon flour
2 cups shredded Swiss cheese

Bring milk in large saucepan to a simmer. Add broccoli and onion. Cook until tender. Melt butter in small saucepan. Blend in flour. Stir into broccoli mixture. Cook for 3 minutes, stirring constantly. Add cheese and salt to taste. Cook until cheese melts, stirring constantly. Serve immediately.

Approx Per Serving: Cal 499; Prot 29.6 g; T Fat 32.6 g; Chol 113.0 mg;
  Carbo 23.2 g; Sod 353.0 mg; Potas 650.0 mg.

Faye Wilkinson
Hinds Community College, Vicksburg, Mississippi

PICANTE CHEESE AND BROCCOLI SOUP

Yields: 4 servings   *Pan Size: 2 quart*

1 medium onion, coarsely
  chopped
1 clove of garlic, minced
1 tablespoon butter
1 14-ounce can chicken broth
½ cup picante sauce
1 teaspoon Dijon mustard
1 cup chopped red bell pepper

½ cup instant mashed potato
  flakes
1 10-ounce package frozen
  broccoli cuts, thawed
8 ounces process cheese
  spread, cubed
1 cup milk

Sauté onion and garlic in butter in saucepan until tender but not brown. Stir in broth, picante sauce and mustard. Simmer, uncovered, for 5 minutes. Stir in red pepper, potato flakes and broccoli. Simmer for 5 minutes or until vegetables are tender-crisp. Add cheese. Cook until cheese melts, stirring constantly. Add milk. Heat to serving temperature; do not boil. Ladle into soup bowls. Garnish with additional picante sauce.

Approx Per Serving: Cal 377; Prot 19.3 g; T Fat 18.1 g; Chol 48.7 mg;
  Carbo 37.7 g; Sod 1355.0 mg; Potas 725.0 mg.

Doris Poindexter
Mt. Pleasant, Iowa

CREAM CHEESE AND LEEK SOUP

Yields: 8 servings   *Pan Size: 4 quart*

1 pound spinach, chopped	1 teaspoon salt
White portion of 4 large leeks, chopped	16 ounces cream cheese
	2 cups yogurt
5 tablespoons butter	4 egg yolks
6 tablespoons flour	2 cups chopped cooked ham
4½ cups chicken broth	1 cup chopped chives
4½ cups water	

Sauté spinach and leeks in butter in saucepan until tender. Add flour. Cook for 2 minutes, stirring constantly; remove from heat. Stir in broth, water and salt. Cook over low heat until thickened, stirring constantly. Simmer for 15 minutes. Mash cream cheese in small bowl. Add yogurt, egg yolks and salt and pepper to taste; beat until smooth. Stir into soup. Cook over low heat for 5 minutes. Sauté ham in skillet. Stir into soup. Garnish with chives.

Approx Per Serving: Cal 451; Prot 20.2 g; T Fat 35.6 g; Chol 239.0 mg;
    Carbo 13.4 g; Sod 1382.0 mg; Potas 763.0 mg.

Joyce Sandberg
Pittsburgh, Pennsylvania

A.J.'S CATFISH CHOWDER

Yields: 6 servings   *Pan Size: 4 quart*

2 pounds catfish	1 cup chopped celery
2 cups water	1 bay leaf, crumbled
2 ounces salt pork, chopped	1 teaspoon salt
2 onions, sliced	Freshly ground pepper to taste
4 large potatoes, peeled, chopped	1 quart milk
	2 tablespoons butter

Simmer catfish in water in saucepan for 15 minutes. Drain, reserving broth. Bone catfish. Cook salt pork in saucepan until crisp; remove and reserve. Sauté onions in drippings until golden. Add boned catfish, potatoes, celery, bay leaf, salt and pepper. Add enough boiling water to reserved broth to measure 3 cups liquid. Stir into soup. Simmer for 30 minutes. Add milk and butter. Simmer for 5 minutes longer. Garnish with reserved salt pork.

Approx Per Serving: Cal 426; Prot 37.1 g; T Fat 18.1 g; Chol 128.0 mg;
    Carbo 27.7 g; Sod 578.0 mg; Potas 1163.0 mg.

Aaron J. Miller
Columbus, Ohio

CHARLESTON SHE-CRAB SOUP

Yields: 4 servings   *Pan Size: double boiler*

2 tablespoons melted butter
2 teaspoons flour
2 cups milk
1/2 cup cream
1/2 teaspoon mace
1/4 teaspoon celery salt

1 tablespoon Worcestershire
  sauce
1 pound lump crab meat
  with roe
1/4 cup (about) Sherry, warmed

Blend butter and flour in double boiler. Stir in milk and cream gradually. Add mace, celery salt, Worcestershire sauce and salt and pepper to taste. Fold in crab meat gently. Heat to serving temperature. Ladle into bowls; add Sherry to taste.

Approx Per Serving: Cal 367; Prot 28.2 g; T Fat 22.3 g; Chol 174.0 mg;
    Carbo 8.5 g; Sod 660.0 mg; Potas 655.0 mg.

The Honorable Ernest Hollings
U.S. Senator, South Carolina
Washington, District of Columbia

GROUND BEEF SOUP

Yields: 10 servings   *Pan Size: 4 quart*

2 pounds ground beef
1 46-ounce can tomato juice
1 6-ounce can minced clams
1 8-ounce can stewed tomatoes
1 4-ounce can mushroom
   pieces
1 16-ounce can French-style
   green beans
2 cups chopped celery

2 cups sliced cabbage
1 cup sliced carrots
2 tablespoons chopped onion
1 tablespoon Worcestershire
  sauce
1 tablespoon garlic powder
2 teaspoons basil
2 teaspoons oregano
1 bay leaf

Brown ground beef in soup pot, stirring until crumbly; drain. Add tomato juice, clams, undrained canned vegetables, fresh vegetables and seasonings. Bring to a boil; reduce heat. Simmer, covered, until vegetables are tender. Discard bay leaf. Soup freezes and reheats well for cold weather meals.

Approx Per Serving: Cal 329; Prot 25.4 g; T Fat 20.5 g; Chol 91.8 mg;
    Carbo 14.2 g; Sod 801.0 mg; Potas 867.0 mg.

Frances G. Bliven
Oneonta, New York

LOBSTER SOUP

Yields: 4 servings   *Pan Size: 3 quart*

1 8-ounce rock lobster tail	1 cup thin noodles, broken
2 tablespoons butter	1 4-inch zucchini, thinly sliced
6 cups fresh chicken broth	2 eggs, beaten

Cut lobster tail into halves lengthwise. Cook cut side down in butter in saucepan for 1 minute. Add broth. Bring to a boil. Remove lobster. Remove lobster meat from shell; cut into chunks and set aside. Add noodles and zucchini. Cook for 3 minutes or until noodles are tender. Add lobster. Pour eggs in fine stream into simmering soup, swirling soup constantly. Add salt and pepper to taste. Ladle into soup bowls. Garnish each with spoonful of hot cooked rice.

Approx Per Serving: Cal 361; Prot 17.9 g; T Fat 11.2 g; Chol 181.0 mg; Carbo 46.2 g; Sod 2396.0 mg; Potas 351.0 mg.

Roberta Null
Pomona, California

POTATO SOUP

Yields: 8 servings   *Pan Size: pressure cooker*

5 medium potatoes, peeled, chopped	1 teaspoon salt
1 small onion, chopped	1/8 teaspoon thyme
1 cup chopped celery	1/4 teaspoon celery seed
2 cups water	2 cups milk
1 can cream of celery soup	3 tablespoons melted butter
1 can New England clam chowder	3 tablespoons flour
	1 cup milk

Combine potatoes, onion, celery and water in pressure cooker. Cook using manufacturer's instructions for 8 minutes. Add celery soup, clam chowder and seasonings. Cook over medium-low heat until heated through. Add 2 cups milk. Blend butter and flour in small saucepan. Stir in 1 cup milk gradually. Cook until thickened, stirring constantly. Stir a small amount of hot soup into white sauce; stir white sauce into hot soup. Cook until thickened, stirring constantly.

Approx Per Serving: Cal 233; Prot 8.8 g; T Fat 12.0 g; Chol 31.2 mg; Carbo 28.5 g; Sod 773.5 mg; Potas 538.8 mg.

Francie Soliday, President
Oklahoma Vocational Association
Shawnee, Oklahoma

BAVARIAN SPINACH SOUP

Yields: 25 servings   *Pan Size: 2 gallon*

1 gallon medium cream sauce
24 ounces American cheese,
 shredded
1 20-ounce package fresh
 spinach

1 cup chopped green onions
1/4 cup chopped pimento
8 ounces canned crab meat
1 cup beer

Heat cream sauce in double boiler; do not overheat. Add cheese. Heat until cheese melts. Wash spinach; drain well and chop. Sauté spinach and green onions in small skillet until tender. Add to soup. Add pimento, crab meat and beer. Heat to serving temperature. Add desired amount of milk or cream if necessary to make of desired consistency.

Approx Per Serving: Cal 266; Prot 15.8 g; T Fat 15.4 g; Chol 55.9 mg;
 Carbo 16.4 g; Sod 1240.0 mg; Potas 544.0 mg.

Jerry Cote
Hartford Area Vocational Center
White River Junction, Vermont

MICROWAVE VEGETABLE CHOWDER

Yields: 2 servings   *Pan Size: 2 quart*   *≈M≈*

6 slices bacon
1/4 cup chopped onion
1 can cream of potato soup
1/2 cup milk

1 15-ounce can mixed
 vegetables, drained
1/4 cup water

Microwave bacon in glass casserole on High for 5 minutes or until crisp; drain and crumble. Stir onion into bacon drippings. Microwave for 2 minutes or until tender. Add soup, milk, vegetables, water and crumbled bacon; mix well. Microwave to 170 degrees on Microwave probe.

Approx Per Serving: Cal 337; Prot 15.5 g; T Fat 14.6 g; Chol 31.6 mg;
 Carbo 37.1 g; Sod 1775.0 mg; Potas 978.0 mg.

*Harvey and Gale Link
*AVA Vice President, Region V
Wahpeton, North Dakota

ZESTY VEGETABLE AND RICE SOUP

Yields: 6 servings 　　　*Pan Size: 3 quart*

2 cups coarsely chopped onion
1 cup ¼-inch celery pieces
2 cloves of garlic, minced
1 tablespoon oil
2 14-ounce cans beef broth
1 16-ounce can whole tomatoes
1 cup ¼-inch carrot slices

½ cup uncooked rice
½ cup picante sauce
2 teaspoons basil leaves,
　crushed
1 large leek
¼ cup chopped fresh parsley

Sauté onion, celery and garlic in oil in saucepan for 4 minutes. Add broth, undrained chopped tomatoes, carrots, rice, picante sauce and basil. Simmer, covered, for 15 minutes. Slice white and light green portion of leek ¼ inch thick and separate into rings. Add to soup. Simmer, covered, for 10 minutes. Stir in parsley. Serve with additional picante sauce.

Approx Per Serving: Cal 147; Prot 4.7 g; T Fat 3.2 g; Chol 0.6 mg;
　　Carbo 26.1 g; Sod 688.0 mg; Potas 571.0 mg.

Trisha Verdal
Moscow, Idaho

APPLE SALAD

Yields: 12 servings 　　　*Pan Size: large bowl*

1 20-ounce can sliced
　pineapple
3 eggs, beaten
1 cup sugar
2 tablespoons flour
2 tablespoons melted butter

12 Jonathan apples
Juice of 1 lemon
1 pound red seedless grapes
1 cup whipping cream,
　whipped

Drain pineapple, reserving juice. Bring reserved juice to a boil in small saucepan. Beat eggs with mixture of sugar and flour in medium saucepan. Stir in boiling juice. Cook until thickened, stirring constantly. Cool. Blend in butter. Chop apples; sprinkle with lemon juice. Cut grapes into halves and pineapple into small pieces. Combine fruit in bowl. Add dressing; mix gently. Chill in refrigerator. Fold in whipped cream just before serving.

Approx Per Serving: Cal 317; Prot 2.8 g; T Fat 11.4 g; Chol 101.0 mg;
　　Carbo 55.6 g; Sod 43.8 mg; Potas 313.0 mg.

Constance Handy Spohn
Cobleskill, New York

APRICOT SALAD

Yields: 15 servings   *Pan Size: 9x13 inch*

1 28-ounce can crushed
   pineapple
1 28-ounce can apricots
3 6-ounce packages orange
   gelatin
2 cups boiling water
3/4 cup miniature
   marshmallows

1/2 cup sugar
2 tablespoons flour
1 egg, beaten
2 tablespoons margarine
1 cup whipping cream,
   whipped
1/2 cup shredded Cheddar
   cheese

Drain pineapple and apricots, reserving juice. Add enough water to reserved juice to measure 3 cups. Chop apricots. Dissolve gelatin in boiling water in large bowl. Add 2 cups juice mixture. Add fruit and marshmallows. Pour into dish. Chill until firm. Mix sugar and flour in saucepan. Add egg and remaining 1 cup juice mixture; mix well. Cook until thickened, stirring constantly. Add margarine. Cool. Fold in whipped cream. Spread whipped cream mixture over gelatin; sprinkle with cheese.

Approx Per Serving: Cal 365; Prot 5.7 g; T Fat 9.1 g; Chol 44.0 mg;
        Carbo 69.1 g; Sod 173.0 mg; Potas 152.0 mg.

Betty Stanley
Bryan, Ohio

FROZEN CRANBERRY SALAD

Yields: 12 servings   *Pan Size: 6 cup*

6 ounces cream cheese,
   softened
1/2 cup mayonnaise
1 cup jellied cranberry sauce,
   mashed

1 20-ounce can crushed
   pineapple, drained
1/2 cup chopped pecans
1/2 cup whipping cream,
   whipped

Blend cream cheese and mayonnaise in bowl. Add cranberry sauce and salt to taste; mix well. Stir in pineapple and pecans. Fold in whipped cream. Spoon into mold. Freeze until firm. Let stand at room temperature for several minutes before inverting onto serving plate.

Approx Per Serving: Cal 242; Prot 1.9 g; T Fat 19.4 g; Chol 34.5 mg;
        Carbo 17.2 g; Sod 105.0 mg; Potas 103.0 mg.

*K. Otto and Patty Logan
*AVA President 1965-1966
Mesa, Arizona

JIFFY LIME SALAD

Yields: 6 servings   *Pan Size: 1½ quart*

1 4-ounce package lime gelatin
1 cup miniature marshmallows
1 cup boiling water
1 cup crushed pineapple

1 cup cottage cheese
¼ cup sugar
1 cup chopped pecans

Dissolve gelatin and marshmallows in boiling water in bowl. Cool. Stir in remaining ingredients. Pour into mold. Chill until firm. Unmold onto serving plate. Garnish with whipped cream and cherries.

Approx Per Serving: Cal 423; Prot 8.6 g; T Fat 15.0 g; Chol 5.2 mg;
    Carbo 68.7 g; Sod 236.0 mg; Potas 154.0 mg.

Roberta Looper, Chairman
AVA Cookbook Committee
Monterey, Tennessee

PINEAPPLE AND CREAM CHEESE SALAD

Yields: 8 servings   *Pan Size: 6 cup*

1 3-ounce package lemon
   gelatin
1 3-ounce package lime gelatin
2 tablespoons sugar
4 cups boiling water
10 large marshmallows,
   chopped

3 ounces cream cheese
1 16-ounce can crushed
   pineapple, drained
¼ cup mayonnaise
1 cup whipping cream,
   whipped
1 cup crushed pecans

Dissolve gelatins and sugar in boiling water in large bowl. Add marshmallows and cream cheese; beat until well blended. Cool. Add pineapple, mayonnaise, whipped cream and pecans; mix well. Pour into mold. Chill until firm. Unmold onto serving plate.

Approx Per Serving: Cal 435; Prot 5.0 g; T Fat 30.5 g; Chol 56.4 mg;
    Carbo 40.0 g; Sod 158.0 mg; Potas 161.0 mg.

Alice Karen Hite, Executive Director
Ohio Vocational Association
Worthington, Ohio

WHITE FRUIT SALAD

Yields: 12 servings   Pan Size: 11x14 inch

2 8-ounce cans crushed
   pineapple
1 envelope unflavored gelatin
1 6-ounce package lemon
   gelatin
2 cups boiling water
1 4-ounce jar maraschino
   cherries, chopped

4 bananas, chopped
4 ounces pecans, chopped
8 ounces cream cheese,
   softened
1 cup mayonnaise
2 cups whipping cream,
   whipped

Drain pineapple, reserving juice. Soften unflavored gelatin in a small amount of reserved juice. Add enough water to remaining juice to measure 2 cups. Dissolve unflavored gelatin and lemon gelatin in boiling water in large bowl. Add juice mixture. Chill until partially set. Add fruit and pecans; mix well. Blend cream cheese and mayonnaise in bowl. Fold in whipped cream. Add to gelatin mixture; mix well. Pour into glass dish. Chill for several hours or until firm.

Approx Per Serving: Cal 485; Prot 5.6 g; T Fat 40.2 g; Chol 75.6 mg;
    Carbo 30.0 g; Sod 220.0 mg; Potas 298.0 mg.

Dana Q. Markham
Roanoke, Virginia

CHICKEN SALAD

Yields: 6 servings   Pan Size: medium bowl

2 cups chopped cooked
   chicken
1 cup shredded American
   cheese
1/2 cup slivered blanched
   almonds

1/2 cup chopped celery
1 9-ounce can crushed
   pineapple, drained
1/2 cup mayonnaise
1 teaspoon salt
1 teaspoon soy sauce

Combine chicken, cheese, almonds, celery and pineapple in bowl. Mix mayonnaise, salt and soy sauce in bowl. Add to chicken mixture; mix well.

Approx Per Serving: Cal 380; Prot 20.4 g; T Fat 30.0 g; Chol 70.5 mg;
    Carbo 8.8 g; Sod 837.0 mg; Potas 311.0 mg.

Elizabeth H. Mettling
Lewis, Kansas

CRAB MEAT SALAD

Yields: 4 servings　　　　*Pan Size: medium bowl*

2 cups crab meat
1 cup chopped celery
4 sweet pickles, chopped
1 white onion, chopped
Juice of 1 lemon
1 clove of garlic, minced

¼ teaspoon salt
¼ teaspoon pepper
¼ teaspoon paprika
¼ cup (about) mayonnaise
2 ripe avocados

Combine crab meat, celery, pickles, onion, lemon juice, garlic and seasonings in bowl. Add enough mayonnaise to moisten; mix gently. Peel avocados; cut into halves and discard seed. Place on lettuce-lined plates. Spoon salad into avocados.

Approx Per Serving: Cal 292; Prot 15.8 g; T Fat 21.2 g; Chol 68.1 mg;
　　　Carbo 12.4 g; Sod 572.0 mg; Potas 753.0 mg.

Kristin Robinson
AVA Cookbook Committee
Washington, District of Columbia

SHRIMP SALAD

Yields: 4 servings　　　　*Pan Size: 6 cup*

1 cup tomato soup
9 ounces cream cheese,
　softened
2 tablespoons unflavored
　gelatin

1 cup chopped celery
½ cup chopped onion
1 green bell pepper, chopped
1 cup mayonnaise
1 cup chopped cooked shrimp

Heat soup in saucepan. Add cream cheese; heat until cheese melts. Soften gelatin in a small amount of cold water. Stir into soup mixture until dissolved. Remove from heat. Stir in celery, onion, green pepper, mayonnaise and shrimp. Spoon into mold. Chill until firm. Unmold onto serving plate. Serve with crackers.

Approx Per Serving: Cal 725; Prot 17.3 g; T Fat 67.7 g; Chol 158.0 mg;
　　　Carbo 15.0 g; Sod 1022.0 mg; Potas 436.0 mg.

Catherine Lyons
Owensboro, Kentucky

BROCCOLI AND CAULIFLOWER SALAD

Yields: 6 servings	*Pan Size: 1 quart*

1 cup frozen peas, blanched
2 cups chopped fresh broccoli
1 cup cauliflowerets
1/2 cup chopped celery
1/2 cup chopped red bell
  pepper
1/2 cup chopped green bell
  pepper

2 tablespoons chopped red
  onion
1 cup reduced-calorie
  mayonnaise
1/2 cup sour cream
2 tablespoons sugar
3/4 cup peanuts

Combine peas, broccoli, cauliflower, celery, bell peppers and onion in bowl. Blend mayonnaise, sour cream and sugar in small bowl. Add to vegetables; toss lightly to coat. Chill in refrigerator for 6 hours or until serving time. Add peanuts; toss lightly.

Approx Per Serving: Cal 292; Prot 8.1 g; T Fat 20.9 g; Chol 18.2 mg; Carbo 21.9 g; Sod 258.0 mg; Potas 418.0 mg.

Joyce M. Leimbach
Sandusky, Ohio

CABBAGE SLAW

Yields: 20 servings	*Pan Size: large bowl*

1 large head cabbage,
  shredded
2 white onions, sliced
14 to 16 tablespoons sugar
3/4 cup oil

1 cup vinegar
2 teaspoons sugar
1 teaspoon dry mustard
1 teaspoon celery seed
1 tablespoon salt

Alternate 2 inch thick layers of cabbage with onions in bowl. Sprinkle 14 to 16 tablespoons sugar over top. Combine oil, vinegar, 2 teaspoons sugar, dry mustard, celery seed and salt in saucepan. Bring to a full rolling boil. Pour over cabbage. Chill, lightly covered, for 4 hours. Mix well; spoon into covered jars. Store in refrigerator for up to 2 months.

Approx Per Serving: Cal 119; Prot 0.4 g; T Fat 8.3 g; Chol 0.0 mg; Carbo 12.1 g; Sod 324.0 mg; Potas 78.7 mg.

Lynn A. Wagner
Newton, Mississippi

FRESH VEGETABLE SALAD

Yields: 6 servings   *Pan Size: medium bowl*

1 cup golden raisins
3 cups broccoli flowerets
3 cups cauliflowerets
1/2 cup onion slices
3 slices crisp-fried bacon,
  crumbled

1/2 cup mayonnaise-type salad
  dressing
1/2 cup sugar
2 tablespoons red wine
  vinegar

Soak raisins in water to cover until softened and plumped; drain well. Combine with broccoli, cauliflower, onion and bacon in bowl. Blend salad dressing, sugar and vinegar in small bowl. Pour over vegetables; toss lightly. Chill in refrigerator for 3 to 4 hours before serving.

Approx Per Serving: Cal 232; Prot 4.4 g; T Fat 5.8 g; Chol 7.5 mg;
    Carbo 45.1 g; Sod 169.0 mg; Potas 562.0 mg.

Christine Smith
Troy, Michigan

JALAPEÑO FRITO SALAD

Yields: 10 servings   *Pan Size: large bowl*

1 head iceberg lettuce
2 tablespoons chopped seeded
  tomato
1 large avocado, chopped
1/3 cup finely chopped onion
3 tablespoons evaporated milk

8 ounces Velveeta cheese,
  cubed
1 or 2 jalapeño peppers,
  seeded, finely chopped
1 7-ounce package regular
  corn chips

Tear lettuce into bite-sized pieces; place in bowl. Add tomato, avocado and onion. Combine evaporated milk, cheese and jalapeño peppers in double boiler. Heat over medium heat until cheese melts, stirring frequently. Toss corn chips with lettuce mixture. Add cheese mixture gradually, tossing gently; do not crush lettuce. Serve immediately. Wonderful with spaghetti or hamburgers.

Approx Per Serving: Cal 240; Prot 7.7 g; T Fat 16.9 g; Chol 22.9 mg;
    Carbo 15.0 g; Sod 511.0 mg; Potas 293.0 mg.

Betty Weissinger
Abilene, Texas

MARINATED VEGETABLE SALAD

Yields: 15 servings	Pan Size: large bowl

1 16-ounce can French-style green beans	1/2 cup chopped onion
1 16-ounce can white Shoe Peg corn	1/2 cup chopped cucumber
	11/2 cups vinegar
1 16-ounce can small early peas	2/3 cup sugar
	2/3 cup oil
1 4-ounce jar chopped pimento	1/2 cup water
1/2 cup chopped celery	1/2 teaspoon ground cloves
	1/2 teaspoon pepper

Drain canned vegetables well. Layer celery, onion, cucumber, green beans, corn, peas and pimento in large bowl. Combine vinegar, sugar, oil, water, cloves and pepper in bowl. Pour over vegetable layers; do not stir. Chill in refrigerator for 24 hours. Stir gently and serve. Salad may be refrigerated for up to 1 week.

Approx Per Serving: Cal 179; Prot 2.8 g; T Fat 9.8 g; Chol 0.0 mg; Carbo 22.8 g; Sod 148.0 mg; Potas 184.0 mg.

Daisy Stewart
Blacksburg, Virginia

SPINACH AND BACON SALAD

Yields: 10 servings	Pan Size: plastic bag

2 bunches fresh spinach	1 teaspoon dry mustard
1 head lettuce	1 tablespoon poppy seed
1/3 cup cider vinegar	8 ounces bacon, crisp-fried,
1 cup oil	crumbled
1/4 cup sugar	1 red onion, sliced into rings
1 teaspoon salt	1 cup large curd cottage cheese

Wash spinach well. Alternate layers of spinach and damp paper towels in plastic bag. Tear lettuce into bite-sized pieces. Alternate layers of lettuce and damp paper towels in plastic bag. Combine vinegar, oil, sugar, salt, dry mustard and poppy seed in jar; shake to mix. Chill spinach, lettuce and dressing in refrigerator overnight. Tear spinach into bite-sized pieces. Combine with lettuce, bacon and onion in large plastic bag. Add half the salad dressing; toss gently. Mix remaining salad dressing with cottage cheese. Add to greens; toss lightly.

Approx Per Serving: Cal 385; Prot 11.1 g; T Fat 34.5 g; Chol 22.5 mg; Carbo 8.7 g; Sod 688.0 mg; Potas 352.0 mg.

Jane McEllhiney Stein
AVA Building Fund Committee
AVA Cookbook Committee
San Diego, California

VIP TOSSED SALAD WITH DRESSING

Yields: 8 servings   *Pan Size: salad bowl*

1 clove of garlic
1 head lettuce
1/2 bunch romaine
1 bunch watercress
1/4 cup slivered toasted
   almonds

Flowerets of 1 small head
   cauliflower
1 or 2 avocados, chopped
1 or 2 tomatoes, peeled,
   chopped

Rub bowl with garlic. Tear greens into bowl. Add almonds, cauliflower, avocados and tomatoes. Toss with Dressing just before serving.

Approx Per Serving: Cal 221; Prot 4.9 g; T Fat 19.3 g; Chol 0.0 mg;
   Carbo 11.3 g; Sod 301.0 mg; Potas 847.0 mg.

DRESSING

1 clove of garlic
1 teaspoon salt
2 tablespoons fresh lemon
   juice
1/4 teaspoon sugar

1/4 teaspoon pepper
1/2 teaspoon celery seed
1/2 teaspoon paprika
3/4 teaspoon dry mustard
1/3 cup oil

Mash garlic with salt. Combine with lemon juice and remaining ingredients in covered jar; shake vigorously. Chill until serving time.

Joan M. Gehee
Emily Griffith Opportunity School
Denver, Colorado

JULIA'S ASPARAGUS DRESSING

Yields: 24 tablespoons   *Pan Size: small bowl*

1 16-ounce can cut asparagus
4 green onions, minced
1/2 cup mayonnaise

1/4 cup lemon juice
1/2 teaspoon salt
Pepper to taste

Drain asparagus, reserving 3 tablespoons juice. Mash asparagus with green onions in bowl. Add remaining ingredients; mix well. Chill until serving time. Serve dressing over favorite green salad.

Approx Per Tablespoon: Cal 37; Prot 0.5 g; T Fat 3.8 g; Chol 2.7 mg;
   Carbo 1.1 g; Sod 115.0 mg; Potas 46.7 mg.

Julia Jenkins
Little Rock, Arkansas

Artist: *Rod Farley*—Putnam County Vo Tech; Lynne McNiel, Teacher;
         Eleanor, West Virginia
Artist: *Shannon Allison*—Lawrence County AVTS; Gerald Zona, Teacher;
         New Castle, Pennsylvania

MAIN
DISHES

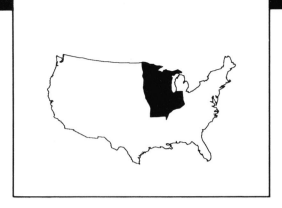

Hearty Midwestern Supper
Region III

Ham and Sauerkraut Balls
page 19

Lettuce Wedges with Favorite Dressing

Minnesota Stew with Biscuits
page 62

or

Barbecued Steak with Onion Pull-Aparts
page 57 and page 134

Chocolate Pecan Caramel Torte
page 167

or

Fruit Pizza
page 169

BARBECUED BRISKET

Yields: 16 servings   *Pan Size: 9x13 inch*   *Preheat: 275 degrees*

1 4-pound beef brisket	5 tablespoons Worcestershire
Liquid smoke	sauce
1/4 teaspoon celery salt	1 cup packed brown sugar
1/4 teaspoon onion salt	2 tablespoons margarine
1/4 teaspoon garlic salt	1 tablespoon mustard
1 32-ounce bottle of catsup	Dash of hot sauce

Place brisket in glass baking dish. Add 2/3 bottle of liquid smoke. Sprinkle with celery salt, onion salt and garlic salt. Marinate, tightly covered, in refrigerator overnight. Bake, covered, in marinade for 5 hours. Combine catsup, 5 to 6 tablespoons liquid smoke, Worcestershire sauce, brown sugar, margarine, mustard and hot sauce in saucepan. Heat until smooth, stirring constantly. Pour juices from baking pan, leaving just enough to cover bottom of pan. Cut brisket into thin slices. Return to pan. Pour barbecue sauce over top. Bake for 30 minutes longer. Serve on homemade bread as sandwiches. Do not use corned beef brisket.

Approx Per Serving: Cal 436; Prot 36.4 g; T Fat 19.0 g; Chol 120.0 mg;
Carbo 28.5 g; Sod 852.0 mg; Potas 590.0 mg.

Cindy Olson
Clatonia, Nebraska

BARBECUED STEAK

Yields: 8 servings   *Pan Size: roaster*   *Preheat: 325 degrees*

4 pounds round steak	1 1/2 tablespoons
1 cup catsup	Worcestershire sauce
1/4 cup vinegar	2 tablespoons brown sugar
1/4 cup chopped onion	1/2 cup water
1/4 cup chopped green bell	1/2 teaspoon salt
pepper	1/8 teaspoon pepper
1 tablespoon mustard	

Cut steak into serving-sized pieces. Place in large roasting pan. Combine catsup, vinegar, onion, green pepper, mustard, Worcestershire sauce, brown sugar, water, salt and pepper in saucepan. Bring to a boil; reduce heat. Simmer for 5 minutes. Pour over steak. Bake for 2 hours.

Approx Per Serving: Cal 594; Prot 73.5 g; T Fat 22.2 g; Chol 216.0 mg;
Carbo 21.1 g; Sod 1074.0 mg; Potas 1219.0 mg.

Sara Jo Robinson
Indianapolis, Indiana

BEEF FILETS WELLINGTON WITH GOLDEN TARRAGON SAUCE

Yields: 8 servings *Pan Size: shallow* *Preheat: 450 degrees*

8 5-ounce beef filets
2 tablespoons oil
1 pound ground sirloin
1/2 teaspoon salt
Pepper to taste

1 clove of garlic, crushed
1 tablespoon chopped parsley
9 frozen puff pastry shells,
  thawed
1 egg white, slightly beaten

Chill filets in freezer for 20 minutes. Brush with oil. Sprinkle with salt and pepper to taste. Sear in skillet over high heat for 5 minutes on each side. Chill in refrigerator. Combine ground sirloin with 1/2 teaspoon salt, pepper, garlic and parsley in bowl. Spoon onto tops of filets. Return to refrigerator. Roll 8 pastry shells to 5x9-inch rectangles on lightly floured surface. Invert 1 filet onto each rectangle. Fold sides over filet. Place seam side down in baking pan. Roll remaining pastry shell on floured surface. Cut out designs as desired. Place on pastry bundles. Chill until time to bake. Brush with egg white. Bake for 10 minutes for rare, 12 minutes for medium-rare and 15 minutes for medium. Serve with Golden Tarragon Sauce. This recipe cannot be frozen.

Approx Per Serving: Cal 731; Prot 60.7 g; T Fat 39.1 g; Chol 176.0 mg;
    Carbo 30.5 g; Sod 774.0 mg; Potas 873.0 mg.

Golden Tarragon Sauce

Yields: 8 servings *Pan Size: 1/2 quart*

3 egg yolks
1/2 cup melted butter
2 tablespoons lemon juice
2 tablespoons hot water

1/4 teaspoon salt
Chopped parsley to taste
1/8 teaspoon tarragon

Beat egg yolks with wire whisk in double boiler until smooth but not fluffy. Add butter, lemon juice, hot water and salt. Place over hot water. Cook until sauce begins to thicken, beating constantly. Stir in parsley and tarragon. Add ice cube if sauce begins to separate, stirring until smooth again; remove unmelted ice cube.

Approx Per Serving: Cal 126; Prot 1.2 g; T Fat 13.6 g; Chol 133.0 mg;
    Carbo 0.4 g; Sod 166.0 mg; Potas 14.8 mg.

Cynthia Lyon
AVA Vice President, Region II
Alpharetta, Georgia

SOUR CREAM STEAK

Yields: 4 servings   *Pan Size: electric skillet*

1/4 cup flour
Garlic powder to taste
1 pound beef steak
3 tablespoons oil
3/4 cup chopped onion
1 cup beef broth
1/2 teaspoon thyme

1 8-ounce can sliced
  mushrooms
1 10-ounce package frozen
  peas
1/2 cup sour cream
3 cups hot cooked rice

Season flour with salt, pepper and garlic powder to taste. Cut steak into serving pieces. Roll in flour mixture to coat. Brown on both sides in oil in skillet. Add onion, broth, thyme and mushroom liquid. Simmer, covered, for 20 minutes. Add mushrooms and peas. Simmer, covered, for 8 minutes. Stir in sour cream. Heat just to serving temperature. Serve over rice.

Approx Per Serving: Cal 633; Prot 41.7 g; T Fat 26.2 g; Chol 106.0 mg;
    Carbo 55.9 g; Sod 529.0 mg; Potas 869.0 mg.

Suanne Knopf
AVA Cookbook Committee
Gainesville, Florida

FAJITAS CON AVOCADO

Yields: 6 servings   *Pan Size: 10 inch skillet*

3 tablespoons corn oil
1/4 cup Tequila
2 tablespoons fresh lime juice
1 clove of garlic, minced
1 1/2 teaspoons onion salt
1 1/2 teaspoons oregano
1/2 teaspoon chili powder
1/2 teaspoon paprika
1/2 teaspoon pepper
1 pound beef skirt steak, cut
  into strips

1/2 cup chopped fresh cilantro
1/2 cup chopped onion
1/2 cup chopped seeded tomato
1/2 cup sliced green onions
3 tablespoons corn oil
6 8-inch flour tortillas,
  warmed
1/2 cup salsa
2 medium avocados, sliced

Combine 3 tablespoons oil, Tequila, lime juice, garlic, onion salt, oregano, chili powder, paprika and pepper in bowl; mix well. Add beef, cilantro, onion and tomato. Marinate for several hours. Drain. Stir-fry beef and green onions in 3 tablespoons oil in skillet for 5 minutes. Spoon into tortillas. Add salsa and avocados.

Nutritional information not available.

Barbara Kline Taylor, Executive Director
New Mexico Vocational Association
Silver City, New Mexico

ITALIAN BEEF

Yields: 18 servings   *Pan Size: Crock•Pot*

1 5-pound beef rump roast
¼ cup pickling spices
4 cups water
1 clove of garlic, minced
2 tablespoons savory

1 teaspoon salt
1 teaspoon pepper
1 envelope dry Italian salad
   dressing mix

Brown roast on all sides in skillet. Place in Crock•Pot. Tie pickling spices in cheesecloth bag. Add spice bag, water, garlic, savory, salt, pepper and dry salad dressing mix to Crock•Pot. Cook for 5 to 6 hours or until tender. Let stand for 20 minutes. Slice thinly. Serve on Italian or hard rolls. May bake in oven at 350 degrees for 3 hours if preferred.

Approx Per Serving: Cal 304; Prot 34.1 g; T Fat 17.8 g; Chol 91.9 mg;
      Carbo 0.1 g; Sod 193.0 mg; Potas 457.0 mg.
      Nutritional information does not include salad dressing mix.

Margaret Bankey
Bowling Green, Ohio

BEEF STROGANOFF

Yields: 6 servings   *Pan Size: electric skillet*   *Preheat: 350 degrees*

2 pounds round steak or
   sirloin steak
2 4-ounce cans mushroom
   pieces
1 large onion, sliced
1 teaspoon garlic salt
2 teaspoons oil
1½ cups sour cream

½ 8-ounce can tomato sauce
2 beef bouillon cubes
1 cup hot water
1 tablespoon Worcestershire
   sauce
1 teaspoon salt
⅛ teaspoon pepper
½ cup Sherry

Cut beef into strips or 1-inch cubes. Drain 1 can mushrooms. Sauté onion with garlic salt in 2 teaspoons oil in electric skillet; remove with slotted spoon. Add beef to skillet. Cook until brown. Return onions to skillet. Add drained and undrained mushrooms, sour cream, tomato sauce, beef bouillon cubes dissolved in hot water, Worcestershire sauce, salt and pepper; mix well. Simmer for 2 hours or until beef is tender. Add Sherry just before serving. Serve over wide egg noodles with a green salad and fruit for dessert. May make ahead and reheat to serve.

Approx Per Serving: Cal 575; Prot 48.1 g; T Fat 36.2 g; Chol 170.0 mg;
      Carbo 6.9 g; Sod 981.0 mg; Potas 771.0 mg.

Mary Anne Sagraves
New Britain, Connecticut

COWBOY STEW

Yields: 6 servings   *Pan Size: stockpot*

1 pound stew beef
1 envelope meat marinade
  mix, prepared
2 beef bouillon cubes
2 tablespoons steak sauce
1 large smoked sausage, cut
  into 1-inch pieces
1 29-ounce can whole tomatoes
1/4 teaspoon garlic powder
4 large potatoes, cut into
  quarters
6 carrots, cut into 1-inch pieces

1 large onion, cut into quarters
1 large green bell pepper,
  sliced into 1-inch strips
1 12-ounce can button
  mushrooms
1 16-ounce can whole green
  beans, drained
1 pound smoked ham, cut into
  1-inch pieces
1 12-ounce can beer
1 pound egg noodles

Combine stew beef, meat marinade mix, bouillon cubes and steak sauce in saucepan. Simmer for 2 to 3 hours or until beef is tender. Add sausage, tomatoes and garlic powder. Simmer for 2 hours. Add vegetables and ham. Cook for 1 hour. Stir in beer, noodles and salt to taste. Simmer for 30 minutes. Refrigerate overnight. Reheat over low heat at serving time.

Nutritional information not available.

Marlene Free
Alexandria, Virginia

JANUARY STEW

Yields: 8 servings   *Pan Size: heavy 4 quart*

2 pounds stew beef
Leaves of 2 stalks celery
4 cups water
1 medium onion, chopped
1 cup sauerkraut
2 tablespoons butter

1 teaspoon brown sugar
Nutmeg to taste
4 medium carrots, chopped
3 medium potatoes, chopped
2 stalks celery, chopped

Cook stew beef and celery leaves in water in saucepan until beef is tender; drain. Sauté onion and sauerkraut in butter in heavy saucepan until onion is transparent. Add brown sugar and nutmeg, stirring until brown sugar is melted. Return beef to saucepan. Bring to a boil. Add carrots, potatoes and celery. Season with salt and pepper to taste. Simmer for 2 hours or longer.

Approx Per Serving: Cal 529; Prot 30.5 g; T Fat 37.6 g; Chol 124.0 mg;
      Carbo 16.3 g; Sod 314.0 mg; Potas 625.0 mg.

Birdie H. Holder
Lincoln, Nebraska

MINNESOTA STEW with Biscuit Topping

Yields: 6 servings   *Pan Size: 9x13 inch*   *Preheat: 450 degrees*

2 pounds boneless stew beef	1/4 teaspoon pepper
2 tablespoons shortening	1 cup chopped celery
1 onion, chopped	3 cups chopped potatoes
2 teaspoons sugar	1/2 cup chopped carrots
3 1/2 cups water	1/2 cup peas
2 teaspoons Worcestershire	1/4 cup flour
sauce	1/2 cup cold water
1 bay leaf	Kitchen Bouquet to taste
1/2 teaspoon paprika	2 cups buttermilk baking mix
1 tablespoon salt	2/3 cup milk

Brown stew beef in shortening in heavy saucepan. Add onion, sugar, 3 1/2 cups water, Worcestershire sauce, bay leaf, paprika, salt and pepper. Simmer, covered, for 1 1/2 hours. Remove bay leaf. Add celery, potatoes, carrots and peas. Simmer until tender. Strain mixture, reserving liquid. Place beef and vegetable mixture in baking dish. Blend flour and 1/2 cup water in saucepan. Add reserved cooking liquid. Cook until thickened, stirring constantly. Stir in Kitchen Bouquet. Pour over beef mixture. Bake until bubbly. Combine baking mix and milk in bowl; mix to form dough. Roll on floured surface. Cut with biscuit cutter. Place on stew. Bake for 10 minutes longer or until golden brown.

Approx Per Serving: Cal 963; Prot 46.0 g; T Fat 57.6 g; Chol 158.0 mg;
    Carbo 63.1 g; Sod 1748.0 mg; Potas 999.0 mg.

Charlotte Christensen
Moorhead, Minnesota

CORNED BEEF CASSEROLE

Yields: 6 servings   *Pan Size: 2 1/2 quart*   *Preheat: 350 degrees*

2 12-ounce cans corned beef	9 ounces noodles, cooked,
8 ounces Velveeta cheese	drained
2 cans cream of chicken soup	1 cup bread crumbs
2 cups milk	1/4 cup melted butter
1/3 cup chopped onion	

Cut corned beef and cheese into cubes. Combine with soup, milk, onion and noodles in bowl; mix well. Spoon into lightly greased baking dish. Sprinkle with mixture of bread crumbs and butter. Bake for 30 minutes. This can be frozen before or after baking.

Approx Per Serving: Cal 811; Prot 50.4 g; T Fat 45.5 g; Chol 173.0 mg;
    Carbo 47.7 g; Sod 2562.0 mg; Potas 508.0 mg.

Margo DeLucca
Millersville, Pennsylvania

BARBECUED MEATBALLS and Sauce

Yields: 12 servings *Pan Size: two 9x11 inch* *Preheat: 350 degrees*

3 pounds ground beef
1   12-ounce can evaporated
   milk
2 cups oats
2 eggs
1 cup chopped onion
3/4 teaspoon garlic salt
2 tablespoons chili powder

1 teaspoon salt
1/2 teaspoon pepper
2 cups catsup
1 1/2 cups packed brown sugar
2 tablespoons liquid smoke
1/2 teaspoon garlic salt
1/2 cup chopped onion

Combine ground beef, evaporated milk, oats, eggs, 1 cup onion, 3/4 teaspoon garlic salt, chili powder, salt and pepper in bowl; mix well. Shape by 1/4 cupfuls into balls. Place in baking dishes. Combine catsup, brown sugar, liquid smoke, 1/2 teaspoon garlic salt and 1/2 cup onion in bowl; mix well. Pour over meatballs. Bake for 1 hour, basting twice. Meatballs can be frozen without sauce.

Approx Per Serving: Cal 592; Prot 33.0 g; T Fat 28.2 g; Chol 155.0 mg;
   Carbo 52.1 g; Sod 1034.0 mg; Potas 791.0 mg.

Bonnie Sibert
Nebraska Dept. of Education
Lincoln, Nebraska

BARBECUED SAUERKRAUT

Yields: 10 servings *Pan Size: 2 quart* *Preheat: 350 degrees*

1 pound ground beef
1 tablespoon dried onion
   flakes
2 cups (about) tomato juice

1   16-ounce can sauerkraut,
   drained
1 cup packed brown sugar

Brown ground beef with onion flakes in skillet, stirring until crumbly. Combine with remaining ingredients in bowl; mix well. Spoon into baking dish. Bake for 1 hour. This easy recipe can be made ahead and freezes well.

Approx Per Serving: Cal 231; Prot 11.5 g; T Fat 9.6 g; Chol 40.6 mg;
   Carbo 25.5 g; Sod 523.0 mg; Potas 398.0 mg.

Don Bright, AVA President 1989-1990
AVA Building Fund Committee
Bowling Green, Ohio

WYOMING FIFTY-DOLLAR HAMBURGER

Yields: 6 servings   *Pan Size: 2 quart*

1 pound ground beef
1/3 cup ground onion
1 can chicken gumbo soup
2 tablespoons mustard

2 tablespoons catsup
1 teaspoon Worcestershire
sauce

Brown ground beef with onion in saucepan, stirring until ground beef is crumbly; drain. Add remaining ingredients; mix well. Simmer for 1 to 1½ hours. Serve in hamburger buns.

Approx Per Serving: Cal 242; Prot 18.8 g; T Fat 16.4 g; Chol 68.6 mg;
Carbo 4.2 g; Sod 380.0 mg; Potas 283.0 mg.
Nutritional information does not include hamburger buns.

Ellie Noonan
Rawlins High School
Rawlins, Wyoming

Jeff Goughler

PITA BURGERS

Yields: 6 servings   *Pan Size: 10 inch skillet*

1/2 cup chopped onion
1/2 cup chopped celery
1 tablespoon oil
1 pound ground beef
1 medium red Delicious
 apple, chopped

1/4 cup dark raisins
1 teaspoon curry powder
 (optional)
1 teaspoon salt
6 small pita rounds
8 ounces plain yogurt

Sauté onion and celery in oil in skillet. Add ground beef. Cook until crumbly but still barely pink, stirring constantly; drain. Stir in apple, raisins, curry powder and salt. Simmer for several minutes or just until apple is tender-crisp. Cut 1-inch slice from top of pita rounds. Spoon filling into rounds. Top with yogurt. This easy filling can be made ahead. Ground turkey can be substituted for beef.

Approx Per Serving: Cal 473; Prot 26.3 g; T Fat 19.1 g; Chol 69.9 mg;
    Carbo 36.0 g; Sod 567.0 mg; Potas 460.0 mg.

Tricia Boucher-Wallace
Leominster Trade High School
Fitchburg, Massachusetts

CINCINNATI CHILI

Yields: 6 servings   *Pan Size: 4 quart*

2 pounds lean ground beef
2 large onions, chopped
1 clove of garlic, minced
35 whole allspice
4 large red peppers
5 bay leaves
2 quarts water
1 7-ounce can tomato paste

1 1/2 tablespoons vinegar
1 teaspoon cinnamon
1 teaspoon cumin
1 tablespoon chili powder
1 teaspoon red pepper
1 1/2 tablespoons salt
1 teaspoon pepper

Brown ground beef with onions and garlic in saucepan, stirring until crumbly; drain. Tie allspice, red peppers and bay leaves in cheesecloth bag. Add spice bag and remaining ingredients to saucepan; mix well. Simmer for 3 to 4 hours or to desired consistency. Remove spice bag. May serve over spaghetti with shredded sharp cheese and chopped onions if desired.

Approx Per Serving: Cal 469.0; Prot 39.8 g; T Fat 29.3 g; Chol 132.0 mg;
    Carbo 13.1 g; Sod 1752.0 mg; Potas 948.0 mg.

Rosemary Kolde
AVA President 1985-1986
AVA Cookbook Committee
Cincinnati, Ohio

GORDO'S INDUSTRIAL STRENGTH VOC ED CHILI

Yields: 8 servings   *Pan Size: stockpot*

2 large onions, chopped
2 large green bell peppers,
  chopped
1/4 cup chopped celery
2 tablespoons minced garlic
1 tablespoon oil
3 16-ounce cans pinto beans
3 15-ounce cans tomato sauce
1 pound ground beef
1 pound ground pork
1 pound flank steak or round
  steak, chopped

1 tablespoon oil
3 jalapeño peppers, chopped
5 tablespoons chili pepper
1 teaspoon each cumin and
  oregano
2 tablespoons salt
1 teaspoon each pepper, red
  pepper and white pepper
2 tablespoons masa flour
1 teaspoon instant coffee
  powder

Sauté onions, green peppers, celery and garlic in 1 tablespoon oil in skillet. Set aside. Drain beans, reserving liquid. Combine reserved liquid and tomato sauce in saucepan; mix well. Simmer over low heat, stirring occasionally. Brown ground beef, ground pork and steak in 1 tablespoon oil in stockpot, stirring constantly; drain. Add sautéed vegetables and tomato sauce mixture. Stir in jalapeño peppers and seasonings. Simmer, covered, for 1 hour. Blend masa flour with enough water to form a paste. Stir into meat mixture. Add beans; mix well. Skim grease. Simmer for 20 minutes, stirring occasionally. Stir in coffee powder. Simmer for 10 minutes longer. Serve with shredded cheese and chopped onions.

Approx Per Serving: Cal 817; Prot 64.2 g; T Fat 34.7 g; Chol 159.0 mg;
  Carbo 63.0 g; Sod 2740.0 mg; Potas 2098.0 mg.

Gordon Raley
AVA Assistant Executive Director of Government Relations
Alexandria, Virginia

CARLA'S MEAT LOAF

Yields: 8 servings   *Pan Size: 4x8 inch*   *Preheat: 350 degrees*

1 1/2 pounds ground beef
1/4 cup chopped onion
1/4 cup chopped green bell
  pepper

2 eggs, slightly beaten
1/2 cup oats
1/4 cup Worcestershire sauce

Combine ground beef, onion, green pepper, eggs, oats and Worcestershire sauce in bowl; mix well. Pack into loaf pan. Bake for 1 hour.

Approx Per Serving: Cal 293; Prot 22.6 g; T Fat 19.6 g; Chol 145.0 mg;
  Carbo 5.4 g; Sod 161.0 mg; Potas 356.0 mg.

Carla King
Owensboro, Kentucky

MEAT LOAF

Yields: 10 servings   Pan Size: 9x11 inch   Preheat: 350 degrees

2 pounds ground beef
2 eggs
1 medium onion, minced
1/2 cup chopped celery
3/4 cup chili sauce
24 crackers, crushed

1 tablespoon finely chopped
  parsley
1 teaspoon salt
1/4 teaspoon pepper
3 slices bacon
1/4 cup chili sauce

Combine ground beef, eggs, onion, celery, 3/4 cup chili sauce, cracker crumbs, parsley, salt and pepper in bowl; mix well. Shape into loaf in greased baking dish. Top with bacon slices. Spread with 1/4 cup chili sauce. Bake for 1 1/2 hours.

Approx Per Serving: Cal 356; Prot 24.5 g; T Fat 23.5 g; Chol 138.0 mg;
  Carbo 12.8 g; Sod 775.0 mg; Potas 429.0 mg.

Dr. Martin W. Essex, Exec. Dir. Emeritus
Ohio Council on Voc Education
Columbus, Ohio

BAKED LASAGNA SUPREME

Yields: 8 servings   Pan Size: 3 quart   Preheat: 350 degrees

1 pound ground beef
1 large onion, chopped
1 clove of garlic, minced
1/2 cup olive oil
1 29-ounce can tomatoes
1 6-ounce can tomato paste
1 tablespoon chopped parsley
2 bay leaves
1 teaspoon sweet basil

1/4 teaspoon crushed red
  pepper
1 16-ounce package lasagna
  noodles
2 cups shredded mozzarella
  cheese
8 ounces ricotta cheese
4 ounces Parmesan cheese

Brown ground beef with onion and garlic in olive oil in skillet, stirring until crumbly; drain. Combine tomatoes, tomato paste, parsley, bay leaves, basil and red pepper in heavy saucepan. Simmer for several minutes. Add beef mixture. Simmer for 3 hours. Remove bay leaves. Cook noodles according to package directions; drain. Alternate layers of meat sauce, noodles, mozzarella cheese, ricotta cheese and Parmesan cheese in baking dish until all ingredients are used, ending with noodles and meat sauce. Bake for 30 minutes. May substitute cottage cheese for ricotta if preferred.

Approx Per Serving: Cal 731; Prot 37.0 g; T Fat 40.2 g; Chol 97.9 mg;
  Carbo 54.7 g; Sod 622.0 mg; Potas 813.0 mg.

The Honorable Gerald L. Baliles
Governor of Virginia
Richmond, Virginia

MEATSEE PIE

Yields: 6 servings   *Pan Size: baking sheet*   *Preheat: 350 degrees*

1¹/₂ **pounds ground beef**	¹/₄ **teaspoon oregano**
¹/₄ **cup dry bread crumbs**	**Minced garlic to taste**
¹/₂ **cup chopped onion**	**1 teaspoon salt**
1 egg, beaten	**1 can tomato soup**

Combine ground beef, bread crumbs, onion, egg, oregano, garlic, salt and ¹/₄ cup tomato soup in bowl; mix well. Pat into 10-inch circle on foil-lined baking sheet, shaping 1-inch rim. Spread with remaining soup. Top with favorite pizza toppings. Bake for 20 minutes, draining grease if necessary during cooking time. Cut into wedges to serve.

Approx Per Serving: Cal 382; Prot 28.8 g; T Fat 25.5 g; Chol 147.0 mg;
     Carbo 8.2 g; Sod 798.0 mg; Potas 464.0 mg.
     Nutritional information does not include pizza toppings.

Kathy White
Indianapolis, Indiana

SPAGHETTI PIE

Yields: 10 servings   *Pan Size: 9x13 inch*   *Preheat: 350 degrees*

8 ounces spaghetti	**1 16-ounce jar thick spaghetti**
2 tablespoons butter	**sauce**
¹/₃ **cup Parmesan cheese**	**1 teaspoon sugar**
1 egg, beaten	¹/₂ **teaspoon oregano**
¹/₂ **teaspoon salt**	1¹/₂ **teaspoon garlic salt**
¹/₄ **teaspoon pepper**	**16 ounces cottage cheese**
1¹/₂ **pounds ground beef**	**6 ounces mozzarella cheese,**
1 medium onion, chopped	**shredded**
2 tablespoons oil	

Break spaghetti into 2-inch pieces. Cook according to package directions; drain. Add butter, Parmesan cheese, egg, salt and pepper; mix well. Spoon into baking dish. Brown ground beef and onion in oil in skillet, stirring until ground beef is crumbly; drain. Add spaghetti sauce, sugar, oregano and garlic salt. Layer cottage cheese and meat sauce over spaghetti. Bake for 30 minutes. Top with mozzarella cheese. Bake for 10 minutes longer.

Approx Per Serving: Cal 510; Prot 31.1 g; T Fat 28.5 g; Chol 116.0 mg;
     Carbo 30.7 g; Sod 1032.0 mg; Potas 492.0 mg.

*Niel and Carol Edmunds
*AVA President 1988-1989
Columbia, Missouri

TACOS BY RODGER

Yields: 4 servings   *Pan Size: large griddle*   *Preheat: 325 degrees*

1 pound lean ground beef
1 large onion, chopped
1   29-ounce can tomato sauce
Tabasco sauce to taste
1 cup flour
1 cup cornmeal
5 tablespoons cornstarch
1 teaspoon salt
2 eggs

2 cups milk
¼ cup oil
1 head lettuce, chopped
2 large tomatoes, chopped
1 green bell pepper, chopped
1 large onion, chopped
2 pounds sharp Cheddar
   cheese, shredded

Brown ground beef with 1 onion in saucepan, stirring until ground beef is crumbly; drain. Add tomato sauce and season to taste with Tabasco, salt and pepper. Simmer for 2 to 3 hours or cook in Crock•Pot overnight. Combine flour, cornmeal, cornstarch and 1 teaspoon salt in bowl. Add eggs, milk and oil; mix well. Heat oiled griddle to 325 degrees. Spoon ½ cup batter at a time onto griddle, spreading evenly from inside to outside. Bake until slightly dry on top. Turn with spatula. Bake quickly on second side. Remove to serving plates. Spoon meat sauce into middle of taco shells. Top with chopped vegetables, cheese and Tabasco sauce. Fold taco over. Note: Tacos by Rodger have been demonstrated several times on television and were recently served at several AVA Building Fund Raisers.

Approx Per Serving: Cal 1872; Prot 102.0 g; T Fat 121.0 g; Chol 494.0 mg;
     Carbo 95.4 g; Sod 3380.0 mg; Potas 2063.0 mg.

Rodger E. Palmer
Duluth, Minnesota

Jeff Goughler

SOPA DE FIDEO

Yields: 6 servings   *Pan Size: large skillet*

1 pound ground beef	1 16-ounce can tomatoes
1 small onion, chopped	1 teaspoon chili powder
6 ounces vermicelli	1 cup water
1 17-ounce can corn	6 slices American cheese

Brown ground beef with onion and salt and pepper to taste in skillet, stirring until ground beef is crumbly. Break vermicelli into skillet. Cook until slightly browned. Add undrained corn and tomatoes, chili powder and water; mix well. Simmer, covered, for 10 minutes, stirring occasionally. Top with cheese slices. Let stand, covered, until cheese is partially melted. Cut into squares to serve.

Approx Per Serving: Cal 496; Prot 30.0 g; T Fat 25.6 g; Chol 94.5 mg;
    Carbo 37.7 g; Sod 799.0 mg; Potas 637.0 mg.

Joanne Whelchel
Dodge City, Kansas

VERY EASY STUFFED CABBAGE

Yields: 6 servings   *Pan Size: large saucepan*

1 head cabbage	2 small cans Arturo sauce
1¹/₂ pounds ground beef	2 cans whole cranberry sauce

Place cabbage in freezer overnight. Hold cabbage under running water, removing leaves as they thaw. Brown ground beef in skillet, stirring until crumbly; drain. Place 1 heaping tablespoonful ground beef on each cabbage leaf. Roll cabbage leaf to enclose filling; secure with toothpick. Spread Arturo sauce and cranberry sauce in large saucepan. Place cabbage rolls over sauces. Simmer for 2¹/₂ hours. May bake stuffed cabbage at 350 degrees for 1 hour if preferred.

Nutritional information not available.

Dorothy Posner
Springfield, Massachusetts

BAKED PORK CHOPS AND RICE

Yields: 4 servings   *Pan Size: 9x13 inch*   *Preheat: 350 degrees*

4 pork chops
2 tablespoons shortening
1/4 teaspoon salt
1/8 teaspoon pepper
2/3 cup uncooked rice
3 1/2 cups boiling water

1/2 cup chopped green bell
  pepper
1/2 cup chopped onion
1 teaspoon minced parsley
Chili powder to taste
2 teaspoons salt

Brown pork chops on both sides in shortening in skillet. Sprinkle with 1/4 teaspoon salt and pepper. Remove to baking dish. Drain most of the drippings from skillet. Sauté rice in drippings in skillet. Add water, green pepper, onion, parsley, chili powder and 2 teaspoons salt. Cook for 15 minutes or until rice is tender. Spoon over browned pork chops. Bake, covered, for 1 hour.

Approx Per Serving: Cal 438; Prot 21.7 g; T Fat 26.4 g; Chol 73.0 mg;
    Carbo 26.7 g; Sod 1248.0 mg; Potas 330.0 mg.

Teresa Paige
St. Petersburg, Florida

FRENCH ONION PORK CHOPS AND RICE

Yields: 4 servings   *Pan Size: electric skillet*   *Preheat: 350 degrees*

4 large pork chops
1/2 cup flour
1/4 teaspoon salt
Pepper to taste
1/4 cup corn oil

2 cans French onion soup
1/2 cup water
1/4 teaspoon celery seed
1 cup instant rice

Coat pork chops with a mixture of flour, salt and pepper. Heat oil to 350 degrees in electric skillet. Brown pork chops on both sides in oil; drain skillet. Add soup. Rinse soup cans with 1/2 cup water. Add to skillet. Sprinkle with celery seed. Bring to a boil; reduce heat. Simmer for 3 to 4 hours or until pork chops are tender. Remove to serving plate; keep warm. Bring mixture in skillet to a boil. Stir in rice. Turn off skillet. Let stand, covered, for 5 minutes; fluff with fork. May sauté pork chops in skillet and then cook in Crock•Pot if preferred.

Approx Per Serving: Cal 593; Prot 27.1 g; T Fat 35.6 g; Chol 73.0 mg;
    Carbo 40.9 g; Sod 1399.0 mg; Potas 382.0 mg.

Judith A. Perryman
Department of Elementary and Secondary Ed.
Jefferson City, Missouri

PORK CHOP MARINADE

Yields: 6 servings   *Pan Size: broiler pan*   *Preheat: broiler*

3 slices bacon	2 tablespoons honey
1 cup chopped onion	1 tablespoon curry powder
2 cloves of garlic, minced	2 tablespoons chili powder
1/2 cup soy sauce	2 tablespoons rum
1/3 cup lemon juice	6 1¼-inch thick pork chops

Fry bacon in skillet; drain and crumble. Sauté onion and garlic in drippings. Stir in soy sauce, lemon juice, honey, curry powder and chili powder. Simmer for 2 minutes. Add rum. Let stand for 2 hours. Pour over chops in shallow dish. Marinate in refrigerator for 3 hours to overnight. Drain, reserving marinade. Place chops on rack in broiler pan. Broil 4 inches from heat source for 10 to 15 minutes on each side, brushing frequently with marinade. Serve with heated marinade. Top with bacon.

Approx Per Serving: Cal 348; Prot 22.4 g; T Fat 22.0 g; Chol 75.7 mg;
    Carbo 13.3 g; Sod 1496.0 mg; Potas 433.0 mg.

Betty Stanley
Bryan, Ohio

GREEN CHILI FOR SMOTHERED BURRITOS

Yields: 10 servings   *Pan Size: large saucepan*

2 pounds pork cubes	1 4-ounce can whole green
1 tablespoon oil	chilies, cut into strips
1 teaspoon garlic salt	2 quarts water
1 teaspoon salt	2 tablespoons cornstarch
Pepper to taste	1 16-ounce can refried beans
1 small onion, chopped	10 flour tortillas
1 hot chili pepper, crushed	1 cup shredded Cheddar
1 28-ounce can tomatoes	cheese

Brown pork in oil in large saucepan. Sprinkle with seasonings. Add onion and hot chili pepper. Sauté for 4 to 5 minutes. Purée undrained tomatoes in blender container. Add tomato purée, green chilies and water to saucepan. Simmer for 2 to 3 hours, adding water if necessary. Stir in mixture of cornstarch and a small amount of water. Cook until thickened, stirring constantly. Spread warmed refried beans on tortillas. Sprinkle with cheese. Spoon several pieces of pork onto each tortilla. Roll tortilla to enclose filling. Place on serving plate. Spoon remaining sauce over top.

Approx Per Serving: Cal 258; Prot 10.8 g; T Fat 10.0 g; Chol 18.1 mg;
    Carbo 34.0 g; Sod 964.0 mg; Potas 464.0 mg.

Joan M. Gehee
Emily Griffith Opportunity School
Denver, Colorado

HAM CASSEROLE

Yields: 8 servings   *Pan Size: 2 quart*   *Preheat: 325 degrees*

1/2 cup milk	1 teaspoon green onion flakes
1 can mushroom soup	4 ounces noodles
1 cup sour cream	2 cups chopped cooked ham
2 teaspoons prepared mustard	1/4 cup slivered almonds

Combine milk, soup, sour cream, mustard, green onion flakes and salt in bowl; mix well. Cook noodles according to package directions. Layer noodles, ham and sour cream mixture 1/2 at a time in baking dish. Top with almonds. Bake for 30 minutes.

Approx Per Serving: Cal 185; Prot 11.1 g; T Fat 8.8 g; Chol 17.3 mg; Carbo 15.3 g; Sod 685.0 mg; Potas 235.0 mg.

Elizabeth H. Mettling
Lewis, Kansas

DONNA'S HAM CASSEROLE

Yields: 10 servings   *Pan Size: 1 1/2 quart*   *Preheat: 350 degrees*

4 ounces noodles	2 cups sour cream
1 teaspoon oil	1/2 cup cornflake crumbs
3 cups ground ham	1 tablespoon melted butter

Cook noodles with oil in boiling water in saucepan until tender; drain. Combine with ham and sour cream in bowl; mix gently. Spoon into baking dish. Top with mixture of cornflake crumbs and butter. Place baking dish in larger pan of hot water. Bake for 40 minutes.

Approx Per Serving: Cal 337; Prot 14.1 g; T Fat 25.4 g; Chol 72.1 mg; Carbo 12.7 g; Sod 894.0 mg; Potas 303.0 mg.

Donna Holmquist
University of Nebraska at Omaha
Omaha, Nebraska

HAM LOAF with Mustard Sauce

Yields: 12 servings   *Pan Size: 5x9 inch*   *Preheat: 350 degrees*

2 pounds fresh ham, ground
1 pound smoked ham, ground
1 cup milk
1 teaspoon prepared mustard
3 cups cornflakes
2 teaspoons flour
1/3 cup packed brown sugar

1 tablespoon prepared
  mustard
1/3 cup hot water
1/3 cup vinegar
1 egg, beaten
1 tablespoon butter

Combine fresh ham, smoked ham, milk, 1 teaspoon mustard and cornflakes in large bowl; mix well. Pack into loaf pan. Bake for 1½ hours. Mix flour, brown sugar and 1 tablespoon mustard in double boiler. Stir in hot water and vinegar. Cook until thickened, stirring constantly. Stir a small amount of hot mixture into beaten egg; stir egg into hot mixture. Add butter. Cook until heated through. Invert ham loaf onto serving plate. Serve with hot mustard sauce.

Approx Per Serving: Cal 254; Prot 30.2 g; T Fat 8.5 g; Chol 90.5 mg;
   Carbo 12.6 g; Sod 1633.0 mg; Potas 428.0 mg.

Virginia B. Duell
Ellis, Kansas

HAM LOAVES

Yields: 12 servings   *Pan Size: two 5x9 inch*   *Preheat: 325 degrees*

1½ pounds cured ham, ground
1 pound pork shoulder,
  ground
2 eggs
1/2 cup tomato juice
2/3 cup milk
1 cup cracker crumbs

1/2 teaspoon salt
1/8 teaspoon pepper
1 cup packed brown sugar
1 teaspoon dry mustard
1/3 cup vinegar
1/2 cup water

Combine ham, pork, eggs, tomato juice, milk, cracker crumbs, salt and pepper in bowl; mix well. Shape into loaves in 2 loaf pans. Mix brown sugar, dry mustard, vinegar and water in bowl. Pour over loaves. Bake for 1 hour.

Approx Per Serving: Cal 438; Prot 24.5 g; T Fat 22.3 g; Chol 130.0 mg;
   Carbo 33.1 g; Sod 1092.0 mg; Potas 367.0 mg.

Alice Karen Hite, Executive Director
Ohio Vocational Association
Worthington, Ohio

KIELBASA BOILED DINNER

Yields: 10 servings   *Pan Size: stockpot*

3 pounds carrots, cut into
  2-inch pieces
5 medium onions, sliced
1 pound pork kielbasa, cut
  into 2-inch pieces

1 to 2 teaspoons crushed red
  pepper
10 medium potatoes, chopped
1 medium cabbage, cut into
  quarters

Combine carrots, onions, kielbasa, red pepper and salt and pepper to taste with water to cover in stockpot. Simmer for 1 hour. Add unpeeled potatoes and cabbage. Simmer for 1 hour longer.

Approx Per Serving: Cal 334; Prot 10.5 g; T Fat 12.9 g; Chol 29.7 mg;
  Carbo 45.8 g; Sod 549.0 mg; Potas 1136.0 mg.

Gail Cancelliere
Leominster, Massachusetts

MICROWAVE LASAGNA

Yields: 10 servings   *Pan Size: 9x13 inch*   ≈M≈

1 pound Italian sausage
1 32-ounce jar spaghetti sauce
1 8-ounce jar mushroom pieces
16 ounces ricotta cheese
1 tablespoon chopped parsley

1 egg
8 ounces lasagna noodles
12 ounces mozzarella cheese,
  shredded
1/2 cup Parmesan cheese

Microwave crumbled sausage in glass dish on High for 7 minutes, stirring frequently; drain. Stir in spaghetti sauce and undrained mushrooms. Mix ricotta cheese, parsley and egg in small bowl. Spread 1/2 of the meat sauce in baking dish. Layer 1/2 of the noodles, 1/2 of the ricotta mixture, 1/3 of the mozzarella cheese and 1/2 of the Parmesan cheese in prepared dish. Add remaining noodles, pressing into sauce. Top with remaining ricotta mixture, 1/2 of the remaining mozzarella cheese, remaining Parmesan cheese and remaining meat sauce. Microwave, covered, on High for 15 minutes or on Medium for 30 minutes. Sprinkle with remaining mozzarella cheese. Let stand for 15 to 20 minutes.

Approx Per Serving: Cal 536; Prot 28.0 g; T Fat 30.9 g; Chol 115.0 mg;
  Carbo 35.6 g; Sod 1118.0 mg; Potas 704.0 mg.

Abby Flynn
St. Petersburg, Florida

SAUSAGE AND BEAN POLENTA

Yields: 8 servings　　　*Pan Size: large saucepan*

4 ounces pork sausage
4 ounces ground beef
1 cup chopped onion
1 16-ounce can red kidney
  beans
1 16-ounce can tomatoes
1 8-ounce can tomato sauce
1/2 teaspoon oregano
1/2 teaspoon salt

1/4 teaspoon garlic salt
1/8 teaspoon pepper
3 cups water
1 teaspoon salt
1 cup cornmeal
1 cup cold water
1/4 cup shredded Cheddar
  cheese

Brown sausage and ground beef with onion in saucepan, stirring until meat is crumbly; drain. Add undrained beans, tomatoes, tomato sauce, oregano, 1/2 teaspoon salt, garlic salt and pepper. Simmer for 2 hours or longer. Bring 3 cups water and 1 teaspoon salt to a boil in saucepan. Mix cornmeal and 1 cup cold water in bowl. Add cornmeal mixture to boiling water, stirring constantly. Stir in cheese. Spoon cornmeal mixture onto serving platter, making well in center. Spoon meat into center. Serve with green salad.

Approx Per Serving: Cal 249; Prot 11.3 g; T Fat 10.5 g; Chol 26.1 mg;
　　Carbo 28.1 g; Sod 1055.0 mg; Potas 501.0 mg.

Ray D. Ryan, Executive Director
Center on Ed. and Training for Employment
Columbus, Ohio

FROGMORE STEW

Yields: 10 servings　　　*Pan Size: 15 gallon*

1 green bell pepper, chopped
2 large onions, chopped
2 lemons, sliced
1/4 cup seafood seasoning
1/4 cup vinegar
8 gallons water

5 pounds Hillshire smoked
  sausage links
5 ears of corn, broken into
  halves
5 pounds peeled shrimp

Bring green pepper, onions, lemons, seafood seasoning, vinegar, water and salt and pepper to taste to a boil in stockpot. Simmer for 30 minutes. Cut sausage into 1 1/2 to 2-inch pieces. Combine with water to cover in saucepan. Cook for 5 minutes. Drain and rinse sausage. Add to stockpot. Simmer for 5 minutes. Stir in corn. Cook for 7 minutes longer. Add shrimp. Cook for 1 minute; do not overcook. Drain and serve immediately with Texas Pete cocktail sauce.

Approx Per Serving: Cal 1164; Prot 97.7 g; T Fat 76.3 g; Chol 498.0 mg;
　　Carbo 16.8 g; Sod 3740.0 mg; Potas 1316.0 mg.

Erwin W. Hooker
Walterboro, South Carolina

VENISON SPECIAL

Yields: 10 servings   *Pan Size: 9x13 inch*   *Preheat: 350 degrees*

1 3-pound venison roast
2 tablespoons steak sauce

1 envelope dry onion soup mix
1 can cream of mushroom soup

Place roast in baking pan lined with foil extending over edges of pan. Top with steak sauce, dry soup mix and mushroom soup. Bring up edges of foil; seal tightly. Bake for 2 hours for rare or for 3 hours for well done. Serve thinly sliced with pan juices. May substitute antelope roast for venison.

Approx Per Serving: Cal 233; Prot 40.8 g; T Fat 5.2 g; Chol 88.8 mg;
    Carbo 3.0 g; Sod 387.0 mg; Potas 481.0 mg.

Billie Lou Arnott
Utica, Montana

VERMONT VENISON MARINADE

Yields: 2 servings   *Pan Size: 12 inch*

2 8-ounce venison steaks
1/4 cup maple syrup
1/4 cup honey
11/2 cups apple cider vinegar
Onion powder, garlic powder,
    parsley flakes and pepper to
    taste

1 tablespoon soy sauce
2 bay leaves
1 large yellow onion, chopped
1 tablespoon oil
1 can mushroom soup
1/2 cup water

Combine steaks, maple syrup, honey, vinegar, seasonings, soy sauce and bay leaves in airtight container. Marinate for 6 to 12 hours, shaking every hour. Drain, reserving 1/3 of the marinade. Sauté onion and venison in oil in skillet until venison is brown on all sides. Add reserved marinade, soup and water. Simmer for 30 minutes. Remove bay leaves. May substitute beef, pork or chicken breasts for venison if desired.

Approx Per Serving: Cal 818; Prot 70.7 g; T Fat 22.7 g; Chol 149.0 mg;
    Carbo 88.2 g; Sod 1832.0 mg; Potas 1250.0 mg.

Hank Stopinski
Area Vo-Tech Center
Springfield, Vermont

ALASKAN CURRIED MOOSE AND LENTIL STEW

Yields: 6 servings   *Pan Size: 4 quart*

1 cup sliced mushrooms
1½ pounds moose meat, cubed
3 tablespoons curry powder
1 cup lentils

1 cup chopped carrots
2 quarts water
1   14-ounce can stewed
   tomatoes

Sauté mushrooms in large skillet. Add moose meat and curry powder. Cook until browned on all sides, stirring constantly. Bring lentils, carrots and water to a boil in saucepan. Cook for 30 minutes. Stir in meat mixture and tomatoes. Simmer for 30 minutes.

Approx Per Serving: Cal 300; Prot 36.2 g; T Fat 1.6 g; Chol 82.2 mg;
     Carbo 27.4 g; Sod 126.0 mg; Potas 650.0 mg.

Colleen Doherty
Kotzebue Technical Center
Kotzebue, Alaska

VENISON STEW

Yields: 8 servings   *Pan Size: Crock•Pot*

6 slices bacon
3 pounds venison, cubed
2 large carrots, chopped
1 medium onion, chopped
¼ cup margarine
1 can beef broth
1 tablespoon tomato paste
3 tablespoons flour

1 teaspoon minced garlic
1 teaspoon thyme
1½ teaspoons salt
½ teaspoon pepper
1   8-ounce can mushrooms
1 bay leaf
¼ cup red wine

Fry bacon in skillet until crisp. Remove to paper towel to drain. Brown venison in bacon drippings in skillet. Remove to Crock•Pot. Sauté carrots and onions in remaining drippings and margarine in skillet. Add beef broth, tomato paste, flour, garlic, thyme, salt and pepper. Cook until thickened, stirring constantly. Pour into Crock•Pot. Crumble bacon over top. Stir in mushrooms, bay leaf and wine. Cook on Low for 8 hours. Remove bay leaf. Serve over egg noodles.

Approx Per Serving: Cal 364; Prot 53.3 g; T Fat 12.0 g; Chol 115.0 mg;
     Carbo 6.6 g; Sod 906.0 mg; Potas 752.0 mg.

Delores W. Stroup
Scottsboro, Alabama

BARBECUE SAUCE FOR CHICKEN

Yields: 4 cups	Pan Size: 2½ quart

1 cup vinegar	1 tablespoon Worcestershire
1 cup margarine	sauce
2 cups water	1 teaspoon pepper
¼ cup salt	Paprika and Tabasco sauce to
2 tablespoons sugar	taste

Combine vinegar, margarine, water, salt, sugar, Worcestershire sauce, pepper, paprika and Tabasco sauce in saucepan; mix well. Simmer for 30 minutes. Brush on chicken to grill. This recipe is enough for 4 chickens.

Approx Per Cup: Cal 442; Prot 0.6 g; T Fat 45.5 g; Chol 0.0 mg;
    Carbo 11.0 g; Sod 6968.0 mg; Potas 115.0 mg.

Nancy Clem
Princeton, Indiana

MICROWAVE GOLDEN CHICKEN IMPERIAL

Yields: 4 servings	Pan Size: 8x12 inch	≈M≈

¼ cup butter	3 pounds chicken pieces
1 tablespoon Dijon-style	⅓ cup dry bread crumbs
mustard	2 teaspoons parsley flakes
1 teaspoon Worcestershire	1 teaspoon garlic salt
sauce	⅛ teaspoon pepper

Microwave butter on High in glass dish for ½ to 1 minute or until melted. Stir in mustard and Worcestershire sauce. Wash chicken and pat dry. Brush with butter mixture. Place chicken skin side up in baking dish with thicker parts toward outside. Sprinkle with mixture of bread crumbs, parsley flakes, garlic salt and pepper. Microwave, covered with paper towel, on High for 20 to 25 minutes or until tender, turning dish several times. Broil 3 inches from heat source for 2 to 4 minutes or until brown.

Approx Per Serving: Cal 410; Prot 53.3 g; T Fat 19.5 g; Chol 174.0 mg;
    Carbo 2.3 g; Sod 841.0 mg; Potas 446.0 mg.

Jean H. Goad
Salem, Virginia

OVEN-FRIED CHICKEN

Yields: 6 servings   *Pan Size: 9x13 inch*   *Preheat: 350 degrees*

3/4 cup Parmesan cheese
1 3-ounce can French-fried
  onions, crushed
1/4 cup dry bread crumbs
1 teaspoon paprika
1/2 teaspoon salt

1 teaspoon pepper
1 egg, beaten
1 tablespoon milk
6 chicken breasts, skinned
1/4 cup melted butter

Combine Parmesan cheese, onion crumbs, bread crumbs, paprika, salt and pepper in bowl. Mix egg and milk in small bowl. Wash chicken and pat dry. Dip in egg mixture. Roll in crumb mixture, coating well. Place in baking dish. Drizzle with butter. Bake for 1 hour or until golden brown.

Approx Per Serving: Cal 376; Prot 41.3 g; T Fat 19.6 g; Chol 175.0 mg;
    Carbo 6.7 g; Sod 564.0 mg; Potas 309.0 mg.

Nadine F. Marcum
Little Rock, Arkansas

CHICKEN AMARETTO

Yields: 6 servings   *Pan Size: large skillet*

6 chicken breast filets
Garlic powder and curry
  powder to taste
1/2 cup flour
1/4 cup margarine
8 ounces fresh mushrooms,
  sliced

1/4 cup Amaretto
Juice and grated rind of 1
  lemon
1 1/2 cups chicken broth
1 tablespoon cornstarch
6 baked individual pastry
  shells

Wash chicken and pat dry. Cut into 1-inch strips. Sprinkle with garlic powder, curry powder and salt and pepper to taste. Roll in flour, coating well. Brown in margarine in skillet. Add mushrooms, Amaretto, lemon juice and lemon rind. Simmer for 5 minutes. Stir in mixture of broth and cornstarch. Cook until thickened, stirring constantly. Spoon into pastry shells. Garnish with parsley and chopped tomato. May serve over hot cooked rice if preferred.

Approx Per Serving: Cal 603; Prot 43.0 g; T Fat 25.4 g; Chol 109.0 mg;
    Carbo 43.1 g; Sod 825.0 mg; Potas 559.0 mg.

Judy Ward
Naples, Florida

CHICKEN À LA BARRY

Yields: 1 serving   *Pan Size: 10 inch*

1 4 to 6-ounce chicken breast filet
2 tablespoons flour
1½ ounces clarified butter
1 tablespoon chopped shallots
Freshly ground pepper to taste
4 medium mushrooms, thinly sliced

8 green seedless grapes, cut into halves
½ teaspoon Dijon-style mustard
1½ ounces white wine
2 ounces heavy cream

Wash chicken and pat dry. Coat with flour seasoned with salt and pepper to taste. Brown on both sides in butter in hot skillet. Remove to plate; keep warm. Sauté shallots with freshly ground pepper in skillet. Stir in mushrooms, grapes and mustard. Cook for 1 to 2 minutes. Add wine, stirring to deglaze skillet. Stir in cream. Cook until reduced to desired consistency. Add chicken. Serve over rice.

Approx Per Serving: Cal 885; Prot 49.2 g; T Fat 62.6 g; Chol 290.0 mg; Carbo 26.1 g; Sod 460.0 mg; Potas 822.0 mg.

Barry Ferraro
Florence, Vermont

CHICKEN TORTILLA CASSEROLE

Yields: 8 servings   *Pan Size: 9x13 inch*   *Preheat: 400 degrees*

4 chicken breasts
12 corn tortillas
1 10-ounce can green chili sauce
1 can cream of mushroom soup

1 can cream of chicken soup
1 cup milk
1 onion, grated
2 cups shredded Cheddar cheese

Wash chicken and pat dry. Season with salt to taste. Wrap in foil. Bake for 1 hour. Pour cooking juices into buttered baking dish. Bone chicken, cutting into bite-sized pieces. Cut tortillas into 1-inch strips. Alternate layers of tortillas and chicken in prepared dish until all ingredients are used. Combine chili sauce, soups, milk and onion in bowl; mix well. Pour over layers. Top with cheese. Chill in refrigerator for 24 hours. Preheat oven to 300 degrees. Bake casserole, covered, for 30 minutes. Bake, uncovered, for 30 minutes longer. Serve with frozen cranberry salad.

Approx Per Serving: Cal 435; Prot 31.0 g; T Fat 19.4 g; Chol 84.9 mg; Carbo 35.6 g; Sod 1273.0 mg; Potas 458.0 mg.

*K. Otto and Patty Logan
*AVA President 1965-1966
Mesa, Arizona

CHINESE CHICKEN WITH WALNUTS

Yields: 6 servings   *Pan Size: 10 inch*   *Preheat: wok or skillet*

1½ pounds chicken breast
  filets
3 tablespoons soy sauce
2 teaspoons cornstarch
2 tablespoons dry Sherry
1 teaspoon sugar
½ teaspoon salt
1 teaspoon grated fresh
  gingerroot

½ teaspoon crushed red
  pepper
2 medium green bell peppers,
  cut into ¾-inch pieces
4 green onions, cut diagonally
  into 1-inch pieces
2 tablespoons (about) oil
½ cup walnut halves

Wash chicken and pat dry. Cut into 1-inch pieces. Blend soy sauce and cornstarch in small bowl. Stir in Sherry, sugar, salt, gingerroot, and red pepper; set aside. Stir-fry green peppers and green onions in hot oil in wok for 2 minutes. Remove with slotted spoon. Stir-fry walnuts for 1 to 2 minutes or until golden. Remove with slotted spoon. Stir-fry chicken ½ at a time for 2 minutes, adding additional oil if necessary. Combine chicken and soy sauce mixture in wok. Cook until thickened, stirring constantly. Stir in vegetables and walnuts. Simmer covered, for 1 minute.

Approx Per Serving: Cal 309; Prot 36.8 g; T Fat 14.9 g; Chol 95.6 mg;
  Carbo 4.5 g; Sod 781.0 mg; Potas 366.0 mg.

Senator Albert Gore, Jr.
U.S. Senator, Tennessee
Washington, District of Columbia

CREAMY CHICKEN

Yields: 8 servings   *Pan Size: 9x13 inch*   *Preheat: 350 degrees*

1 can cream of chicken soup
1 can cream of mushroom soup
½ cup chicken broth
½ cup evaporated milk
8 ounces cream cheese,
  softened

6 ounces Escort crackers,
  crushed
½ cup melted butter
8 chicken breasts, cooked,
  chopped

Combine soups, broth, evaporated milk and cream cheese in bowl; mix well. Mix cracker crumbs and butter in bowl. Layer half the crumb mixture, all the chicken, all the soup mixture and remaining crackers in baking dish. Bake for 30 minutes. Serve hot or cold.

Approx Per Serving: Cal 596; Prot 41.7 g; T Fat 39.4 g; Chol 166.0 mg;
  Carbo 22.7 g; Sod 1111.0 mg; Potas 454.0 mg.

Emily M. Richardson
Columbia, South Carolina

MICROWAVE HERB AND CHEESE CHICKEN BREASTS

Yields: 6 servings   *Pan Size: shallow glass dish*   ≈*M*≈

8 chicken breasts, boned, skin
  left on
8 ounces cream cheese,
  softened
2 tablespoons milk
2 green onions, minced
1 small clove of garlic, crushed

2 tablespoons chopped parsley
1/2 teaspoon thyme
1/2 teaspoon salt
1/4 teaspoon pepper
1/3 cup dry bread crumbs
1 teaspoon paprika

Wash chicken and pat dry. Combine cream cheese, milk, green onions, garlic, parsley, thyme, salt and pepper in bowl; mix well. Spoon into pockets between chicken breasts and skin. Coat chicken with mixture of bread crumbs and paprika. Arrange in baking dish. Microwave on High for 15 minutes, rotating dish once. May bake in oven at 350 degrees for 30 minutes if preferred.

Approx Per Serving: Cal 404; Prot 50.0 g; T Fat 20.3 g; Chol 169.0 mg;
  Carbo 2.8 g; Sod 422.0 mg; Potas 439.0 mg.

Susan N. Donar
Augusta, Maine

CHICKEN PARMESAN

Yields: 8 servings   *Pan Size: 9x13 inch*   *Preheat: 350 degrees*

8 chicken breast filets
1/8 teaspoon garlic salt
1/2 cup melted butter

1/3 cup Parmesan cheese
1 cup crushed cornflake
  crumbs

Wash chicken and pat dry. Sprinkle with garlic salt. Dip in butter. Roll in mixture of cheese and cornflake crumbs, coating well. Roll filets as for jelly roll. Arrange in baking dish. Bake for 1 hour.

Approx Per Serving: Cal 324; Prot 36.8 g; T Fat 17.6 g; Chol 129.0 mg;
  Carbo 2.6 g; Sod 315.0 mg; Potas 289.0 mg.

The Honorable Arthur Ravenel, Jr.
U.S. House of Representatives, South Carolina
Charleston, South Carolina

CHICKEN BREASTS PIQUANT

Yields: 3 servings *Pan Size: 9x13 inch* *Preheat: 375 degrees*

3 chicken breasts	1 teaspoon tarragon
1 tablespoon oil	1 teaspoon salt
1/2 cup grapefruit juice	1/8 teaspoon pepper

Wash chicken and pat dry. Place skin side down in baking dish. Combine oil, grapefruit juice, tarragon, salt and pepper in bowl; mix well. Brush over chicken. Bake for 40 to 50 minutes, basting occasionally. Serve chicken breasts hot or cold.

Approx Per Serving: Cal 252; Prot 35.3 g; T Fat 9.7 g; Chol 95.6 mg; Carbo 3.8 g; Sod 798.0 mg; Potas 346.0 mg.

Kristin Robinson
AVA Cookbook Committee
Washington, District of Columbia

POPPY SEED CHICKEN

Yields: 4 servings *Pan Size: 1 quart* *Preheat: 350 degrees*

8 ounces sour cream	Poppy seed to taste
1 can cream of chicken soup	1 1/2 cups cornflakes
4 chicken breasts, cooked, chopped	1/4 cup margarine

Combine sour cream and soup in bowl; mix well. Layer chicken, soup mixture and poppy seed 1/2 at a time in baking dish. Top with cornflakes and margarine. Bake for 20 minutes. May freeze without cornflake topping. Add topping before baking.

Approx Per Serving: Cal 518; Prot 39.6 g; T Fat 32.5 g; Chol 126.0 mg; Carbo 15.1 g; Sod 914.0 mg; Potas 424.0 mg.

Carolyn Thomas
Tupelo, Mississippi

SAUTÉED CHICKEN RASPBERRY

Yields: 4 servings	Pan Size: 10 inch

4 8-ounce boneless chicken
  breasts
1/2 cup butter
1/2 cup white wine
2 teaspoons minced garlic

1/4 cup raspberry vinegar
1 12-ounce package frozen
  whole raspberries
4 ounces honey

Wash chicken and pat dry. Sauté on both sides in butter in skillet until golden brown. Add wine, stirring to deglaze skillet. Stir in garlic, vinegar and raspberries. Reduce heat to medium. Simmer for 4 minutes. Stir in honey. Place chicken on serving platter. Pour sauce over top. Garnish with whole raspberries.

Approx Per Serving: Cal 792; Prot 71.2 g; T Fat 33.4 g; Chol 253.0 mg;
   Carbo 47.3 g; Sod 373.0 mg; Potas 718.0 mg.

Charles J. Izzi, Jr.
Capital Area Regional Voc Center
Augusta, Maine

CHICKEN AND BROCCOLI CASSEROLE

Yields: 6 servings	Pan Size: 9x13 inch	Preheat: 350 degrees

3 10-ounce packages frozen
  broccoli spears
3 cups chopped cooked
  chicken
2 cans cream of chicken soup
1 cup mayonnaise
1 teaspoon lemon juice

1/2 teaspoon (heaping) curry
  powder
2 cups shredded Cheddar
  cheese
1/2 cup bread crumbs
2 tablespoons melted butter

Cook broccoli according to package directions; drain. Place in greased baking dish. Layer chicken over broccoli. Combine soup, mayonnaise, lemon juice, curry powder and salt and pepper to taste in bowl; mix well. Spoon over layers. Top with cheese and mixture of bread crumbs and butter. Bake for 30 minutes or until bubbly.

Approx Per Serving: Cal 719; Prot 37.2 g; T Fat 56.9 g; Chol 142.0 mg;
   Carbo 17.8 g; Sod 1335.0 mg; Potas 752.0 mg.

*Niel and Carol Edmunds
*AVA President 1988-1989
Columbia, Missouri

CHICKEN CASSEROLE

Yields: 6 servings   *Pan Size: 2 quart*   *Preheat: 350 degrees*

1 7-ounce can chunky chicken
1 can cream of chicken soup
1 can cream of mushroom soup
2 tablespoons minced onion

1 15-ounce can evaporated
milk
1 8-ounce can chow mein
noodles

Combine chicken, soups, onion, evaporated milk, and noodles in bowl; mix well. Spoon into baking dish. Bake for 30 minutes. May add green pepper or pimento if desired.

Approx Per Serving: Cal 431; Prot 22.1 g; T Fat 22.6 g; Chol 57.2 mg;
        Carbo 36.2 g; Sod 1233.0 mg; Potas 393.0 mg.

Lynn A. Wagner
Newton, Mississippi

BRUNSWICK STEW

Yields: 16 servings   *Pan Size: 8 quart*

2½ to 3 pounds chicken
2 stalks celery
1 small onion
4 cups water
2 quarts tomatoes
3 medium potatoes, peeled
1 cup chopped onion

4 cups drained green butter
beans
4 cups drained whole kernel
corn
5 tablespoons sugar
Red and black pepper to taste

Wash chicken and pat dry. Combine with celery, small onion and water in stockpot. Simmer until chicken is very tender. Remove chicken; bone and chop. Strain cooled broth. Combine broth, tomatoes, whole potatoes and chopped onion in stockpot. Cook over medium heat until potatoes are tender. Remove potatoes and chop. Add chopped potatoes, chicken, butter beans, corn and sugar to stew. Season with salt and red and black pepper to taste. Simmer, covered, for 3 to 5 hours or until tomatoes have cooked to pieces, stirring occasionally. If stew is to be frozen, mash potatoes rather than chopping.

Approx Per Serving: Cal 295; Prot 29.6 g; T Fat 7.2 g; Chol 75.9 mg;
        Carbo 29.0 g; Sod 193.0 mg; Potas 708.0 mg.

H.B. Brockwell
Lawrenceville, Virginia

EASY CHICKEN PIE

Yields: 6 servings   *Pan Size: 2 quart*   *Preheat: 350 degrees*

1/4 cup butter
1 8-count package refrigerator
   crescent rolls
2 1/2 cups chopped cooked
   chicken

3 hard-cooked eggs, sliced
1 10-ounce can chicken stock
1 can cream of chicken soup

Melt butter in baking dish. Line prepared dish with roll dough. Layer chicken and eggs over dough. Combine chicken stock, soup and salt and pepper to taste in bowl; mix well. Pour over layers. Bake for 30 minutes or until bubbly and crust is brown.

Approx Per Serving: Cal 403; Prot 24.2 g; T Fat 25.2 g; Chol 214.0 mg;
    Carbo 18.6 g; Sod 975.0 mg; Potas 333.0 mg.

Sarah W. Hallman
Autaugaville, Alabama

FLORIDA CHICKEN PIE

Yields: 8 servings   *Pan Size: 9x15 inch*   *Preheat: 350 degrees*

1 1/2 pounds chopped cooked
   chicken
1 can cream of chicken soup
1 cup chicken broth
1/2 cup cooked chopped carrots
1/2 cup cooked chopped celery

1/2 cup cooked chopped
   potatoes
1/2 cup cooked peas
2 recipes buttermilk baking
   mix biscuits

Combine chicken, soup, broth, vegetables and seasonings in bowl; mix well. Spoon into baking dish. Prepare biscuit dough according to package directions. Cut 16 biscuits 5/8 inch thick. Arrange over filling. Bake for 30 minutes or until biscuits are brown on top and firm on bottom.

Approx Per Serving: Cal 412; Prot 31.2 g; T Fat 14.8 g; Chol 79.1 mg;
    Carbo 35.2 g; Sod 2385.0 mg; Potas 483.0 mg.

Maxine Felts
Lake County Area Vo-Tech Center
Eustis, Florida

HOT CHICKEN SALAD

Yields: 12 servings *Pan Size: 9x13 inch* *Preheat: 350 degrees*

1 8-ounce package seasoned bread stuffing mix
1/2 cup melted margarine
1 cup very warm water
2 1/2 cups chopped cooked chicken
1/2 cup chopped onion
1/4 cup chopped chives
1/2 cup chopped celery

1/2 cup mayonnaise-type salad dressing
3/4 teaspoon salt
2 eggs, slightly beaten
1 1/2 cups milk
1 can cream of mushroom soup
1 cup shredded Cheddar cheese

Combine stuffing mix, margarine and water in bowl; mix well. Place half the mixture in baking dish. Mix chicken, onion, chives, celery, salad dressing and salt in bowl. Spoon over stuffing. Top with remaining stuffing mix. Beat eggs with milk in bowl. Pour over layers. Chill in refrigerator overnight. Let stand at room temperature for 1 hour before baking. Spread mushroom soup over top. Bake for 40 minutes. Sprinkle with Cheddar cheese. Bake for 10 minutes longer.

Approx Per Serving: Cal 330; Prot 15.9 g; T Fat 20.6 g; Chol 88.5 mg; Carbo 20.3 g; Sod 920.0 mg; Potas 179.0 mg.

Donna Lord
Springfield, Ohio

TURKEY CASSEROLE

Yields: 8 servings *Pan Size: 4 quart* *Preheat: 375 degrees*

1 cup sour cream
2 tablespoons flour
3 cups chopped cooked turkey
1/4 cup chopped black olives
1 4-ounce can mushroom pieces, drained

1 1/2 tablespoons chopped onion
1 can cream of mushroom soup
1 teaspoon salt
Pepper to taste
2 1/2 cups cooked noodles

Blend sour cream and flour in saucepan. Heat just until heated through; do not boil. Combine sour cream mixture, turkey, olives, mushrooms, onion, soup, salt and pepper in bowl; mix well. Add noodles; toss to mix well. Spoon into baking dish. Bake for 30 to 40 minutes or until bubbly. May top with strips of pimento before baking if desired.

Approx Per Serving: Cal 269; Prot 19.5 g; T Fat 13.2 g; Chol 53.3 mg; Carbo 18.6 g; Sod 720.0 mg; Potas 269.0 mg.

Jane King
AVA Vice President, Region I
AVA Cookbook Committee
Newark, Ohio

GROUND TURKEY LASAGNA

Yields: 8 servings   *Pan Size: 7x12 inch*   *Preheat: 350 degrees*

3 tablespoons chopped onion
2 teaspoons olive oil
1 pound ground turkey
1 1/2 tablespoons oregano
1 1/2 teaspoons garlic powder
1 tablespoon salt
1 1/2 teaspoon red pepper
1 32-ounce can tomato purée

1/4 cup red wine
12 ounce lasagna noodles,
  cooked
1 pound skim mozzarella
  cheese, sliced
1 pound skim ricotta cheese
1/4 cup Parmesan cheese

Sauté onion in oil in saucepan. Add ground turkey. Cook until no longer pink. Stir in seasonings, tomato purée and wine. Simmer for 20 minutes, stirring occasionally. Layer 1/4 of the meat sauce, 1/3 of the noodles, 1/3 of the mozzarella and 1/3 of the ricotta in baking dish. Repeat layers 2 more times. Top with remaining meat sauce and Parmesan cheese. Bake for 20 to 30 minutes or until bubbly. Let stand for 5 minutes before serving. Serve with hot garlic bread and tossed salad.

Approx Per Serving: Cal 598; Prot 44.8 g; T Fat 23.8 g; Chol 97.1 mg;
    Carbo 48.7 g; Sod 1306.0 mg; Potas 852.0 mg.

Marie A. Allen
Newark, Delaware

GROUND TURKEY SPAGHETTI SAUCE

Yields: 6 servings   *Pan Size: electric skillet*

2 pounds ground turkey
2 quarts drained tomatoes
1 16-ounce can low-salt
  tomato sauce
2 6-ounce cans low-salt
  tomato paste
1 cup chopped onion

1 cup chopped green bell
  pepper
3/4 cup grape jelly
1 bay leaf
1/4 to 1/2 teaspoon red pepper
Garlic and oregano to taste

Brown ground turkey in electric skillet; drain. Stir in tomatoes, tomato sauce, tomato paste, onion, green pepper, jelly and seasonings. Simmer for 2 to 3 hours or to desired consistency, stirring occasionally. Remove bay leaf. Serve over spaghetti with Parmesan cheese.

Approx Per Serving: Cal 584; Prot 45.9 g; T Fat 21.2 g; Chol 127.0 mg;
    Carbo 58.1 g; Sod 1197.0 mg; Potas 1977.0 mg.
    Nutritional information does not include spaghetti or cheese.

Kathy A. Eschenmann
Blacksburg, Virginia

STIR-FRY TURKEY DINNER

Yields: 4 servings   *Pan Size: 10 inch*

8 ounces ground turkey	1/2 cup sliced mushrooms
1 tablespoon oil	1/2 cup sliced water chestnuts
1 carrot, sliced	3 tablespoons soy sauce
1 stalk of celery, sliced	1 tablespoon cornstarch
1/2 cup sliced green bell pepper	1 teaspoon sugar

Stir-fry ground turkey in oil in skillet over medium-high heat. Add vegetables. Stir-fry until tender-crisp. Stir in mixture of soy sauce, cornstarch and sugar. Cook until heated through, stirring constantly. Serve over rice. May substitute chicken breast strips or shrimp for ground turkey, adding shrimp at the end of cooking time. May substitute broccoli, bean sprouts, green onions or other vegetables of choice for vegetables listed.

Approx Per Serving: Cal 207; Prot 16.2 g; T Fat 11.0 g; Chol 47.6 mg;
    Carbo 10.9 g; Sod 855.0 mg; Potas 392.0 mg.

Chris Wyatt
Seabeck, Washington

CORNISH HENS WITH PINEAPPLE-WILD RICE STUFFING

Yields: 4 servings   *Pan Size: roasting pan*   *Preheat: 325 degrees*

4 Cornish game hens	1 1/2 cups cooked wild rice
2/3 cup chopped canned mushrooms	1 1/2 cups cooked rice
1/4 cup chopped onion	1/2 cup drained crushed pineapple
2 tablespoons chopped green bell pepper	3/4 teaspoon salt
1 1/2 tablespoons butter	1/8 teaspoon pepper
	1/2 cup butter

Wash hens and pat dry inside and out. Sprinkle cavities with salt to taste. Sauté mushrooms, onion and green pepper in 1 1/2 tablespoons butter in large skillet. Add wild rice, rice, pineapple, 3/4 teaspoon salt and pepper; toss to mix well. Spoon stuffing into hens. Secure openings with toothpicks. Place breast side up in roasting pan. Brush with 1/2 cup butter. Bake uncovered, for 1 hour. Bake, covered, for 1 hour longer. May bake stuffing in baking dish if preferred.

Approx Per Serving: Cal 959; Prot 87.3 g; T Fat 48.8 g; Chol 327.0 mg;
    Carbo 39.3 g; Sod 984.0 mg; Potas 848.0 mg.

*Ron and Deanna McCage, *AVA Vice President
New and Related Services Division
Lawrenceville, Georgia

CHEESE BAKED PHEASANT

Yields: 4 servings	*Pan Size: 2 quart*	*Preheat: 350 degrees*

5 slices bacon, chopped
1/2 onion, chopped
10 mushrooms, sliced
1 pheasant, cut up

1/2 cup flour
1 can Cheddar cheese soup
2/3 cup white wine

Cook bacon, onion and mushrooms in skillet, stirring until bacon is crisp. Remove with slotted spoon. Wash pheasant and pat dry. Coat lightly with mixture of flour and salt and pepper to taste. Brown in drippings in skillet. Remove to baking dish. Spoon bacon mixture over top. Mix soup and wine in small bowl. Pour over casserole. Bake for 30 minutes. Serve with rice.

Approx Per Serving: Cal 421; Prot 32.3 g; T Fat 19.9 g; Chol 103.0 mg; Carbo 20.8 g; Sod 702.0 mg; Potas 603.0 mg.

Marty McFarland, President
California Business Ed. Association
Redding, California

CROCK•POT CREAMED PHEASANT

Yields: 5 servings	*Pan Size: Crock•Pot*

1 pheasant, cut up
1 tablespoon oil
1 can cream of chicken soup

1 tablespoon crumbled
chicken bouillon

Wash pheasant and pat dry. Brown on both sides in oil in 12-inch skillet. Place in Crock•Pot. Spoon soup over pheasant. Sprinkle bouillon over soup. Cook on High just until heated. Cook on Low for 6 to 9 hours. Serve with hot cooked rice.

Approx Per Serving: Cal 194; Prot 21.9 g; T Fat 9.2 g; Chol 64.0 mg; Carbo 4.6 g; Sod 938.0 mg; Potas 337.0 mg.

Pat Bortnem
Volga, South Dakota

BAKED FISH IN VINEGAR SAUCE

Yields: 8 servings   Pan Size: shallow baking dish   Preheat: 350 degrees

3 pounds whitefish fillets
1/2 cup flour
2 large yellow onions, thinly
    sliced
2 tablespoons butter
1/2 cup olive oil
1/2 cup white wine vinegar

2 cloves of garlic, crushed
1 teaspoon oregano
2 teaspoons dry mustard
1/4 cup chopped parsley
1/2 teaspoon coriander
1 tablespoon lemon juice
1/4 cup dry white wine

Roll fish in mixture of flour and salt to taste, coating well. Arrange in baking dish. Sauté onions in butter in skillet until tender. Spread over fish. Combine olive oil, vinegar, garlic, oregano, dry mustard, parsley, coriander, lemon juice and wine in bowl; mix well. Pour over fish. Bake for 45 minutes.

Approx Per Serving: Cal 401; Prot 35.1 g; T Fat 23.4 g; Chol 74.1 mg;
        Carbo 10.3 g; Sod 180.0 mg; Potas 595.0 mg.

Gail Cancelliere
Leominster, Massachusetts

Marjorie A. Adcock

JASPER'S BAG-SHOOK CATFISH

Yields: 6 servings   *Pan Size: deep fryer*   *Preheat: 375 degrees*

10 6-ounce fresh or frozen
   catfish fillets
1 cup yellow cornmeal

1 tablespoon salt
1 tablespoon pepper
Peanut oil for deep frying

Wash fillets and pat dry. Combine cornmeal, salt and pepper in large paper bag. Add catfish. Shake to coat well. Deep-fry in 375 to 400-degree oil for 7 minutes or until golden brown. Drain on paper towel. Serve with hush puppies, French fries, slaw, onion slices and corn salad.

Approx Per Serving: Cal 413; Prot 53.4 g; T Fat 12.4 g; Chol 164.0 mg;
    Carbo 18.0 g; Sod 1245.0 mg; Potas 1017.0 mg.
    Nutritional information does not include oil for deep frying.

Jasper S. Lee
Mississippi State, Mississippi

OVEN-FRIED ORANGE ROUGHY

Yields: 4 servings   *Pan Size: shallow baking pan*   *Preheat: 350 degrees*

1 pound orange roughy fillets
2 egg whites, slightly beaten
1 cup low-sodium butter
   crackers, crushed

2 tablespoons fresh lemon
   juice
Butter-flavored granules

Wash fillets and pat dry. Dip in egg whites. Roll in cracker crumbs, coating well. Place on rack in baking pan. Drizzle with lemon juice. Sprinkle with butter-flavored granules. Bake for 20 to 25 minutes or until fish flakes easily.

Approx Per Serving: Cal 431; Prot 28.1 g; T Fat 22.8 g; Chol 44.2 mg;
    Carbo 41.2 g; Sod 694.0 mg; Potas 434.0 mg.
    Nutritional information does not include butter-flavored granules.

Sara Jo Robinson
Indianapolis, Indiana

PACIFIC BAKED SALMON SUPREME

Yields: 8 servings   *Pan Size: baking sheet*   *Preheat: 450 degrees*

1 5-pound salmon
1/2 cup sour cream
1/2 cup chopped cucumber
1/4 cup sliced green olives
1 tablespoon chopped parsley

1/2 teaspoon chopped lemon
  rind
1/4 teaspoon salt
1/4 teaspoon dillweed

Wash salmon and pat dry inside and out. Combine remaining ingredients in bowl; mix well. Spread in cavity and over top of salmon. Wrap in heavy foil; place on baking sheet. Bake for 12 to 15 minutes per pound. Remove skin; place on serving platter.

Approx Per Serving: Cal 444; Prot 56.8 g; T Fat 22.1 g; Chol 162.0 mg;
    Carbo 1.2 g; Sod 370.0 mg; Potas 1437.0 mg.

Thelma Clemons
Eugene, Oregon

ITALIAN SALMON

Yields: 6 servings   *Pan Size: 9x13 inch*   *Preheat: 350 degrees*

1 16-ounce can tomatoes
1 large onion, cut into quarters
1 clove of garlic
1/4 cup flour
1/4 teaspoon rosemary
1 teaspoon oregano
1 teaspoon salt
1/4 cup margarine

1/2 cup milk
1/2 cup shredded Cheddar
  cheese
1 16-ounce can salmon
8 ounces macaroni, cooked
1/2 cup bread crumbs
2 tablespoons melted butter

Combine tomatoes, onion, garlic, flour and seasonings in blender container. Process until smooth. Melt margarine in saucepan. Add puréed ingredients and milk; mix well. Cook until thickened, stirring constantly. Stir in Cheddar cheese and salmon. Place macaroni in baking dish. Pour salmon sauce over macaroni. Top with mixture of bread crumbs and butter. Bake for 30 minutes or until bubbly.

Approx Per Serving: Cal 505; Prot 24.6 g; T Fat 21.5 g; Chol 50.0 mg;
    Carbo 40.9 g; Sod 963.0 mg; Potas 522.0 mg.

Joyce L. Comfort
North Pole, Alaska

POACHED SALMON WITH RASPBERRY BEURRE BLANC

Yields: 6 servings   *Pan Size: fish poacher*

2 cups dry white wine
1/2 cup water
2 stalks celery, chopped
2 carrots, sliced
1 onion, sliced
2 parsley sprigs
4 peppercorns
1 bay leaf

1/4 teaspoon salt
6 8-ounce salmon fillets
1/2 cup raspberry vinegar
1/4 cup minced shallots
8 ounces unsalted butter,
   sliced
2 tablespoons strained
   raspberry jam

Combine wine, water, celery, carrots, onion, parsley, peppercorns, bay leaf and salt in fish poacher. Bring to the simmering point. Add salmon. Poach over medium-low heat just until tender; do not boil. Combine vinegar and shallots in saucepan. Cook until liquid is reduced to 2 tablespoons. Remove from heat. Whisk in half the butter 1 tablespoon at a time. Return to low heat. Add remaining butter 1 tablespoon at a time, whisking until mixture is consistency of mayonnaise. Whisk in jam. Place fish on serving platter. Strain poaching liquid, reserving vegetables; discard peppercorns and bay leaf. Spoon vegetables over fish. Serve with raspberry butter.

Approx Per Serving: Cal 688; Prot 46.1 g; T Fat 45.1 g; Chol 208.0 mg;
   Carbo 11.5 g; Sod 219.0 mg; Potas 1367.0 mg.

The Honorable Butler Derrick
U.S. House of Representatives, South Carolina
Washington, District of Columbia

POACHED SALMON

Yields: 8 servings   *Pan Size: large skillet*

8 6-ounce fresh or frozen
   salmon steaks
1/2 cup white wine
1 cup water
2 tablespoons wine vinegar
1/2 cup chopped celery leaves

1/4 bay leaf
7 peppercorns
1 teaspoon dillweed
5 whole allspice
2 teaspoons salt

Wash salmon and pat dry. Combine wine, water, vinegar and seasonings in skillet. Add salmon. Simmer, tightly covered, over medium heat for 8 to 10 minutes or until fish flakes easily. Drain well. Serve on heated platter garnished with watercress or parsley.

Approx Per Serving: Cal 255; Prot 33.8 g; T Fat 10.9 g; Chol 93.6 mg;
   Carbo 1.2 g; Sod 610.0 mg; Potas 860.0 mg.

Joan M. Gehee
Emily Griffith Opportunity School
Denver, Colorado

HOT TUNA MELTS

Yields: 10 servings   *Pan Size: baking sheet*   *Preheat: broiler*

2 7-ounce cans tuna
1/3 cup mayonnaise
2 tablespoons minced onion
2 tablespoons minced parsley
2 teaspoons lemon juice

Pepper to taste
3/4 cup shredded Cheddar
  cheese
5 English muffins, split

Drain and flake tuna. Combine with mayonnaise, onion, parsley, lemon juice and pepper in bowl; toss gently to mix. Add 1/2 cup cheese; mix gently. Spread over muffin halves. Sprinkle with remaining 1/4 cup cheese. Broil 6 inches from heat for 3 to 4 minutes or until cheese is golden brown.

Approx Per Serving: Cal 209; Prot 16.2 g; T Fat 9.4 g; Chol 35.6 mg;
    Carbo 13.7 g; Sod 425.0 mg; Potas 309.0 mg.

Shirley W. Stacey
Venice, Florida

MICROWAVE TUNA AND RICE CASSEROLE

Yields: 6 servings   *Pan Size: 1 1/2 quart*   ≈M≈

3 ounces cream cheese,
  softened
1 can cream of mushroom soup
1 6-ounce can tuna, drained
2 cups cooked rice

1/4 cup chopped green onions
1 tablespoon chopped parsley
1/8 teaspoon pepper
1/4 cup Parmesan cheese
Paprika to taste

Blend cream cheese and soup in bowl. Add tuna, rice, green onions, parsley and pepper; mix well. Spoon into glass baking dish. Top with cheese and paprika. Microwave on High for 4 to 6 minutes or until heated through.

Approx Per Serving: Cal 207; Prot 12.5 g; T Fat 7.8 g; Chol 25.4 mg;
    Carbo 21.0 g; Sod 554.0 mg; Potas 178.0 mg.

Martha Atchley
O.T. Autry Area Vocational Technical Center
Enid, Oklahoma

SEAFOOD NEWBURG

Yields: 20 servings   *Pan Size: stockpot*

12 cups milk
2 teaspoons salt
3/4 teaspoon white pepper
2 teaspoons Accent
2 ounces paprika
1 1/2 cups butter
2 1/4 cups flour

20 ounces scallops
20 ounces shrimp
20 ounces sealegs
2 tablespoons butter
8 ounces Sauvignon Blanc
20 ounces haddock, cut into
    1-inch cubes

Heat milk in double boiler until bubbly. Whisk in seasonings. Melt 1 1/2 cups butter in stockpot. Whisk in flour. Cook for 3 minutes, stirring constantly. Add hot milk. Cook until thickened, stirring constantly. Cook scallops, shrimp and sealegs in 2 tablespoons butter and wine in saucepan. Strain, reserving liquid. Add seafood to cream sauce. Add enough reserved cooking liquid to make of desired consistency. Bring haddock to a boil in water to just cover in saucepan. Drain well. Add to seafood mixture. Heat just to serving temperature.

Approx Per Serving: Cal 391; Prot 26.5 g; T Fat 21.3 g; Chol 141.0 mg;
    Carbo 21.5 g; Sod 1181.0 mg; Potas 486.0 mg.

James F. Cole, Sr.
Dexter Regional Vocational Center
Dexter, Maine

HARRY BECK'S CRAB CAKES

Yields: 6 servings   *Pan Size: 10 inch skillet*

1 pound crab meat
2 eggs, beaten
1/2 cup fine cracker crumbs
3 tablespoons mayonnaise
2 tablespoons finely minced
    onion

1 tablespoon finely minced
    green bell pepper
1 tablespoon Dijon-style
    mustard
2 tablespoons butter

Combine crab meat, eggs, cracker crumbs, mayonnaise, onion, green pepper, mustard and salt and pepper to taste in bowl; mix well. Shape into patties. Brown on both sides in butter in skillet.

Approx Per Serving: Cal 285; Prot 18.9 g; T Fat 18.7 g; Chol 181.0 mg;
    Carbo 14.3 g; Sod 527.0 mg; Potas 306.0 mg.

Harry Beck
Dover, Delaware

MARY'S-LAND CRAB CAKES

Yields: 6 servings   *Pan Size: 10 inch skillet*

1 cup bread crumbs	1/2 teaspoon honey
2 eggs, beaten	1/2 cup chopped celery
1/2 cup plain yogurt	1/2 cup chopped shallots
1/2 cup milk	1/2 cup chopped parsley
2 teaspoons Dijon-style	2 tablespoons butter
mustard	2 pounds lump crab meat
1/2 teaspoon Old Bay	1/3 cup Brandy
seasoning	2 tablespoons oil

Combine bread crumbs, eggs, yogurt, milk, mustard, seasoning and honey in bowl; mix well. Sauté celery, shallots and parsley in butter in skillet. Add sautèed vegetables, crab meat and Brandy to bread crumb mixture; mix well. Shape into patties. Brown patties on both sides in oil in skillet.

Approx Per Serving: Cal 345; Prot 35.2 g; T Fat 14.6 g; Chol 258.0 mg;
     Carbo 13.9 g; Sod 566.0 mg; Potas 679.0 mg.

*Phil and Mary Wagner
*AVA Director of Advertising
Annapolis, Maryland

NORFOLK CRAB CAKES

Yields: Variable

Fresh onions, chopped	Eggs
(preferably 2 kinds for	Bread crumbs
variety and flavor)	Pepper
Green bell peppers, chopped	Vegetable salt
Butter	Heavy cream
Fresh Chesapeake Bay blue	Butter
crab meat	Parsley, chopped

Sauté onions and green peppers lightly in butter in skillet. Combine onions, green peppers, crab meat, eggs, bread crumbs, pepper and salt to taste in bowl; mix well. Add enough cream to make of desired consistency. Melt butter in skillet. Heat until light brown. Add parsley. Sauté just until flavor of parsley is released. Shape crab mixture into cakes. Brown lightly on both sides in butter in skillet. Serve immediately. This recipe is infinitely variable to reflect your own tastes.

Nutritional information not available.

The Honorable John Warner
U.S. Senator, Virginia
Washington, District of Columbia

CRAB CASSEROLE

Yields: 4 servings	Pan Size: 1½ quart	Preheat: 350 degrees

8 ounces crab meat
1 cup cooked rice
5 hard-cooked eggs, chopped
1½ cups mayonnaise
6 ounces evaporated milk

½ teaspoon salt
⅛ teaspoon pepper
¼ teaspoon red pepper
½ cup shredded Cheddar
cheese

Combine crab meat, rice and eggs in bowl; mix well. Add mayonnaise, evaporated milk, salt, pepper and red pepper. Spoon into baking dish. Sprinkle with cheese. Bake for 20 minutes. Serve as main dish or appetizer.

Approx Per Serving: Cal 918; Prot 27.4 g; T Fat 81.7 g; Chol 475.0 mg;
    Carbo 19.8 g; Sod 1107.0 mg; Potas 451.0 mg.

The Honorable Gerald L. Baliles
Governor of Virginia
Richmond, Virginia

JEAN'S CRAB CASSEROLE

Yields: 10 servings	Pan Size: 9x13 inch	Preheat: 325 degrees

8 slices bread
1 pound crab meat
1 cup chopped celery
1 green bell pepper, chopped
1 medium onion, finely
chopped
½ cup mayonnaise

½ teaspoon salt
4 eggs, slightly beaten
1¾ cups milk
1 can cream of mushroom soup
½ cup shredded Cheddar
cheese

Trim crusts from bread. Cut into cubes. Sprinkle half the bread in baking dish. Combine flaked crab meat, celery, green pepper, onion, mayonnaise and salt in bowl; mix well. Spread over bread. Top with remaining bread. Mix eggs and milk in bowl. Pour over layers. Chill in refrigerator overnight. Bake for 15 minutes. Spread soup over top. Sprinkle with cheese. Bake for 1 hour longer.

Approx Per Serving: Cal 285; Prot 16.6 g; T Fat 17.9 g; Chol 174.0 mg;
    Carbo 14.1 g; Sod 699.0 mg; Potas 337.0 mg.

Jean Holbrook
Roanoke, Virginia

SEAFOOD MORNAY

Yields: 8 servings   *Pan Size: 2 quart*

1 small bunch green onions, chopped	2 cups half and half
1/2 cup finely chopped parsley	2 cups shredded Swiss cheese
1/2 cup butter	1 tablespoon Sherry
2 tablespoons flour	Red pepper to taste
	1 pound crab meat

Sauté green onions and parsley in butter in saucepan. Stir in flour, half and half and cheese. Cook until sauce is thickened and cheese is melted. Add wine, red pepper and salt to taste. Fold in crab meat. Cook until heated through. Serve in pastry shells. May serve from chafing dish with melba rounds as appetizer.

Approx Per Serving: Cal 359; Prot 21.9 g; T Fat 27.3 g; Chol 136.0 mg; Carbo 6.0 g; Sod 355.0 mg; Potas 352.0 mg.

Faye Wilkinson
Hinds Community College
Vicksburg, Mississippi

STUFFED LOBSTER À LA RALPH

Yields: 2 servings   *Pan Size: 10x15 inch*   *Preheat: 425 degrees*

2 1-pound lobsters, split	Juice of 1 lemon
4 slices bread, cubed	1 onion, chopped
3 tablespoons Parmesan cheese	1/4 cup butter
8 ounces crab meat	1/4 cup Sherry
1 tablespoon chopped parsley	1 tablespoon toasted bread crumbs
1 egg, beaten	2 tablespoons butter

Wash cleaned lobsters and reserve roe. Place cut side up in baking pan. Combine bread, cheese, crab meat, parsley, and salt and pepper to taste in bowl; mix well. Stir in egg and lemon juice. Sauté onion in 1/4 cup butter in skillet. Add reserved lobster roe. Cook until heated through. Stir in Sherry. Simmer for several minutes; remove from heat. Add stuffing mixture; mix well. Stuff into cavities of lobsters. Sprinkle with bread crumbs. Dot with 2 tablespoons butter. Bake for 30 to 40 minutes. Broil for several minutes for crisp topping if desired.

Nutritional information not available.

Dolores Palladino
Sarasota, Florida

OYSTER CASSEROLE

Yields: Variable   *Preheat: 350 degrees*

¹/₂ cup margarine	Worcestershire sauce
Salted crackers	Margarine
Unsalted crackers	Milk
Oysters	Paprika

Melt ¹/₂ cup margarine in baking dish. Alternate layers of salted crackers, unsalted crackers and oysters in dish until all ingredients are used, ending with crackers. Sprinkle with Worcestershire sauce and additional margarine. Pour milk over layers. Sprinkle with paprika. Bake for 30 minutes.

Nutritional information not available.

Nancy Raynor, AVA Vice President
Health Occupation Education Division
Raleigh, North Carolina

FRIED OYSTERS

Yields: 4 servings   *Pan Size: deep fryer*

2¹/₂ cups flour	2 eggs
¹/₄ teaspoon garlic powder	¹/₂ cup evaporated milk
¹/₄ teaspoon onion salt	2 dozen oysters
¹/₄ teaspoon Accent	Oil for deep frying

Mix flour with garlic powder, onion salt, Accent and salt and pepper to taste in large bowl. Beat eggs with milk in bowl. Dip oysters in egg mixture. Roll in flour mixture, coating well. Deep-fry in hot oil just until light brown; do not overcook.

Approx Per Serving: Cal 312; Prot 16.1 g; T Fat 7.8 g; Chol 193.0 mg;
Carbo 42.5 g; Sod 565.0 mg; Potas 369.0 mg.
Nutritional information does not include oil for deep frying.

Ted Ardoin
Lafayette, Louisiana

SHRIMP ETOUFFÉE

Yields: 6 servings   *Pan Size: 4 quart*

2 large onions, chopped
3/4 cup butter
1 1/2 pounds fresh shrimp,
  peeled
1 28-ounce can whole tomatoes

1/2 cup white wine
1/4 cup chopped green onion
  tops
Pepper and red pepper to taste

Sauté onions in butter in saucepan until transparent. Add shrimp. Cook, covered, over low heat for 15 to 20 minutes. Add tomatoes, wine, green onion tops, pepper and red pepper. Add salt to taste. Simmer for 15 to 20 minutes. Serve over rice.

Approx Per Serving: Cal 384; Prot 25.3 g; T Fat 25.5 g; Chol 234.0 mg;
    Carbo 11.4 g; Sod 579.0 mg; Potas 635.0 mg.

Kenneth Harmon
Washington, District of Columbia

LIME AND GINGER SHRIMP

Yields: 4 servings   *Preheat: grill*

1 1/2 pounds large shrimp,
  peeled
2 limes, cut into wedges
3/4 cup fresh lime juice
1 tablespoon minced fresh
  ginger
2 small shallots, chopped
2 cloves of garlic, minced
1 1/2 teaspoons lemon or lime
  marmalade
3 tablespoons finely chopped
  cilantro

1/2 teaspoon salt
1/8 teaspoon pepper
1/8 teaspoon crushed red
  pepper flakes
1/3 cup olive oil
1 large cucumber, peeled,
  shredded
4 large carrots, peeled,
  shredded
1 head leaf lettuce, shredded
3 tablespoons finely chopped
  cilantro

Thread shrimp and lime wedges onto 4 skewers. Place in shallow glass dish. Combine lime juice, ginger, shallots, garlic, marmalade, 3 tablespoons cilantro, salt, pepper and red pepper in bowl. Whisk in olive oil gradually. Pour half the mixture over shrimp. Let stand for 30 minutes, turning several times. Place cucumber, carrots, lettuce and 3 tablespoons cilantro on large platter. Pour remaining marinade over top, tossing lightly to coat well. Grill shrimp over medium heat for 5 minutes or just until cooked through, turning once. Place skewers on vegetable mixture. Serve immediately.

Approx Per Serving: Cal 425; Prot 37.4 g; T Fat 21.3 g; Chol 259.0 mg;
    Carbo 23.5 g; Sod 557.0 mg; Potas 949.0 mg.

Kristin Robinson
AVA Cookbook Committee
Washington, District of Columbia

ANN MCDERMOTT'S SHRIMP WITH BLACK-EYED PEAS

Yields: 2 servings   *Pan Size: 1¹/₂ quart*

1/2 cup chopped onion
3 cloves of garlic, crushed
2 tablespoons olive oil
1 16-ounce can black-eyed
   peas

1/2 cup catsup
Tabasco sauce to taste
1/2 teaspoon crushed red
   pepper
8 ounces shrimp, peeled

Sauté onion and garlic in olive oil in saucepan. Add peas, catsup, Tabasco sauce and red pepper. Simmer for 10 minutes. Cut shrimp into halves. Add to saucepan. Simmer for 5 minutes.

Approx Per Serving: Cal 506; Prot 35.8 g; T Fat 17.1 g; Chol 172.0 mg;
    Carbo 53.6 g; Sod 1559.0 mg; Potas 928.0 mg.

Ann McDermott
Washington, District of Columbia

COQUILLES SAINT JACQUES

Yields: 10 servings   *Pan Size: individual shells*   *Preheat: 400 degrees*

1/4 cup butter
3 tablespoons flour
1/4 teaspoon dry mustard
1/2 teaspoon grated lemon rind
1/2 teaspoon MSG
1/2 teaspoon powdered
   horseradish
2 cups half and half
1¹/₂ cups sliced mushrooms

2 teaspoons instant onion
   flakes
2 tablespoons butter
8 ounces scallops
8 ounces shrimp, peeled,
   cooked
4 ounces crab meat
2 tablespoons dry Sherry
1/4 cup bread crumbs

Melt 1/4 cup butter in saucepan. Stir in flour, dry mustard, lemon rind, MSG and horseradish. Add half and half. Cook until thickened, stirring constantly. Sauté mushrooms and onion in 2 tablespoons butter in skillet. Remove to sauce with slotted spoon. Cut scallops into bite-sized pieces. Add to skillet. Sauté for 3 minutes. Add to sauce with shrimp, crab meat and Sherry; mix well. Spoon into individual shells or ramekins. Top with bread crumbs. Bake for 10 minutes. Broil just until light brown.

Approx Per Serving: Cal 198; Prot 12.8 g; T Fat 13.3 g; Chol 89.7 mg;
    Carbo 5.9 g; Sod 400.0 mg; Potas 265.0 mg.

Joan M. Gehee
Emily Griffith Opportunity School
Denver, Colorado

SEAFOOD CASSEROLE

Yields: 8 servings   *Pan Size: 2 quart*   *Preheat: 350 degrees*

1 pound shrimp, peeled	1 can cream of mushroom soup
1 large onion, chopped	2 cups crab meat
1 green bell pepper, chopped	1 cup cooked rice
2 stalks celery, chopped	1 teaspoon Tabasco sauce
2 tablespoons butter	1 tablespoon garlic salt
8 ounces cream cheese	1/2 teaspoon red pepper
1/2 cup butter	1/2 cup shredded sharp
1 8-ounce can mushrooms	Cheddar cheese

Sauté shrimp, onion, green pepper and celery in 2 tablespoons butter in skillet. Melt cream cheese and 1/2 cup butter in double boiler; mix until smooth. Combine with sautéed vegetables in bowl. Add drained mushrooms, soup, crab meat, rice, Tabasco sauce and seasonings; mix well. Spoon into baking dish. Top with cheese. Bake for 20 to 30 minutes or until bubbly.

Approx Per Serving: Cal 431; Prot 24.4 g; T Fat 31.1 g; Chol 198.0 mg;
    Carbo 14.1 g; Sod 1646.0 mg; Potas 412.0 mg.

Kenneth Harmon
Washington, District of Columbia

EASY SEAFOOD PASTA

Yields: 4 servings   *Pan Size: large skillet*

1 cup chopped scallions	1 tablespoon fresh lemon juice
1/4 cup butter	1 tablespoon chopped parsley
1/4 cup olive oil	1/2 teaspoon oregano
1 clove of garlic, minced	1 teaspoon basil
1 7-ounce can minced clams	9 ounces fresh angel hair pasta
1 7-ounce can medium shrimp	3 tablespoons Parmesan
1 tomato, peeled, chopped	cheese

Sauté scallions in butter and olive oil in skillet. Add garlic. Sauté lightly. Drain seafood, reserving liquid. Add reserved liquid, tomato, lemon juice and herbs to skillet. Simmer for several minutes. Add seafood and salt and freshly ground pepper to taste. Simmer for several minutes; do not boil. Cook pasta *al dente* using package directions; drain. Toss with cheese and several tablespoons sauce. Place on serving plates. Top with sauce.

Approx Per Serving: Cal 623; Prot 34.6 g; T Fat 29.0 g; Chol 153.0 mg;
    Carbo 54.5 g; Sod 313.0 mg; Potas 705.0 mg.

Joyce Sandberg
Pittsburgh, Pennsylvania

Artist: *Daniel R. Johnson*—Olympus High School; Dick Powell, Teacher
Salt Lake City, Utah
Artist: *Noah Tietze*—Warwick Area Vo-Tech Center; Mr. Corrigan, Teacher
Warwick, Rhode Island

VEGETABLES
&
SIDE DISHES

Deep South Chicken and Fish Fry
Region IV

Cheddar Crackers with Pepper Jelly
page 15 and page 20

Jalapeno Frito Salad or Cabbage Slaw
page 52 and page 51

Oven-Fried Chicken
page 80

Jasper's Bag-Shook Catfish
page 93

Fried Oysters
page 101

Spicy Hush Puppies
page 151

Hominy Casserole
page 118

Shoe Peg Corn Relish
page 122

Oatmeal Cake with Topping or Caramel Pie
page 179 and page 191

ASPARAGUS CASSEROLE

Yields: 8 servings	Pan Size: 2 quart	Preheat: 350 degrees

2 16-ounce cans asparagus,
   drained
1 pound Velveeta cheese,
   thinly sliced
1 16-ounce can English peas,
   drained

1 can cream of mushroom soup
2 7-ounce cans sliced water
   chestnuts, drained
6 slices bread, crusts trimmed
3/4 cup melted butter

Layer asparagus, half the cheese, mixture of peas and soup, water chestnuts and remaining cheese in greased casserole. Cut bread slices into fourths; dip in melted butter to coat. Arrange over layers. Bake for 35 to 45 minutes or until bread is brown.

Approx Per Serving: Cal 527; Prot 19.9 g; T Fat 39.2 g; Chol 101.0 mg;
Carbo 27.1 g; Sod 1842.0 mg; Potas 467.0 mg.

Kay Clayton
AVA President-Elect
Kingsville, Texas

BROCCOLI CASSEROLE

Yields: 8 servings	Pan Size: 9x13 inch	Preheat: 375 degrees

1 10-ounce package frozen
   broccoli
6 eggs
24 ounces creamed small curd
   cottage cheese

6 tablespoons flour
8 ounces shredded American
   cheese
1/2 cup butter, softened
2 green onions, chopped

Thaw broccoli in colander under running hot water; separate pieces and drain. Combine broccoli, eggs, cottage cheese, flour, American cheese, butter and green onions in bowl; mix well. Spoon into greased casserole. Bake, covered, for 1 hour. This may be cooked in Crock•Pot on Low for 6 to 8 hours if preferred.

Approx Per Serving: Cal 332; Prot 20.2 g; T Fat 23.8 g; Chol 263.0 mg;
Carbo 9.4 g; Sod 704.0 mg; Potas 220.0 mg.

Dorothy Johnson
Mountain View, Wyoming

BROCCOLI AND ONION DELUXE

Yields: 10 servings   *Pan Size: 1½ quart*   *Preheat: 350 degrees*

2 10-ounce packages frozen
   cut broccoli
2 cups frozen whole small
   onions
2 tablespoons butter
2 tablespoons flour
¼ teaspoon salt

Dash of pepper
1 cup milk
3 ounces cream cheese
2 tablespoons butter
1 cup soft bread crumbs
¼ cup Parmesan cheese

Cook broccoli and onions in separate saucepans using package directions for each; drain. Melt 2 tablespoons butter in saucepan. Stir in flour, salt and pepper. Add milk. Cook until thickened, stirring constantly. Reduce heat to low. Add cream cheese. Cook until cream cheese melts, stirring constantly. Add vegetables. Pour into casserole. Bake for 20 minutes. Melt remaining 2 tablespoons butter in saucepan. Stir in bread crumbs and cheese. Sprinkle over casserole. Bake until crumbs are brown.

Approx Per Serving: Cal 141; Prot 4.9 g; T Fat 9.3 g; Chol 26.6 mg;
    Carbo 10.9 g; Sod 205.0 mg; Potas 201.0 mg.

Betty Albee
Leominster, Massachusetts

BROCCOLI AND RICE CASSEROLE

Yields: 6 servings   *Pan Size: 2 quart*   *Preheat: 300 degrees*

2 10-ounce packages frozen
   chopped broccoli
1½ cups rice
½ medium onion, chopped

2 tablespoons butter
1 can cream of chicken soup
1 16-ounce jar Cheez Whiz

Cook broccoli using package directions; drain. Cook rice using package directions; set aside. Sauté onion in butter in skillet. Add soup, broccoli and rice; mix well. Spoon into baking dish. Spoon Cheez Whiz over top. Bake, covered, for 20 minutes or until cheese melts.

Approx Per Serving: Cal 409; Prot 20.2 g; T Fat 25.3 g; Chol 62.0 mg;
    Carbo 26.9 g; Sod 1323.0 mg; Potas 439.0 mg.

Margie Golding
Belden, Mississippi

BROCCOLI 'N RICE 'R NICE

Yields: 6 servings　　　*Pan Size: 8x8 inch*　　　*Preheat: 350 degrees*

1 onion, finely chopped
1 stalk celery, chopped
1/2 cup butter
1　10-ounce package frozen
　chopped broccoli
1 can cream of chicken soup
1 cup shredded sharp
　Cheddar cheese

1 1/2 cups cooked rice
Tabasco sauce
Pepper to taste
1/2 cup shredded sharp
　Cheddar cheese
1　4-ounce package sliced
　almonds

Sauté onion and celery in butter in skillet. Cook broccoli using package directions; drain. Add soup and 1 cup cheese; mix well. Add broccoli mixture to sautéed vegetables. Stir in rice. Season with Tabasco sauce and salt and pepper to taste. Pour into casserole. Top with 1/2 cup cheese. Bake for 45 minutes. Top with almonds.

Approx Per Serving: Cal 481; Prot 15.0 g; T Fat 37.5 g; Chol 74.9 mg;
　　Carbo 24.3 g; Sod 695.0 mg; Potas 353.0 mg.

Faye Wilkinson
Hinds Community College
Vicksburg, Mississippi

BARBECUED CABBAGE

Yields: 4 servings　　　*Pan Size: 2 1/2 quart*

1　2-pound head cabbage
1/8 teaspoon salt
4 ounces bacon, chopped

1/4 cup sugar
1/4 cup vinegar
1/4 cup catsup

Cut cabbage into wedges. Place in saucepan. Add salt and enough water to cover. Cook until cabbage is tender. Fry bacon in skillet until brown. Add sugar, vinegar and catsup. Simmer for 3 minutes; set aside. Drain cabbage thoroughly. Place in serving dish. Reheat sauce. Pour over cabbage.

Approx Per Serving: Cal 283; Prot 11.7 g; T Fat 14.4 g; Chol 23.9 mg;
　　Carbo 30.0 g; Sod 736.0 mg; Potas 772.0 mg.

Rodney E. and Jean F. Meagher
New Tripoli, Pennsylvania

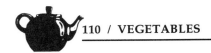

COPPER PENNIES

Yields: 8 servings

2 pounds carrots, sliced
1 medium green bell pepper,
    cut into strips
1 3-inch onion, sliced into
    rings
1 cup tomato juice
1/2 cup oil

1/4 cup sugar
3/4 cup vinegar
2 tablespoons Worcestershire
    sauce
1 tablespoon prepared
    mustard

Cook carrots in a small amount of water in saucepan for 10 minutes or until tender; drain and cool. Layer carrots, green pepper and onion in bowl. Combine tomato juice, oil, sugar, vinegar, Worcestershire sauce and mustard in saucepan. Bring to a boil. Pour hot mixture over layered vegetables. Chill, tightly covered, for 12 hours or longer.

Approx Per Serving: Cal 216; Prot 1.9 g; T Fat 14.0 g; Chol 0.0 mg;
    Carbo 23.3 g; Sod 248.0 mg; Potas 423.0 mg.

Anne E. Lentz
Charlotte, North Carolina

CORN CUSTARD

Yields: 20 servings   *Pan Size: 12x16 inch*   *Preheat: 350 degrees*

2 16-ounce cans creamed corn
6 eggs, beaten
1 1/2 cups cracker crumbs
2/3 cup melted butter
1 1/2 cups cream
2/3 cup finely chopped green
    bell pepper

2/3 cup finely chopped carrots
2/3 cup finely chopped celery
2/3 cup finely chopped onion
2 tablespoons sugar
2 teaspoons salt
16 drops of Tabasco sauce

Combine corn, eggs, cracker crumbs, butter, cream, remaining vegetables and seasonings in large bowl in order listed; mix well. Pour into buttered baking pan. Bake for 50 to 60 minutes or until custard is set.

Approx Per Serving: Cal 267; Prot 4.4 g; T Fat 20.1 g; Chol 123.0 mg;
    Carbo 23.3 g; Sod 599.0 mg; Potas 157.0 mg.

Catherine Bither
Southern Aroostook Vocational Education
Houlton, Maine

CORN PUDDING

Yields: 6 servings   *Pan Size: 1 quart*   *Preheat: 350 degrees*

1 tablespoon melted butter
1 cup milk
2 eggs, beaten

¼ cup sugar
¼ teaspoon salt
1 cup corn

Pour butter into casserole. Combine milk, eggs, sugar, salt and corn in bowl; mix well. Pour into prepared casserole. Bake for 1 hour.

Approx Per Serving: Cal 122; Prot 4.2 g; T Fat 5.4 g; Chol 102.0 mg;
Carbo 15.3 g; Sod 149.0 mg; Potas 146.0 mg.

Ann D. Austin
Carrollton, Virginia

SCALLOPED CORN

Yields: 8 servings   *Pan Size: 9x13 inch*   *Preheat: 350 degrees*

2 tablespoons butter
2 tablespoons flour
1 teaspoon salt
Dash of pepper
1 cup evaporated milk

2 eggs, beaten
2 16-ounce cans whole kernel
corn, drained
½ cup buttered bread crumbs
Paprika to taste

Melt butter in saucepan. Stir in flour, salt and pepper. Add evaporated milk gradually. Cook until thickened, stirring constantly. Add a small amount of hot mixture to eggs; add eggs to hot mixture. Cook for 1 minute longer, stirring constantly. Add corn. Pour into casserole. Top with buttered crumbs and paprika. Place in shallow pan of hot water. Bake for 45 to 50 minutes or until set.

Approx Per Serving: Cal 199; Prot 7.8 g; T Fat 8.2 g; Chol 85.5 mg;
Carbo 27.6 g; Sod 373.0 mg; Potas 424.0 mg.

Jean Holbrook
Roanoke, Virginia

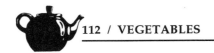

CORN AND BEAN DELIGHT

Yields: 6 servings   *Pan Size: 2 quart*   *Preheat: 350 degrees*

1 16-ounce can French-style
 green beans, drained
1 16-ounce can white Shoe
 Peg corn, drained
1 can cream of celery soup
1/2 cup sour cream
1/4 cup chopped onion

1 cup shredded sharp
 Cheddar cheese
1/2 cup margarine
1 4-ounce tube Ritz crackers,
 crumbled
1/2 cup slivered almonds

Layer green beans and corn in casserole. Combine soup, sour cream, onion and cheese in saucepan. Heat until cheese is partially melted. Pour over beans. Melt margarine in saucepan. Add cracker crumbs and almonds. Sprinkle over casserole. Bake until bubbly.

Approx Per Serving: Cal 526; Prot 12.9 g; T Fat 39.7 g; Chol 33.6 mg;
 Carbo 39.7 g; Sod 1047.0 mg; Potas 406.0 mg.

Cordelia S. Overstreet
Roanoke, Virginia

SHOE PEG CORN AND GREEN BEAN CASSEROLE

Yields: 10 servings   *Pan Size: 2 quart*   *Preheat: 325 degrees*

2 16-ounce cans French-style
 green beans, drained
1 16-ounce can Shoe Peg corn,
 drained
1/2 cup chopped celery
1/2 cup chopped onion
1/4 cup chopped green bell
 pepper

3/4 cup shredded extra-sharp
 cheese
1 can cream of celery soup
3/4 cup sour cream
1/2 cup margarine
6 ounces Ritz crackers,
 crumbled
1/2 cup slivered almonds

Combine green beans, corn, celery, onion, green pepper, cheese, soup and sour cream in bowl; mix well. Pour into casserole. Melt butter in saucepan. Add cracker crumbs. Sprinkle over casserole. Top with almonds. Bake for 30 to 40 minutes or until bubbly.

Approx Per Serving: Cal 357; Prot 8.2 g; T Fat 26.0 g; Chol 19.7 mg;
 Carbo 30.7 g; Sod 790.0 mg; Potas 334.0 mg.

Mary M. McGee
Starr, South Carolina

PEA AND BROCCOLI CASSEROLE

Yields: 6 servings   *Pan Size: medium casserole*   *Preheat: 350 degrees*

1 10-ounce package frozen
   peas
1 10-ounce package frozen
   chopped broccoli
1 can cream of mushroom soup

1 8-ounce jar Cheez Whiz
1/2 cup slivered almonds
1/2 2-ounce jar sliced
   mushrooms, drained

Cook peas and broccoli together in a small amount of water in saucepan until broccoli is tender; drain. Add soup, Cheez Whiz, almonds and mushrooms; mix well. Spoon into casserole. Bake for 20 minutes.

Approx Per Serving: Cal 289; Prot 14.4 g; T Fat 19.0 g; Chol 24.5 mg;
    Carbo 17.8 g; Sod 897.0 mg; Potas 392.0 mg.

Jean Holbrook
Roanoke, Virginia

BAKED POTATO FANS

Yields: 4 servings   *Pan Size: 7x11 inch*   *Preheat: 375 degrees*

4 medium baking potatoes
1/4 cup melted margarine
1/4 teaspoon garlic salt
Pepper to taste

2 tablespoons dry bread
   crumbs
1/4 cup Parmesan cheese
Paprika to taste

Cut potatoes crosswise into 1/8-inch slices, cutting only 3/4 of the way through. Place cut side up in baking dish. Brush with margarine. Sprinkle with garlic salt and pepper. Bake for 45 minutes, brushing several times with butter. Sprinkle with mixture of bread crumbs and cheese. Top with paprika. Bake for 20 to 30 minutes longer or until tender.

Approx Per Serving: Cal 349; Prot 7.0 g; T Fat 13.1 g; Chol 3.9 mg;
    Carbo 52.0 g; Sod 385.0 mg; Potas 857.0 mg.

Sybil B. Murphy
Greensboro, North Carolina

POTATO CASSEROLE

Yields: 12 servings   *Pan Size: 9x13 inch*   *Preheat: 350 degrees*

10 medium potatoes	3/4 cup finely chopped onion
1/2 cup melted margarine	2 cups shredded Cheddar
2 cups sour cream	cheese

Cook potatoes in water to cover in saucepan until tender. Cool, peel and grate potatoes. Combine with margarine, sour cream and onion in bowl. Add salt and pepper to taste; mix well. Spoon into greased baking dish. Sprinkle with cheese. Bake for 25 minutes.

Approx Per Serving: Cal 413; Prot 10.0 g; T Fat 22.1 g; Chol 36.8 mg;
     Carbo 45.2 g; Sod 240.0 mg; Potas 796.0 mg.

Suellen Murphy
Thomasville, North Carolina

JUDY'S POTATO CASSEROLE

Yields: 8 servings   *Pan Size: 9x13 inch*   *Preheat: 300 degrees*

24 ounces frozen hashed brown potatoes	8 ounces sour cream
1/2 cup melted margarine	1 tablespoon salt
1/2 cup chopped onion	1/2 teaspoon pepper
1 can cream of chicken soup	Tabasco sauce to taste
2 cups shredded mild Cheddar cheese	2 cups crushed cornflakes
	1/4 cup melted butter

Combine potatoes, 1/2 cup margarine, onion, soup, cheese, sour cream and seasonings in bowl; mix well. Spoon into buttered baking dish. Top with mixture of cornflakes and 1/4 cup melted butter. Bake for 1 hour. May prepare the day ahead and store in refrigerator until baking time.

Approx Per Serving: Cal 571; Prot 12.3 g; T Fat 44.4 g; Chol 60.7 mg;
     Carbo 33.9 g; Sod 1550.0 mg; Potas 493.0 mg.

Judy Francis
Birmingham, Alabama

POTATO HOLIDAY

Yields: 8 servings   *Pan Size: 9x12 inch*   *Preheat: 350 degrees*

4 pounds frozen hashed
  brown potatoes
1 cup chopped onions
1/4 cup butter

1 can cream of celery soup
2 cups sour cream
1 1/2 cups shredded Cheddar
  cheese

Place potatoes in baking dish. Sauté onions in butter in skillet. Add remaining ingredients; mix well. Spoon over potatoes. Bake, covered, for 50 minutes. Bake, uncovered, for 10 minutes longer. May prepare the day ahead and store in refrigerator until baking time.

Approx Per Serving: Cal 786; Prot 15.0 g; T Fat 52.6 g; Chol 67.3 mg;
    Carbo 70.7 g; Sod 556.0 mg; Potas 1160.0 mg.

Linda Stemper, Executive Director
Wisconsin Vocational Association
Verona, Wisconsin

POTATOES FOR A CROWD

Yields: 12 servings   *Pan Size: 9x11 inch*   *Preheat: 325 degrees*

32 ounces frozen hashed
  brown potatoes
1/4 cup chopped onion
1/2 cup butter

8 ounces sour cream
1 can cream of chicken soup
2 cups shredded American
  cheese

Place potatoes and onion in buttered baking dish. Combine butter, sour cream, soup and cheese in saucepan. Heat until cheese and butter are melted, stirring frequently. Pour over potatoes. Bake for 1 hour or until potatoes are tender.

Approx Per Serving: Cal 367; Prot 7.9 g; T Fat 27.6 g; Chol 48.9 mg;
    Carbo 24.4 g; Sod 556.0 mg; Potas 411.0 mg.

Sally Carder
Arkansas Department of Education
Little Rock, Arkansas

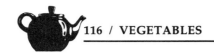

SCALLOPED POTATOES

Yields: 10 servings   *Pan Size: 9x13 inch*   *Preheat: 350 degrees*

32 ounces hashed brown
  potatoes
12 ounces sour cream
1 can cream of chicken soup

1/2 cup chopped onion
1/2 cup melted margarine
2 cups shredded Cheddar
  cheese

Combine potatoes with sour cream, soup, onion, melted margarine and cheese in bowl. Add salt and pepper to taste; mix well. Spoon into baking dish. Bake for 45 minutes.

Approx Per Serving: Cal 472; Prot 10.5 g; T Fat 35.9 g; Chol 41.1 mg;
    Carbo 30.1 g; Sod 519.0 mg; Potas 503.0 mg.

Mary Jacoby
Kent, Ohio

SWISS SPINACH

Yields: 6 servings   *Pan Size: 1 1/2 quart*   *Preheat: 350 degrees*

2 cups cooked elbow macaroni
1 cup shredded Swiss cheese
2 cups chopped spinach
2 tablespoons melted butter

2 tablespoons flour
1 cup milk
1 cup shredded Swiss cheese

Layer macaroni, 1 cup cheese and spinach in baking dish. Blend butter and flour in saucepan. Stir in milk gradually. Cook until thickened, stirring constantly. Pour over layers. Top with 1 cup cheese. Bake for 30 minutes or until golden brown.

Approx Per Serving: Cal 298; Prot 15.6 g; T Fat 16.0 g; Chol 50.5 mg;
    Carbo 23.1 g; Sod 163.0 mg; Potas 247.0 mg.

Rosemary Kolde, AVA President 1985-1986
AVA Cookbook Committee
Cincinnati, Ohio

SWEET POTATO CASSEROLE

Yields: 8 servings   *Pan Size: 2 quart*   *Preheat: 350 degrees*

3 cups mashed cooked sweet
   potatoes
1 cup sugar
1/2 teaspoon salt
2 eggs, slightly beaten
1/2 cup milk
1 teaspoon vanilla extract

3 tablespoons melted
   margarine
1 cup packed brown sugar
1/3 cup flour
3 tablespoons melted
   margarine
1 cup finely chopped pecans

Combine sweet potatoes, sugar and salt in bowl; mix well. Stir in eggs, milk
and vanilla. Blend in 3 tablespoons melted margarine. Spoon into baking
dish. Combine brown sugar, flour, 3 tablespoons melted margarine and
pecans in bowl. Mix with fingers until crumbly. Sprinkle over casserole.
Bake for 30 to 35 minutes or until light brown.

Approx Per Serving: Cal 500; Prot 4.9 g; T Fat 20.2 g; Chol 68.5 mg;
   Carbo 78.5 g; Sod 315.0 mg; Potas 478.0 mg.

Ann H. Lowrey, President
S.C. Vocational Home Economics
Greenville, South Carolina

Amanda Godfrey

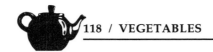

CHEESY VEGETABLE CASSEROLE

Yields: 4 servings   *Pan Size: 1 quart*   *Preheat: 350 degrees*

1 16-ounce package frozen
   mixed broccoli, cauliflower
   and carrots
1/4 cup butter

8 ounces American cheese,
   cubed
1 cup crushed butter crackers
1/4 cup melted butter

Place vegetables in baking dish. Melt 1/4 cup butter and cheese in saucepan, stirring until smooth. Mix with vegetables. Sprinkle mixture of crumbs and melted butter over casserole. Bake for 20 to 25 minutes. Serve immediately.

Approx Per Serving: Cal 485; Prot 16.1 g; T Fat 41.1 g; Chol 116.0 mg;
   Carbo 16.3 g; Sod 1051.0 mg; Potas 292.0 mg.

Mary E. Van Vactor
Daviess County State Voc
Owensboro, Kentucky

HOMINY CASSEROLE

Yields: 8 servings   *Pan Size: 2 quart*   *Preheat: 325 degrees*

3 14-ounce cans hominy,
   drained

1 cup sour cream
1 8-ounce jar Cheez Whiz

Combine hominy, sour cream and Cheez Whiz in casserole; mix well. Add salt and pepper to taste. Bake for 25 minutes or until heated through.

Approx Per Serving: Cal 282; Prot 11.3 g; T Fat 14.7 g; Chol 30.7 mg;
   Carbo 31.5 g; Sod 374.0 mg; Potas 522.0 mg.

Francie Soliday, President
Oklahoma Vocational Association, Shawnee, Oklahoma

GREEN CHILI HOMINY CASSEROLE

Yields: 8 servings   *Pan Size: 2 quart*   *Preheat: 325 degrees*

3 14-ounce cans hominy,
   drained
1 4-ounce can chopped green
   chilies

2 cups sour cream
1 can cream of celery soup
1 cup shredded smoky sharp
   Cheddar cheese

Combine hominy, green chilies, sour cream and soup in bowl; mix well. Spoon into greased casserole. Sprinkle cheese on top. Bake for 1 hour.

Approx Per Serving: Cal 339; Prot 10.9 g; T Fat 20.1 g; Chol 44.3 mg;
   Carbo 34.7 g; Sod 410.0 mg; Potas 582.0 mg.

Martha Atchley
O.T. Autry Area Vocational Technical Center
Enid, Oklahoma

LINGUINI WITH LEMON SAUCE

Yields: 6 servings   *Pan Size: heavy skillet*

8 ounces linguini
2 tablespoons butter
1 tablespoon grated lemon
  rind
1/4 cup whipping cream

2 tablespoons fresh lemon
  juice
2 tablespoons Parmesan
  cheese

Cook linguini in 10 cups boiling salted water for 7 to 9 minutes or until tender; drain. Heat butter in skillet. Add lemon rind and cream. Mix in linguini and lemon juice. Bring to a simmer. Add cheese; toss to mix. Serve with additional Parmesan cheese.

Approx Per Serving: Cal 217; Prot 5.7 g; T Fat 8.5 g; Chol 25.2 mg;
    Carbo 29.4 g; Sod 68.2 mg; Potas 102.0 mg.

Sara Jo Robinson
Indianapolis, Indiana

ARROZ CON JOCOQUI

Yields: 8 servings   *Pan Size: 1 1/2 quart*   *Preheat: 350 degrees*

12 ounces Monterey Jack
  cheese
3 cups sour cream
2 4-ounce cans chopped green
  chilies

3 cups cooked rice
1/2 teaspoon salt
1/4 teaspoon pepper
1/2 cup shredded Cheddar
  cheese

Cut Monterey Jack cheese into strips. Mix sour cream with green chilies. Layer rice seasoned with salt and pepper, sour cream mixture and cheese strips in buttered casserole. Bake for 25 minutes. Top with Cheddar cheese. Bake for 5 minutes longer or until cheese melts.

Approx Per Serving: Cal 467; Prot 17.0 g; T Fat 33.4 g; Chol 84.6 mg;
    Carbo 25.3 g; Sod 453.0 mg; Potas 283.0 mg.

Elizabeth H. Mettling
Lewis, Kansas

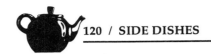

CURRIED RICE WITH RAISINS

Yields: 4 servings   *Pan Size: medium saucepan*

1 cup uncooked rice	1¹/2 teaspoons salt
1/2 cup chopped onion	2 cups chicken broth
6 tablespoons butter	1/2 cup raisins
1 tablespoon curry powder	

Sauté rice and onion in butter in saucepan until golden. Add curry powder, salt, broth and raisins. Bring to a boil; reduce heat. Simmer, covered, for 20 minutes or until rice is tender.

Approx Per Serving: Cal 412; Prot 6.9 g; T Fat 18.5 g; Chol 47.1 mg;
    Carbo 56.5 g; Sod 1338.0 mg; Potas 363.0 mg.

Kenneth Harmon
Washington, District of Columbia

DUTCH RICE

Yields: 5 servings   *Pan Size: 2 quart*   *Preheat: 350 degrees*

1 cup uncooked rice	1 4-ounce can sliced
1 cup chopped onion	mushrooms, drained
1/4 cup chopped green bell	1/2 cup chopped unsalted
pepper	peanuts
1/2 cup butter	2 cups chicken broth
1/2 cup chopped celery	Pepper to taste

Sauté rice, onion and green pepper in butter in skillet until rice is golden. Stir in celery, mushrooms, peanuts, broth and pepper to taste. Pour into baking dish. Bake, uncovered, for 1 hour or until rice is tender.

Approx Per Serving: Cal 414; Prot 9.4 g; T Fat 26.5 g; Chol 50.1 mg;
    Carbo 36.6 g; Sod 482.0 mg; Potas 406.0 mg.

Sandy Turner
Leominster, Massachusetts

ELIZABETH RICE

Yields: 12 servings	Pan Size: bowl

3 cups cooked rice
2 3-ounce packages vanilla
   instant pudding mix
1¼ cups milk

1¼ cups vanilla ice cream,
   softened
½ teaspoon cinnamon
2 cups whipped topping

Rinse rice with cool water after cooking; drain well. Combine pudding mix, milk, ice cream and cinnamon in mixer bowl. Beat for 1 minute. Fold in rice. Chill in refrigerator. Fold in whipped topping just before serving. Serve as side dish, salad or dessert.

Approx Per Serving: Cal 192; Prot 2.5 g; T Fat 5.6 g; Chol 9.6 mg;
   Carbo 33.1 g; Sod 121.0 mg; Potas 78.2 mg.

Pat Bortnem
Volga, South Dakota

FRIED RICE

Yields: 4 servings	Pan Size: skillet

1 cup water
½ teaspoon salt
½ cup uncooked long grain
   rice
1 egg, beaten
1 tablespoon margarine

1 green onion, chopped
2 slices crisp-fried bacon,
   crumbled
1 tablespoon oil
2 teaspoons soy sauce

Combine water, salt and rice in saucepan. Bring to a full rolling boil; reduce heat to low. Cook, covered, for 10 to 15 minutes or until rice is tender. Beat egg with salt and pepper to taste. Melt margarine in skillet. Pour in egg mixture. Cook for 2 to 3 minutes, stirring to break egg into small pieces. Remove to plate to cool. Sauté rice, egg, onion and bacon in oil in skillet for 2 to 3 minutes or until heated through. Add soy sauce; mix well.

Approx Per Serving: Cal 179; Prot 4.3 g; T Fat 9.3 g; Chol 71.2 mg;
   Carbo 19.2 g; Sod 540.0 mg; Potas 63.8 mg.

Dale McKinnie
Greensboro, North Carolina

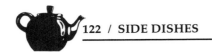

GREEN AND GOLD PILAF

Yields: 8 servings　　　　*Pan Size: 3 quart*

1½ cups uncooked long grain
　rice
3 tablespoons butter
3 cups water
6 chicken bouillon cubes

¼ teaspoon white pepper
3 small carrots
1　10-ounce package frozen
　French-style green beans,
　thawed

Combine rice, butter, water, bouillon cubes and pepper in saucepan. Bring to a boil; reduce heat. Simmer, covered, for 15 minutes or until rice is tender. Cut carrots into short thin sticks. Add carrots and beans to rice. Let stand, covered, for 5 minutes. Season to taste.

Approx Per Serving: Cal 188; Prot 3.6 g; T Fat 4.7 g; Chol 11.6 mg;
　　Carbo 32.8 g; Sod 913.0 mg; Potas 273.0 mg.

Dorothy Rolf
Hastings, Nebraska

SHOE PEG CORN RELISH

Yields: 10 servings　　　　*Pan Size: saucepan*

1　16-ounce can small green
　peas
1　16-ounce can white Shoe
　Peg corn
1　4-ounce jar chopped pimento
1 cup chopped celery
1 medium green bell pepper,
　chopped

1 bunch green onions,
　chopped
1 cup sugar
½ cup apple cider vinegar
1 teaspoon salt
1 teaspoon pepper
¼ cup oil
1 tablespoon water

Drain canned vegetables. Combine with celery, green pepper and green onions in bowl. Mix sugar, vinegar, salt, pepper, oil and water in saucepan. Bring to a boil, stirring until sugar dissolves. Cool. Pour over vegetables. Chill for 24 hours to 1 month. Serve with fried chicken or any meat.

Approx Per Serving: Cal 203; Prot 3.6 g; T Fat 6.2 g; Chol 0.0 mg;
　　Carbo 36.6 g; Sod 429.0 mg; Potas 230.0 mg.

*Francis and Vivian Tuttle
*AVA President 1987-1988
Stillwater, Oklahoma

Artist: *Ava Buck*—Putnam County Vo-Tech; Lynne McNiel, Teacher;
　　Leon, West Virginia

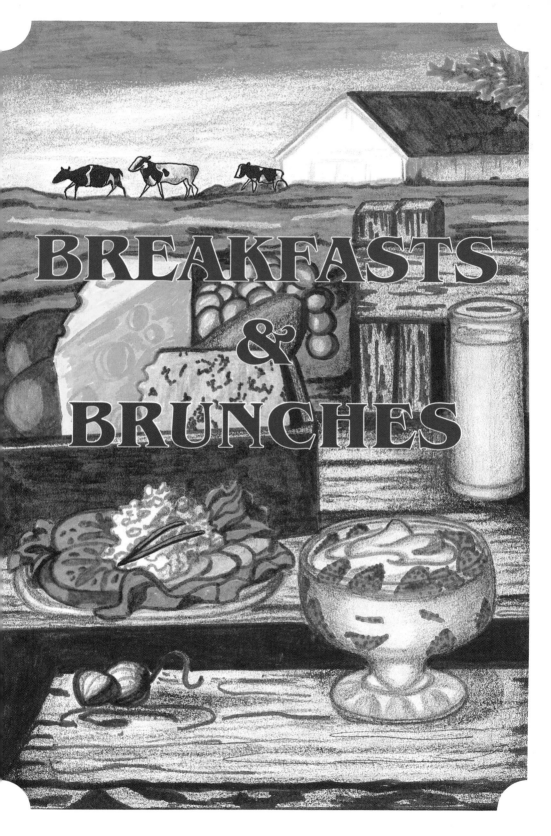

BREAKFASTS & BRUNCHES

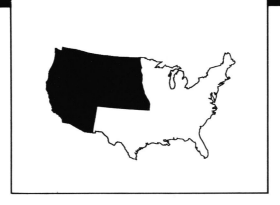

Big West Breakfast Bar
Region V

Fresh Fruit or Fruit Juice

Breakfast Eggs
page 126

Quick Quiche
page 130

Breakfast Pizza
page 127

Sausage Patties and Crisp Bacon

Arroz con Jocoqui
page 119

Swedish Oatmeal Pancakes
page 139

Toasted Dakota Bread
page 154

Coffee or Tea

HOT CURRIED FRUIT

Yields: 10 servings   *Pan Size: 9x13 inch*   *Preheat: 325 degrees*

1 29-ounce can pear halves
1 20-ounce can pineapple
   chunks
1 29-ounce can peach halves
1 29-ounce can apricot halves

1/2 cup butter, softened
1 cup packed brown sugar
1 tablespoon cornstarch
1 1/2 teaspoons curry powder

Drain fruit well. Arrange fruit in baking dish. Combine butter, brown sugar, cornstarch and curry powder in small bowl; blend well. Spoon over fruit. Bake for 1 hour, basting occasionally. May prepare fruit, refrigerate for several hours and bake just before serving.

Approx Per Serving: Cal 401; Prot 1.3 g; T Fat 9.6 g; Chol 24.8 mg;
    Carbo 83.4 g; Sod 100.0 mg; Potas 387.0 mg.

Sherry Baber
Owensboro, Kentucky

JUDY'S FROZEN FRUIT CUPS

Yields: 12 servings   *Pan Size: muffin cups*

1 6-ounce can frozen orange
   juice concentrate
1 6-ounce can frozen
   lemonade concentrate
1 cup sugar
2 1/2 cups water
3 or 4 bananas, sliced

1 10-ounce package frozen
   whole strawberries
1 16-ounce can crushed
   pineapple
1 4-ounce jar maraschino
   cherries

Thaw orange juice and lemonade concentrates. Combine with sugar and water in bowl; stir until sugar dissolves. Add bananas, strawberries, pineapple and cherries. Spoon into foil-lined muffin cups or clear plastic glasses. Freeze until firm.

Approx Per Serving: Cal 183; Prot 1.0 g; T Fat 0.4 g; Chol 0.0 mg;
    Carbo 46.7 g; Sod 2.7 mg; Potas 314.0 mg.

Virginia C. Seal, Past President
Florida Special Needs Association, 1986-1987
Panama City, Florida

APPLE AND SAUSAGE RING

Yields: 6 servings	Pan Size: 9 inch	Preheat: 350 degrees

2 eggs, slightly beaten
1/2 cup milk
1 1/2 cups cracker crumbs
1/3 cup minced onion

2 pounds pork sausage
1 cup chopped peeled apple
2 whole apples
2 tablespoons butter

Combine eggs, milk, crumbs, onion, sausage and chopped apple in bowl; mix well. Press into ring mold; invert onto baking sheet and remove mold. Bake for 1 hour. Core unpeeled apples; slice 1/2-inch thick. Sauté apple slices in butter in skillet until tender-crisp. Place Sausage Ring on serving plate. Spoon apples around ring and in center. Serve with scrambled eggs and Coconut-Orange Toast (page 131). Unbaked Sausage Ring may be tightly wrapped in foil and frozen. Allow extra time for baking.

Approx Per Serving: Cal 1029; Prot 24.5 g; T Fat 85.9 g; Chol 208.0 mg;
Carbo 53.8 g; Sod 1639.0 mg; Potas 524.0 mg.

Betty Weissinger
Abilene, Texas

BREAKFAST EGGS

Yields: 15 servings	Pan Size: 9x13 inch	Preheat: 325 degrees

2 pounds pork sausage
2 1/2 cups plain croutons
2 cups shredded Cheddar
  cheese
5 eggs

3/4 teaspoon dry mustard
2 1/2 cups milk
1 can cream of mushroom soup
1/2 cup milk

Cook sausage in skillet until brown, stirring until crumbly; drain well. Layer croutons, cheese and sausage in greased baking dish. Beat eggs with dry mustard and 2 1/2 cups milk; pour over layers. Chill, covered, in refrigerator for several hours to overnight. Mix soup and 1/2 cup milk in small bowl; spoon over top. Bake for 1 hour. Let stand for 10 to 15 minutes before cutting.

Approx Per Serving: Cal 407; Prot 15.4 g; T Fat 34.5 g; Chol 155.0 mg;
Carbo 8.3 g; Sod 760.0 mg; Potas 246.0 mg.

Barbara Hoff, Vice President
South Dakota Vocational Association
Madison, South Dakota

BREAKFAST PIZZA

Yields: 6 servings   *Pan Size: 12 inch*   *Preheat: 375 degrees*

1 pound ground pork
1 8-count package refrigerator
  crescent rolls
1 cup frozen hashed brown
  potatoes
1/2 cup crumbled crisp-fried
  bacon
1/2 cup sliced fresh mushrooms

1 cup shredded Cheddar
  cheese
1 cup shredded mozzarella
  cheese
5 eggs, beaten
1/4 cup milk
2 tablespoons Parmesan
  cheese

Cook ground pork in skillet until brown, stirring until crumbly; drain well. Separate rolls into triangles; arrange with points toward center in pizza pan and press over bottom and side of pan to form crust. Layer cooked pork, potatoes, bacon, mushrooms and mixture of Cheddar and mozzarella cheeses in prepared pan. Beat eggs with milk; pour over layers. Sprinkle with Parmesan cheese. Bake for 25 to 30 minutes or until set.

Approx Per Serving: Cal 824; Prot 32.0 g; T Fat 65.7 g; Chol 333.0 mg;
    Carbo 24.8 g; Sod 1402.0 mg; Potas 564.0 mg.

Mary Ellen Johnson
Huron, South Dakota

BRUNCH STRATA

Yields: 8 servings   *Pan Size: 9x11 inch*   *Preheat: 350 degrees*

1 pound hot pork sausage
14 slices brown bread, crusts
  removed
1/3 cup melted margarine
10 ounces sharp Cheddar
  cheese, shredded

6 eggs, beaten
2 cups half and half
1 teaspoon salt
1 teaspoon dry mustard
1/4 teaspoon nutmeg

Cook sausage in skillet until brown, stirring until crumbly; drain well. Brush bread slices with margarine. Layer half the bread, half the cheese, all the sausage, remaining bread and remaining cheese in greased baking dish. Beat eggs with half and half and seasonings. Pour over layers. Chill, covered, overnight. Bake, uncovered, for 35 to 40 minutes. Serve with fresh fruit and coffee cake.

Approx Per Serving: Cal 698; Prot 25.9 g; T Fat 54.8 g; Chol 304.0 mg;
    Carbo 26.0 g; Sod 1214.0 mg; Potas 341.0 mg.

Yvonne Harrison
Home Economics Teacher, Cave Spring High School
Roanoke, Virginia

CHILI CHEESE CASSEROLE

Yields: 12 servings   *Pan Size: 9x13 inch*   *Preheat: 350 degrees*

2 8-ounce cans whole green
  chilies
1 pound Monterey Jack
  cheese, shredded

12 eggs, beaten
2 cups sour cream

Rinse chilies; remove seed and pat dry. Alternate layers of chilies and cheese in buttered baking dish. Beat eggs with sour cream. Pour over layers. Bake for 30 minutes or until puffed and golden. Serve with seasonal fresh fruit and sausages.

Approx Per Serving: Cal 317; Prot 17.3 g; T Fat 25.1 g; Chol 326.0 mg;
    Carbo 6.1 g; Sod 294.0 mg; Potas 279.0 mg.

Shirley Chenault
Weatherford, Texas

GREEN CHILI BREAKFAST EGGS

Yields: 6 servings   *Pan Size: 8 inch*   *Preheat: 450 degrees*

5 eggs, slightly beaten
2 tablespoons melted
  margarine
1/4 cup flour
1/2 teaspoon baking powder
Garlic powder to taste
8 ounces small curd cottage
  cheese

1 cup shredded Monterey Jack
  cheese
1 cup shredded Cheddar
  cheese
1 8-ounce can chopped green
  chilies

Combine eggs, margarine, flour, baking powder and garlic powder in bowl; beat until smooth. Add cheeses and green chilies; mix well. Pour into well-greased pie plate. Bake for 10 minutes. Reduce temperature to 350 degrees. Bake for 20 minutes longer. Let stand for 5 minutes before cutting. May arrange thinly sliced tomatoes over top for final 5 minutes of baking.

Approx Per Serving: Cal 304; Prot 19.7 g; T Fat 22.1 g; Chol 271.0 mg;
    Carbo 6.0 g; Sod 501.0 mg; Potas 127.0 mg.

Betty Weissinger
Abilene, Texas

JUDY'S OVEN OMELET

Yields: 6 servings   *Pan Size: 10 inch*   *Preheat: 350 degrees*

12 slices bacon
4 1-ounce slices American
   cheese
8 eggs, beaten
1 cup milk

¹/₄ cup chopped green bell
   pepper
¹/₄ cup sliced fresh mushrooms
¹/₄ cup sautéed chopped onion

Cook bacon in skillet or microwave until crisp; drain. Shape 1 slice into curl, chop 4 slices and reserve remaining slices whole. Cut cheese slices into halves; arrange in lightly buttered pie plate. Beat eggs with milk. Add chopped bacon, green pepper, mushrooms and sautéed onion; mix well. Pour into pie plate. Bake for 30 minutes. Place bacon curl in center; arrange bacon slices spoke-fashion on top. Bake for 10 minutes longer. Let stand for 5 minutes before cutting. Garnish with chopped parsley.

Approx Per Serving: Cal 278; Prot 17.7 g; T Fat 21.0 g; Chol 399.0 mg;
    Carbo 3.9 g; Sod 582.0 mg; Potas 262.0 mg.

Judy White Harris
AVA Teacher of the Year 1987
Sarasota, Florida

POSNER'S FAMOUS SPINACH QUICHE

Yields: 8 servings   *Pan Size: 9 inch*   *Preheat: 350 degrees*

1 10-ounce package frozen
   chopped spinach
1 frozen 9-inch pie shell
2 eggs, beaten
1 cup sour cream
1 teaspoon salt

Pepper to taste
1 2¹/₂-ounce can French-fried
   onions
2 cups shredded Cheddar
   cheese

Cook spinach using package directions; drain well. Prick pie shell with fork. Bake for 7 to 8 minutes. Beat eggs with sour cream. Add spinach, salt, pepper onions and cheese; mix well. Pour into pie shell. Increase temperature to 375 degrees. Bake quiche for 40 minutes or until center is set and crust is golden brown. May substitute broccoli for spinach.

Approx Per Serving: Cal 345; Prot 12.3 g; T Fat 26.1 g; Chol 114.0 mg;
    Carbo 16.1 g; Sod 654.0 mg; Potas 294.0 mg.

Roni Posner
AVA Assistant Executive Director for Professional Development
Washington, District of Columbia

QUICK QUICHE

Yields: 6 servings   *Pan Size: 9 inch*   *Preheat: 350 degrees*

1/2 cup chopped green chilies
1/2 cup chopped ham
1/2 cup shredded Cheddar
   cheese
1/2 cup buttermilk baking mix

1 3/4 cups milk
4 eggs
1/4 teaspoon salt
1/8 teaspoon pepper

Place green chilies, ham and cheese in lightly greased pie plate. Combine baking mix, milk, eggs, salt and pepper in blender container. Process until well mixed. Pour into pie plate. Bake for 50 to 55 minutes or until knife inserted in center comes out clean.

Approx Per Serving: Cal 207; Prot 12.4 g; T Fat 13.6 g; Chol 211.0 mg;
    Carbo 8.6 g; Sod 548.0 mg; Potas 252.0 mg.

Phyllis J. Eshbaugh
Fort Scott, Kansas

SOUTHERN BISCUITS

Yields: 36 biscuits   *Pan Size: baking sheet*   *Preheat: 450 degrees*

10 cups self-rising flour
1/4 cup baking powder
1/4 cup sugar
1 3/4 cups shortening

1 quart buttermilk
2 cups self-rising flour
1/2 cup melted butter

Mix 10 cups flour, baking powder and sugar in large bowl. Cut in shortening until crumbly. Add buttermilk; mix well. Mixture will be sticky. Sift 2 cups flour onto work surface. Pat dough into rectangle on floured surface with floured hands. Fold over left to right and right to left; fold over from top 3 times. Roll to less than 1-inch thickness; cut with biscuit cutter from outside edge. Place 1 inch apart on greased baking sheet. Bake for 10 minutes or until golden brown. Brush with melted butter.

Approx Per Biscuit: Cal 275; Prot 4.9 g; T Fat 13.2 g; Chol 7.9 mg;
    Carbo 34.0 g; Sod 609.0 mg; Potas 81.4 mg.

Pandra Warren
Lexington Vocational Center
Lexington, South Carolina

COCONUT-ORANGE TOAST

Yields: 16 servings   *Pan Size: 10x15 inch*   *Preheat: 400 degrees*

16 slices sandwich bread
1 cup margarine, softened
1 cup orange marmalade
1 teaspoon cinnamon

1/2 teaspoon nutmeg
4 teaspoons grated orange rind
3/4 cup shredded coconut

Spread bread slices with half the margarine. Mix remaining 1/2 cup margarine with marmalade, cinnamon, nutmeg and orange rind in small bowl. Spread bread slices with marmalade mixture; sprinkle with coconut. Place on baking sheet. Bake for 6 to 8 minutes or until toasted. Cut each slice into 4 triangles. Keep warm in 200-degree oven, leaving door ajar.

Approx Per Serving: Cal 222; Prot 1.9 g; T Fat 13.5 g; Chol 0.0 mg;
Carbo 24.7 g; Sod 261.0 mg; Potas 165.0 mg.

Betty Weissinger
Abilene, Texas

Adrienne A. Fulkerson

SOUR CREAM AND PECAN COFFEE CAKE

Yields: 12 servings *Pan Size: 9x13 inch* *Preheat: 325 degrees*

1/2 cup butter, softened
1 cup sugar
2 eggs
1 teaspoon vanilla extract
2 cups flour
1 teaspoon baking powder
1 teaspoon soda

1/2 teaspoon salt
1 cup sour cream
1/3 cup packed brown sugar
1/2 cup sugar
1 teaspoon cinnamon
1 cup chopped pecans

Cream butter and 1 cup sugar in bowl until light and fluffy. Beat in eggs 1 at a time. Add vanilla. Add mixture of flour, baking powder, soda and salt alternately with sour cream, mixing well after each addition. Pour into greased baking pan. Sprinkle mixture of brown sugar, 1/2 cup sugar, cinnamon and pecans over top. Bake for 40 minutes.

Approx Per Serving: Cal 383; Prot 4.7 g; T Fat 19.5 g; Chol 74.9 mg;
    Carbo 49.4 g; Sod 275.0 mg; Potas 122.0 mg.

Suzanne H. Waldrop, Former President
National Assn. of Voc. Home Economics Teachers
Park City, Kentucky

SOUR CREAM COFFEE CAKE

Yields: 10 servings *Pan Size: bundt pan* *Preheat: 350 degrees*

1 cup margarine, softened
2 cups sugar
2 eggs
1 cup sour cream
1/2 teaspoon vanilla extract
2 cups sifted flour

1 teaspoon baking powder
1/4 teaspoon salt
1/2 cup chopped pecans
1/4 cup packed brown sugar
2 teaspoons cinnamon

Cream margarine, sugar and eggs in bowl until light and fluffy. Fold in sour cream and vanilla. Sift in flour, baking powder and salt; mix well. Mix pecans, brown sugar and cinnamon in small bowl. Alternate layers of batter and pecan mixture in greased and floured bundt pan. Bake for 55 to 60 minutes or until cake tests done. Cool in pan. Invert onto serving plate. Serve on second day for improved flavor.

Approx Per Serving: Cal 527; Prot 5.0 g; T Fat 28.4 g; Chol 65.0 mg;
    Carbo 65.1 g; Sod 330.0 mg; Potas 122.0 mg.

Audrey Shafer
St. Petersburg, Florida

CHOCOLATE DOUGHNUTS

Yields: 18 doughnuts   *Pan Size: deep fryer*   *Preheat: 350 degrees*

3¹/2 ounces unsweetened
  baking chocolate
2 tablespoons margarine
3 eggs
1¹/4 cups sugar
1 teaspoon salt

1 teaspoon soda
4 cups flour
1 cup buttermilk
Oil for deep frying
2 cups confectioners' sugar
¹/4 to ¹/3 cup hot water

Melt chocolate and margarine; cool to lukewarm. Beat eggs with sugar in large bowl. Blend in chocolate mixture. Add mixture of salt, soda and 3 cups flour alternately with buttermilk, mixing well after each addition. Add enough remaining 1 cup flour to make medium dough. Roll ³/4-inch thick on floured surface; cut with 2¹/2-inch doughnut cutter. Deep-fry for 2 to 3 minutes on each side; drain. Dip 1 side in mixture of confectioners' sugar and water; place glaze side up to dry.

Approx Per Doughnut: Cal 255; Prot 5.1 g; T Fat 5.5 g; Chol 46.2 mg;
    Carbo 48.2 g; Sod 206.0 mg; Potas 105.0 mg.
    Nutritional information does not include oil for deep frying.

James H. Graves
Randolph, Vermont

BUTTER BRICKLE BREAD

Yields: 24 servings   *Pan Size: 2 loaf pans*   *Preheat: 300 degrees*

1 2-layer package butter
  brickle cake mix
1 4-ounce package vanilla
  instant pudding mix

¹/4 cup oil
4 eggs
2 tablespoons poppy seed
1 cup hot water

Combine cake mix, pudding mix, oil, eggs, poppy seed and water in bowl; mix well. Pour into greased and floured loaf pans. Bake for 1 hour.

Approx Per Serving: Cal 146; Prot 2.1 g; T Fat 5.3 g; Chol 45.7 mg;
    Carbo 22.6 g; Sod 174.0 mg; Potas 16.3 mg.

Alma Bauman
Clark, South Dakota

CINNAMON PULL-APARTS

Yields: 20 servings   *Pan Size: bundt pan*   *Preheat: 350 degrees*

2 10-count packages refrigerator biscuits 1/2 cup melted butter	1/2 cup sugar 1/4 cup cinnamon

Dip each biscuit in butter; coat with mixture of sugar and cinnamon. Arrange biscuits in ungreased bundt pan in 2 layers or stand on edge in fan-like pattern. Bake for 40 minutes. Invert onto serving plate.

VARIATIONS:

Buttered Pull-Aparts—Omit cinnamon-sugar.

Onion Pull-Aparts—Substitute desired amount of onion salt or flakes for cinnamon-sugar.

Mexican Pull-Aparts—Mix desired amount of taco seasoning with butter and omit cinnamon-sugar.

Cheese Pull-Aparts—Mix desired amount of dry cheese powder with butter and omit cinnamon-sugar.

Approx Per Serving: Cal 160; Prot 1.6 g; T Fat 10.1 g; Chol 12.4 mg; Carbo 16.0 g; Sod 269.0 mg; Potas 64.1 mg.
Nutritional information is for basic recipe only.

Judith A. Perryman
Department of Elementary and Secondary Ed.
Jefferson City, Missouri

MONKEY BREAD

Yields: 120 pieces   *Pan Size: bundt pan*   *Preheat: 350 degrees*

3 10-count packages refrigerator biscuits 1 cup sugar 2 tablespoons cinnamon	1/4 cup melted margarine 1 cup packed brown sugar 2 tablespoons cinnamon

Cut each biscuit into 4 pieces. Coat with mixture of sugar and 2 tablespoons cinnamon; place in greased bundt pan. Sprinkle remaining cinnamon mixture over top. Mix margarine, brown sugar and 2 tablespoons cinnamon in saucepan. Pour over biscuits. Bake for 30 minutes.

Approx Per Piece: Cal 42; Prot 0.4 g; T Fat 1.8 g; Chol 0.0 mg; Carbo 6.2 g; Sod 62.8 mg; Potas 22.2 mg.

Ernest H. Powers, Executive Secretary
West Virginia Vocational Association
South Charleston, West Virginia

COFFEE CAN ENGLISH MUFFIN BREAD

Yields: 20 slices   Pan Size: two 1-pound coffee cans   Preheat: 350 degrees

1 package dry yeast
1/2 cup warm (105 to 115
   degrees) water
4 teaspoons sugar
2 tablespoons oil

1 13-ounce can evaporated
   milk
1 1/2 teaspoons salt
4 cups flour

Dissolve yeast in warm water in large mixer bowl. Add 1 teaspoon sugar. Let stand for 15 minutes or until bubbly. Add remaining sugar, oil, evaporated milk and salt. Add 3 cups flour 1 cup at a time, beating well at low speed after each addition. Stir in remaining 1 cup flour. Divide dough between 2 well-greased 1-pound coffee cans; cover with well-greased plastic lids. Let rise until lids pop off. Bake, uncovered, for 40 to 60 minutes or until loaves test done. Remove from cans immediately. Serve hot or toasted.

Approx Per Slice: Cal 132; Prot 4.0 g; T Fat 3.1 g; Chol 5.4 mg;
   Carbo 21.8 g; Sod 180.0 mg; Potas 86.7 mg.

Sandra W. Miller
University of Kentucky
Lexington, Kentucky

SOUTHWEST VIRGINIA BROWN BREAD

Yields: 60 slices   Pan Size: 5 loaf pans   Preheat: 350 degrees

1 cup packed brown sugar
1 cup dark molasses
3 packages dry yeast
2 tablespoons salt
2 cups instant dry milk
   powder

7 cups very warm water
5 tablespoons melted
   shortening
3 eggs, slightly beaten
9 cups whole wheat flour
8 to 9 cups all-purpose flour

Combine brown sugar, molasses, yeast, salt and dry milk powder in large bowl. Add water, shortening, eggs and whole wheat flour; mix well. Let stand for 15 minutes. Add enough all-purpose flour to make slightly sticky but elastic dough. Knead on floured surface for 7 minutes. Place in greased bowl, turning to coat surface. Let rise, covered, until doubled in bulk. Punch dough down. Let rise again until doubled in bulk. Shape into loaves; place in greased loaf pans. Let rise until more than doubled in bulk. Bake for 45 minutes or until loaves test done. Makes wonderful toast and peanut butter and jelly sandwiches.

Approx Per Slice: Cal 176; Prot 5.6 g; T Fat 1.9 g; Chol 14.1 mg;
   Carbo 34.9 g; Sod 237.0 mg; Potas 302.0 mg.

The Honorable Rick Boucher
U.S. House of Representatives, Virginia
Washington, District of Columbia

APPLE OAT BRAN MUFFINS

Yields: 18 muffins   *Pan Size: muffin cups*   *Preheat: 425 degrees*

2 cups oat bran cereal	2 egg whites, slightly beaten
1/4 cup packed brown sugar	1 cup chopped apple
1 tablespoon baking powder	1/2 cup chopped pecans
1 cup skim milk	1/2 cup raisins

Spray bottom of muffin cups with nonstick cooking spray. Combine oat bran, brown sugar, baking powder, milk and egg whites in bowl; mix until moistened. Stir in apple, pecans and raisins. Spoon into muffin cups. Let stand for 3 to 4 minutes before placing in oven. Bake for 17 minutes or until lightly browned.

Approx Per Muffin: Cal 82; Prot 3.1 g; T Fat 2.7 g; Chol 0.2 mg;
      Carbo 16.0 g; Sod 71.8 mg; Potas 150.0 mg.

Charlotte Stephens
Memphis, Tennessee

BLUEBERRY MUFFINS

Yields: 12 muffins   *Pan Size: muffin cups*   *Preheat: 400 degrees*

1 egg, well beaten	1/2 cup sugar
1/2 cup milk	2 teaspoons baking powder
1/4 cup oil	1/2 teaspoon salt
1 1/2 cups flour	3/4 cup blueberries

Grease bottom of muffin cups. Beat egg with milk and oil. Add sifted flour, sugar, baking powder, salt; mix just until moistened. Stir in blueberries. Fill prepared muffin cups 2/3 full. Bake for 20 to 25 minutes or until golden brown. Cool in pan on wire rack.

Approx Per Muffin: Cal 148; Prot 2.5 g; T Fat 5.5 g; Chol 24.2 mg;
      Carbo 22.2 g; Sod 155.0 mg; Potas 43.2 mg.

Beverly Payne
Owensboro, Kentucky

BRAN MUFFINS

Yields: 60 muffins   *Pan Size: muffin cups*   *Preheat: 350 degrees*

2 cups All-Bran cereal
2 cups hot water
1 cup oil
3 cups sugar
4 eggs, beaten

5 teaspoons soda
2 teaspoons salt
1 quart buttermilk
4 cups All-Bran cereal
5 cups flour

Mix 2 cups All-Bran and water in bowl. Let stand for several minutes. Combine oil, sugar and eggs in large bowl. Add soda, salt, buttermilk and All-Bran and water mixture; mix well. Add 4 cups All-Bran and flour; mix well but do not overbeat. Fill each greased muffin cup with 1/4 cup mixture. Bake for 15 minutes.

Approx Per Muffin: Cal 142; Prot 3.3 g; T Fat 4.4 g; Chol 18.9 mg; Carbo 25.1 g; Sod 259.0 mg; Potas 145.0 mg.

Sonia M. Price
Columbus, Ohio

PEABODY HOTEL MUFFINS

Yields: 12 muffins   *Pan Size: muffin cups*   *Preheat: 375 degrees*

1/2 cup margarine, softened
2 cups sugar
2 eggs, slightly beaten
4 cups flour

1 tablespoon baking powder
2 cups milk
1 tablespoon vanilla extract

Cream margarine and sugar in bowl until light and fluffy. Beat in eggs. Add sifted flour and baking powder alternately with mixture of milk and vanilla, mixing well after each addition. Spoon into preheated greased muffin cups. Bake for 25 minutes or until brown.

Approx Per Muffin: Cal 387; Prot 6.8 g; T Fat 10.3 g; Chol 51.2 mg; Carbo 67.2 g; Sod 214.0 mg; Potas 111.0 mg.

Virginia C. Seal, Past President
Florida Special Needs Association, 1986-1987
Panama City, Florida

ZUCCHINI MUFFINS

Yields: 6 muffins   *Pan Size: muffin cups*   *Preheat: 400 degrees*

1/2 **cup grated zucchini**	3/4 **cup flour**
1 **egg**	1/2 **teaspoon baking powder**
2 **tablespoons oil**	1/4 **teaspoon salt**
1/4 **cup honey**	1/4 **teaspoon cinnamon**
1/4 **teaspoon lemon rind**	

Combine zucchini, egg, oil, honey and lemon rind in bowl; mix well. Add mixture of flour, baking powder, salt and cinnamon; mix just until moistened. Spoon into greased muffin cups. Bake for 20 minutes or until golden.

Approx Per Muffin: Cal 155; Prot 2.8 g; T Fat 5.6 g; Chol 45.7 mg;
     Carbo 24.0 g; Sod 129.0 mg; Potas 60.4 mg.

Beverly Payne
Owensboro, Kentucky

BAKED STRAWBERRY PANCAKE

Yields: 4 servings   *Pan Size: 9x9 inch*   *Preheat: 425 degrees*

1/4 **cup margarine**	3/4 **cup milk**
3/4 **cup flour**	1 **10-ounce package frozen**
1/4 **teaspoon salt**	**strawberries, thawed**
3 **eggs**	8 **ounces whipped topping**

Heat margarine in baking pan in oven until hot and bubbly. Combine flour, salt and eggs in bowl; beat until smooth. Beat in milk gradually. Pour into margarine in pan. Bake for 20 to 25 minutes or until puffed and golden brown. Serve with strawberries and whipped topping.

Approx Per Serving: Cal 523; Prot 9.7 g; T Fat 31.8 g; Chol 212.0 mg;
     Carbo 52.0 g; Sod 355.0 mg; Potas 218.0 mg.

Martha L. Gifreda
Columbus, Ohio

SWEDISH OATMEAL PANCAKES

Yields: 27 pancakes   *Pan Size: griddle*

4 cups rolled oats	1/8 teaspoon salt
1 cup flour	1 quart buttermilk
1/4 cup sugar	4 eggs, beaten
2 teaspoons soda	1/2 cup melted butter
2 teaspoons baking powder	2 teaspoons vanilla extract

Combine oats, flour, sugar, soda, baking powder and salt in large bowl. Add buttermilk, eggs, butter and vanilla; mix well. Let stand for 30 to 45 minutes or until batter has thickened to desired consistency. Ladle onto hot buttered griddle. Bake until puffed and brown on both sides, turning once. Serve with warm spiced applesauce and sour cream or peanut butter and applesauce. Store cooled pancakes between waxed paper in refrigerator and reheat in microwave.

Approx Per Pancake: Cal 127; Prot 4.6 g; T Fat 5.4 g; Chol 51.1 mg;
    Carbo 15.2 g; Sod 148.0 mg; Potas 112.0 mg.

Roberta Krause
Bellevue School District
Bellevue, Washington

GINGERBREAD WAFFLES

Yields: 6 waffles   *Pan Size: waffle iron*

3 cups flour	3 eggs, beaten
1 teaspoon soda	1/4 cup sugar
1 teaspoon baking powder	1/2 cup molasses
1/2 teaspoon salt	1 cup buttermilk
1 teaspoon ginger	5 1/3 tablespoons melted
1/2 teaspoon cinnamon	shortening
1/4 teaspoon cloves	

Sift flour, soda, baking powder, salt, ginger, cinnamon and cloves together. Beat eggs until light. Add sugar, molasses and buttermilk; mix well. Add sifted dry ingredients; beat until smooth. Mix in shortening. Bake in preheated waffle iron according manufacturer's instructions. Serve with hot honey and whipped cream.

Approx Per Waffle: Cal 474; Prot 10.9 g; T Fat 15.2 g; Chol 138.0 mg;
    Carbo 72.9 g; Sod 473.0 mg; Potas 936.0 mg.

William L. Hull
Columbus, Ohio

EASY CLUB SODA WAFFLES

Yields: 6 waffles   *Pan Size: waffle iron*

2 cups buttermilk baking mix	**1/2 cup oil**
1 1/2 cups club soda	**1 egg, beaten**

Combine baking mix, club soda, oil and egg in bowl; mix well. Bake in preheated waffle iron according to manufacturer's instructions. This recipe also makes excellent Belgian waffles.

Approx Per Waffle: Cal 355; Prot 4.0 g; T Fat 25.1 g; Chol 45.7 mg;
    Carbo 28.1 g; Sod 553.0 mg; Potas 72.6 mg.

Russell L. Blackman
Former AVA Vice President, Region V
Aurora, Colorado

CINNAMON ROLLS

Yields: 30 rolls   *Pan Size: baking sheet*   *Preheat: 400 degrees*

2 cups flour	**1/2 cup melted margarine**
1/2 cup sugar	**1 cup sugar**
2 packages dry yeast	**2 tablespoons cinnamon**
1/2 cup margarine, softened	**2 cups confectioners' sugar**
1 1/2 cups hot water	**1/4 cup milk**
2 eggs, beaten	**1 teaspoon vanilla extract**
3 to 4 cups flour	

Combine 2 cups flour, 1/2 cup sugar, yeast and softened margarine in bowl. Add hot water; stir until margarine melts. Beat in eggs. Add enough 3 to 4 cups flour to make soft dough. Roll into two 1/2-inch thick rectangles. Spread with melted margarine; sprinkle with mixture of 1 cup sugar and cinnamon. Roll as for jelly roll from long side; cut into 1-inch slices. Arrange on greased baking sheet. Let rise for 30 minutes. Bake until golden brown. Spread hot rolls with mixture of confectioners' sugar, milk and vanilla. May place rolls in cold oven to rise while oven heats or may store in refrigerator and place in 150-degree oven for faster rising.

Approx Per Roll: Cal 217; Prot 3.3 g; T Fat 6.8 g; Chol 18.4 mg;
    Carbo 35.9 g; Sod 82.7 mg; Potas 42.7 mg.

Catherine Wilson
Columbia, Mississippi

Artist: *Jody Tomski*—Lawrence County AVTS; Gerald Zona, Teacher;
New Castle, Pennsylvania
Artist: *Daniel R. Johnson*—Olympus High School; Dick Powell, Teacher;
Salt Lake City, Utah

BREADS

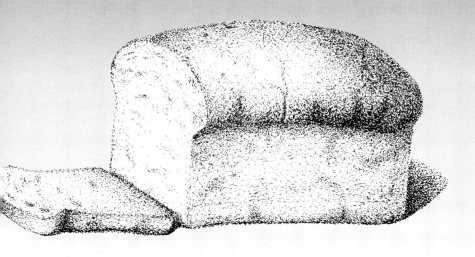

Wine and Cheese Reception for Twenty-Five

Brie in Phyllo
page 24

Pineapple Cheese Sculpture
page 26

Cheese Fondue
page 25

Parmesan Cheese Cubes
page 15

6 to 8 pounds Assorted Cheeses

4 to 5 pounds Assorted Seasonal Fruit

6 to 8 Bottles of Assorted Wines

Unsalted Crackers, Breadsticks or thinly sliced Bread

Wine and Cheese Complements

	Wine List	Cheeses
RED	Beaujolais Bordeaux Burgundy Cabernet Sauvignon Chianti Claret Rosé Zinfandel	Bel Paese Cheddar Edam Monterey Jack Piquant Bleu Roquefort Swiss Tilsit
WHITE	Chablis Chardonnay Chenin Blanc Moselle Pouilly Fuisse Riesling Sauterne Sauvignon Blanc Soave	Boursin Brie Camembert Creamy Bleu Gouda Gruyère Montrachet Port Salut Roquefort
Sparkling	Champagne Sparkling Burgundy Sparkling Rosé	Any of the cheeses listed above would be appropriate complements to any of the sparkling wines.

Presentation:

★ Allow a total of 8 ounces or more wine for each person.
— Serve red wines at room temperature.
— Serve white and sparkling wines chilled but not icy.

★ Allow a total of 4 ounces or more cheese for each person.
— Cut cheeses into bite-sized pieces or place large pieces on cheese boards with cheese servers or knives for slicing as desired.

★ Peel fruit if necessary and cut or slice into bite-sized pieces. Cut grapes into small clusters. Select fruit for visual and taste variety.
— Strawberries, red and white grapes, sweet and tart apples, pears, kiwifruit, pineapple, cantaloupe and other melons, peaches, fresh figs, papayas, nectarines, cherries, plums, dried fruit and nuts.

★ Arrange groupings of wine with appropriate cheeses and an assortment of fruit and crackers.
— Provide an ample supply of small plates, napkins and silverware.
— Glasses should be small for sampling but in ample supply.

FRESH APPLE LOAF

Yields: 24 slices	*Pan Size: two 5x9 inch*	*Preheat: 325 degrees*

4 cups chopped peeled apples	1/4 teaspoon nutmeg
1 cup chopped pecans	1/4 teaspoon cloves
2 cups sugar	3/4 teaspoon cinnamon
3 cups flour	1 cup melted margarine
2 teaspoons soda	2 teaspoons vanilla extract
1/4 teaspoon salt	2 eggs, slightly beaten

Combine apples, pecans and sugar in bowl; mix well. Let stand for 1 hour, stirring frequently. Mix flour, soda, salt and spices in large bowl. Add apple mixture, margarine, vanilla and eggs; mix well. Pour into 2 greased and floured loaf pans. Bake for 1 hour and 15 minutes, or until toothpick inserted in center comes out clean.

Approx Per Slice: Cal 251; Prot 2.7 g; T Fat 11.7 g; Chol 22.8 mg;
Carbo 35.2 g; Sod 187.0 mg; Potas 87.8 mg.

Frances Bishop
Home Economics Teacher, Sr. High School
Denton, Texas

BANANA BREAD

Yields: 12 slices	*Pan Size: 5x9 inch*	*Preheat: 350 degrees*

1/2 cup margarine, softened	2 cups flour
1 cup sugar	1 teaspoon soda
2 eggs, slightly beaten	3 large bananas, mashed
1/8 teaspoon salt	1 cup broken pecans
1 teaspoon vanilla extract	

Cream margarine and sugar in bowl until light and fluffy. Add eggs, salt, bananas and vanilla; mix well. Sift in flour and soda; mix well. Add bananas; mix well. Stir in pecans. Pour into greased and floured loaf pan. Bake for 50 minutes or until bread tests done.

Approx Per Slice: Cal 313; Prot 4.3 g; T Fat 15.6 g; Chol 45.7 mg;
Carbo 41.1 g; Sod 205.0 mg; Potas 186.0 mg.

Lynn A. Wagner
Newton, Mississippi

BUTTERMILK BANANA BREAD

Yields: 12 slices	Pan Size: 5x9 inch	Preheat: 350 degrees

3 medium bananas, mashed
1 tablespoon lemon juice
1/2 cup margarine, softened
1 1/3 cups sugar
2 eggs, beaten
2 cups flour

1 teaspoon salt
1 teaspoon soda
1 teaspoon vanilla extract
1/2 cup buttermilk
1/2 cup chopped pecans

Combine bananas and lemon juice in bowl. Cream margarine and sugar in large bowl until light and fluffy. Add eggs; mix well. Sift flour, salt and soda together. Add to creamed mixture; mix well. Stir in vanilla, buttermilk, pecans and bananas; mix well. Pour into greased and floured loaf pan. Bake until bread tests done.

Approx Per Slice: Cal 306; Prot 4.3 g; T Fat 12.3 g; Chol 46.0 mg;
Carbo 46.2 g; Sod 371.0 mg; Potas 184.0 mg.

Beverly Payne
Owensboro, Kentucky

BROWN BREAD

Yields: 12 slices	Pan Size: 5x9 inch	Preheat: 350 degrees

3 tablespoons butter
3/4 cup packed brown sugar
2 cups buttermilk
3 tablespoons molasses
2 cups whole wheat flour
1 cup all-purpose flour

1/2 cup wheat germ
2 teaspoons soda
1 teaspoon salt
1 cup raisins
1 cup chopped walnuts

Cream butter and brown sugar in large mixer bowl until light and fluffy. Add buttermilk and molasses; mix well. Combine whole wheat flour, all-purpose flour, wheat germ, soda and salt in bowl. Add to buttermilk mixture; mix well. Stir in raisins and chopped walnuts. Spoon into greased loaf pan. Bake for 1 hour and 20 minutes or until bread tests done. Cool in pan for 10 minutes. Remove to wire rack to cool completely. Serve with cream cheese and raspberry preserves.

Approx Per Slice: Cal 325; Prot 7.9 g; T Fat 10.3 g; Chol 9.3 mg;
Carbo 54.3 g; Sod 396.0 mg; Potas 520.0 mg.

Roberta Krause
Bellevue School District
Bellevue, Washington

CHEESE-ONION BREAD

Yields: 12 slices　　　　*Pan Size: 5x9 inch*　　　　*Preheat: 400 degrees*

1 cup chopped onion
2 tablespoons margarine
2 eggs, slightly beaten
2¹/₂ cups buttermilk baking
　mix
²/₃ cup shredded Cheddar
　cheese

1 cup milk
1 tablespoon poppy seed
2 tablespoons margarine,
　softened
¹/₃ cup shredded Cheddar
　cheese

Sauté onion in 2 tablespoons margarine in skillet. Combine eggs, baking mix, ²/₃ cup cheese and milk in bowl; mix well. Add onion; mix well. Pour into greased loaf pan. Combine poppy seed, 2 tablespoons margarine and ¹/₃ cup cheese in small bowl; mix well. Sprinkle over loaf. Bake for 20 to 25 minutes or until bread tests done.

Approx Per Slice: Cal 215; Prot 6.1 g; T Fat 12.3 g; Chol 58.2 mg;
　　Carbo 19.7 g; Sod 457.0 mg; Potas 108.0 mg.

Carolyn Cotton
AVA Teacher of the Year 1989
Bristow, Oklahoma

CHOOSE-A-FLAVOR BREAD

Yields: 12 slices　　　　*Pan Size: 4x8 inch*　　　　*Preheat: 350 degrees*

1 cup all-purpose flour
¹/₂ cup whole wheat flour
¹/₃ cup quick-cooking oats
1 teaspoon soda
¹/₂ cup butter, softened
¹/₂ cup sugar

2 eggs, beaten
2 tablespoons milk
1 teaspoon vanilla extract
¹/₂ teaspoon grated lemon rind
1 cup chopped pears
¹/₂ cup chopped walnuts

Combine first 4 ingredients in bowl. Cream butter and sugar in large mixer bowl until light and fluffy. Mix in eggs, milk, vanilla and lemon rind; beat well. Add flour mixture ¹/₃ at a time, beating at low speed until mixed. Stir in pears and walnuts. Pour into greased loaf pan. Bake for 35 minutes; cover with foil. Bake for 20 to 25 minutes longer or until bread tests done. Cool in pan for 10 minutes. Remove to wire rack to cool completely. Let stand, wrapped, overnight for easier slicing. May substitute 1 cup chopped peaches, zucchini or carrots for pears.

Approx Per Slice: Cal 218; Prot 4.1 g; T Fat 12.2 g; Chol 66.7 mg;
　　Carbo 24.5 g; Sod 147.0 mg; Potas 95.7 mg.

Tricia Boucher-Wallace
Leominster Trade High School
Fitchburg, Massachusetts

DATE BREAD

Yields: 12 slices   *Pan Size: 4x8 inch*   *Preheat: 350 degrees*

1 teaspoon soda
1 cup chopped dates
3/4 cup hot water
3/4 cup sugar
1 egg yolk, beaten
1 egg white, stiffly beaten

1 teaspoon vanilla extract
13/4 cup flour
1/2 teaspoon salt
1/2 cup mixed chopped fruit
1/2 cup chopped walnuts

Sprinkle soda over dates in large bowl. Add water; cool. Combine sugar, egg yolk and vanilla in bowl; add to date mixture. Add stiffly beaten egg white alternately with flour and salt, mixing well after each addition. Stir in fruit and walnuts. Bake for 1 hour or until bread tests done.

Approx Per Slice: Cal 217; Prot 3.7 g; T Fat 3.9 g; Chol 22.7 mg;
    Carbo 44.2 g; Sod 165.0 mg; Potas 220.0 mg.

Charlotte J. O'Mara
Macedon, New York

PEAR-PECAN BREAD

Yields: 12 slices   *Pan Size: 5x9 inch*   *Preheat: 350 degrees*

1 cup sugar
1/2 cup oil
2 eggs
1/4 cup sour cream
1 teaspoon vanilla extract
2 cups sifted flour
1 teaspoon soda

1/2 teaspoon salt
1/4 teaspoon cinnamon
1/4 teaspoon nutmeg
11/2 cups chopped pears
2/3 cup chopped pecans
1/2 teaspoon grated lemon rind

Combine sugar and oil in large mixer bowl; beat well. Add eggs 1 at a time, beating well after each addition. Add sour cream and vanilla; mix well. Sift in flour, soda, salt and spices; beat well. Stir in pears, pecans and lemon rind. Spoon into greased loaf pan. Bake for 1 hour or until bread tests done. Cool in pan for 10 minutes. Remove to wire rack to cool completely.

Approx Per Slice: Cal 294; Prot 3.8 g; T Fat 15.7 g; Chol 47.8 mg;
    Carbo 35.8 g; Sod 172.0 mg; Potas 88.3 mg.

Roberta Krause
Bellevue School District
Bellevue, Washington

PUMPKIN BREAD

Yields: 36 slices   *Pan Size: three 9x11 inch*   *Preheat: 350 degrees*

3¹/₂ cups flour
1 teaspoon nutmeg
1 teaspoon cinnamon
1¹/₂ teaspoons salt
2 teaspoons soda
3 cups sugar

²/₃ cup water
4 eggs
1 cup oil
1¹/₂ cups chopped pecans
2 cups pumpkin purée

Sift flour, spices, salt, soda and sugar into large bowl. Add water, eggs and oil; mix well. Stir in pecans and pumpkin. Pour into 3 greased loaf pans. Bake for 1 hour or until bread tests done.

Approx Per Slice: Cal 207; Prot 2.4 g; T Fat 10.2 g; Chol 30.4 mg;
        Carbo 27.5 g; Sod 143.0 mg; Potas 70.2 mg.

Brenda D. Long
Richlands Middle School
Richlands, Virginia

STRAWBERRY NUT BREAD

Yields: 24 slices   *Pan Size: two 5x9 inch*   *Preheat: 350 degrees*

3 cups flour
1 teaspoon soda
1 teaspoon salt
1 tablespoon cinnamon
2 cups sugar

2 cups thawed sliced frozen
   strawberries
4 eggs, beaten
1¹/₄ cups oil
1¹/₄ cups chopped pecans

Combine flour, soda, salt and cinnamon in large bowl. Add sugar, strawberries, eggs and oil; stir just until moistened. Stir in pecans. Spoon into 2 greased loaf pans. Bake for 60 to 70 minutes or until bread tests done. Cool in pan for 5 minutes. Remove bread to wire rack to cool completely.

Approx Per Slice: Cal 280; Prot 3.2 g; T Fat 16.6 g; Chol 45.7 mg;
        Carbo 30.8 g; Sod 136.0 mg; Potas 69.1 mg.

Suellen Murphy
Thomasville, North Carolina

WALNUT-CRANBERRY BREAD

Yields: 12 slices	Pan Size: 5x9 inch	Preheat: 325 degrees

2 tablespoons butter, softened
1 cup sugar
1 egg, lightly beaten
Grated zest of 2 oranges
3/4 cup orange juice
2 cups flour

1/2 teaspoon salt
1/2 teaspoon soda
1 1/2 teaspoons baking powder
1 cup whole cranberries
3/4 cup chopped walnuts
1 tablespoon flour

Cream butter and sugar in large bowl until light and fluffy. Add egg, orange zest and juice; mix well. Sift in 2 cups flour, salt, soda and baking powder; mix well. Dust cranberries and walnuts with 1 tablespoon flour. Stir into batter. Pour into greased and floured loaf pan. Bake for 1 hour or until bread tests done.

Approx Per Slice: Cal 227; Prot 4.0 g; T Fat 7.3 g; Chol 28.0 mg;
    Carbo 37.6 g; Sod 215.0 mg; Potas 106.0 mg.

The Honorable Mary Sue Terry
Attorney General, Virginia
Richmond, Virginia

ZUCCHINI BREAD

Yields: 24 slices	Pan Size: two 5x9 inch	Preheat: 325 degrees

2 cups chopped zucchini
3 eggs
2 cups sugar
1 cup oil
1/2 cup applesauce
1 tablespoon cinnamon

3 cups flour
1/4 teaspoon baking powder
1 teaspoon soda
1 teaspoon salt
1 cup raisins
1 cup walnuts

Combine zucchini, eggs, sugar, oil, applesauce and cinnamon in large bowl; mix well. Sift in flour, baking powder, soda and salt; mix well. Stir in raisins and walnuts. Pour into 2 greased and floured loaf pans. Bake for 1 hour or until bread tests done.

Approx Per Slice: Cal 268; Prot 3.5 g; T Fat 13.1 g; Chol 34.2 mg;
    Carbo 35.8 g; Sod 137.0 mg; Potas 131.0 mg.

Ernest H. Powers, Executive Secretary
West Virginia Vocational Association
South Charleston, West Virginia

CORN BREAD YOU EAT WITH A FORK

Yields: 10 servings   *Pan Size: 2 quart*   *Preheat: 350 degrees*

1 large onion, chopped	5 to 10 drops of Tabasco sauce
1/2 cup butter	1/2 cup milk
1 cup shredded Cheddar	1 egg
cheese	1 cup cream-style corn
1 cup sour cream	1/2 cup shredded Cheddar
1 7-ounce package corn	cheese
muffin mix	

Sauté onion in butter in skillet until golden. Cool. Add 1 cup cheese and sour cream. Spray casserole with nonstick cooking spray. Combine muffin mix, Tabasco sauce, milk, egg and corn in casserole; mix well. Drop onion mixture by spoonfuls into center of batter; do not stir. Sprinkle remaining 1/2 cup cheese over top. Bake, uncovered, for 30 to 35 minutes or until golden. Let stand for 15 to 30 minutes before serving. Center will be soft.

Approx Per Serving: Cal 277; Prot 7.0 g; T Fat 21.8 g; Chol 81.8 mg;
   Carbo 14.7 g; Sod 372.0 mg; Potas 144.0 mg.

Nola Wade
Little Rock, Arkansas

MEXICAN CORN BREAD

Yield: 24 servings   *Pan Size: two 9x13 inch*   *Preheat: 400 degrees*

3 cups self-rising cornmeal	1 large onion, finely chopped
3 tablespoons sugar	1 8-ounce can cream-style corn
1 teaspoon salt	1 1/2 cups shredded cheese
1 cup oil	2 jalapeño peppers, seeded,
1 1/2 cups milk	chopped
3 eggs, beaten	

Combine cornmeal, sugar, salt, oil, milk and eggs in large bowl; mix well. Add onion, corn, cheese and peppers; mix well. Spoon into 2 greased baking pans. Bake for 45 minutes or until golden brown.

Approx Per Serving: Cal 178; Prot 2.9 g; T Fat 10.6 g; Chol 36.3 mg;
   Carbo 18.1 g; Sod 244.0 mg; Potas 73.8 mg.

Sue Shackelford
Hackleburg High Sschool
Hackleburg, Alabama

FLORIDA'S BEST HUSH PUPPIES

Yields: 36 servings

1 cup self-rising cornmeal	1/2 cup finely chopped green
1/3 cup flour	bell pepper
1 egg, beaten	Buttermilk
1 cup finely chopped onion	Oil for deep frying
1/2 cup cream-style corn	

Combine cornmeal, flour, egg, onion, corn and green pepper in bowl. Add enough buttermilk gradually to make soft ball, mixing well. Drop by teaspoonfuls into hot oil. Deep-fry until golden brown. Drain on paper towels. Note: These hush puppies were served at the Florida Vocational Association August Conference Cookout.

Nutritional information not available.

Gloria Dickson
Gainesville, Florida

SPICY HUSH PUPPIES

Yields: 20 servings

1 cup yellow cornmeal	1 egg, beaten
1/3 cup flour	1/2 cup finely chopped onion
2 teaspoons baking powder	3 dashes of Tabasco sauce
1/2 teaspoon salt	2 tablespoons oil
1/4 teaspoon pepper	1/2 gallon peanut oil
1/2 cup milk	

Sift cornmeal, flour, baking powder, salt and pepper into bowl. Add mixture of milk, egg, onion, Tabasco sauce and 2 tablespoons oil; mix well. Drop by tablespoonfuls into hot peanut oil. Deep-fry until golden brown. Drain on paper towels.

Approx Per Serving: Cal 54; Prot 1.3 g; T Fat 2.0 g; Chol 14.5 mg;
Carbo 7.6 g; Sod 59.5 mg; Potas 27.9 mg.
Nutritional information does not include oil for deep frying.

Jasper S. Lee
Mississippi State, Mississippi

ANGEL BISCUITS

Yields: 48 servings   *Pan Size: baking sheet*   *Preheat: 400 degrees*

1 package dry yeast	1/4 cup sugar
2 tablespoons lukewarm water	1 teaspoon salt
5 to 51/2 cups sifted flour	1 cup shortening
1 teaspoon soda	2 cups buttermilk
3 teaspoons baking powder	

Dissolve yeast in water in small bowl. Sift flour, soda, baking powder, sugar and salt into large bowl. Cut in shortening until crumbly. Add yeast and buttermilk; mix well. Knead dough on floured surface until smooth and elastic. Roll to 1/2 to 3/4-inch thickness. Cut with biscuit cutter. Fold each biscuit in half; place on baking sheet. Bake for 15 to 20 minutes or until golden brown.

Approx Per Serving: Cal 95; Prot 1.8 g; T Fat 4.5 g; Chol 0.4 mg;
     Carbo 11.7 g; Sod 93.2 mg; Potas 31.2 mg.

Hayden Housch
Montgomery, Alabama

CRACKED WHEAT BREAD

Yields: 24 slices   *Pan Size: two 4x8 inch*   *Preheat: 400 degrees*

43/4 to 53/4 cups flour	11/2 cups water
3 tablespoons sugar	1/2 cup milk
4 teaspoons salt	3 tablespoons butter
2 packages dry yeast	1 cup cracked wheat

Combine 2 cups flour, sugar, salt and dry yeast in large bowl; mix well. Heat water, milk and butter in saucepan to 120 to 130 degrees. Stir milk mixture into flour mixture gradually. Pour into food processor container. Process for several seconds or until mixed. Add cracked wheat; process until mixed. Add enough remaining flour 1 cup at a time to make dough soft and elastic, processing for several seconds after each addition. Entire process should take no longer than 1 minute. Place in greased bowl, turning to grease surface. Let rise, covered, in warm place for 1 hour or until doubled in bulk. Punch dough down. Turn onto lightly floured surface. Cover. Let rest for 15 minutes. Divide dough into 2 portions. Roll each into 8x12-inch rectangle. Shape into loaves. Place in greased loaf pans. Let rise, covered, for 1 hour or until doubled in bulk. Bake for 30 minutes or until bread tests done.

Approx Per Slice: Cal 152; Prot 4.3 g; T Fat 2.2 g; Chol 4.6 mg;
     Carbo 28.5 g; Sod 411.0 mg; Potas 59.2 mg.

Janice Wissman
Kansas State University
Manhattan, Kansas

DILLY CASSEROLE BREAD

Yields: 10 servings *Pan Size: 2 quart* *Preheat: 350 degrees*

1 package dry yeast
1/4 cup warm water
1 cup cream-style cottage
  cheese
2 tablespoons sugar
1 tablespoon onion flakes

1 tablespoon butter, softened
2 teaspoons dillseed
1 teaspoon salt
1/4 teaspoon soda
1 egg
21/4 to 21/2 cups flour

Dissolve yeast in water. Combine with next 8 ingredients in mixer bowl. Add enough flour 1/2 cup at a time to make stiff dough, mixing well after each addition. Let rise, covered, in warm place for 50 minutes or until doubled in bulk. Stir dough down. Turn into well-greased round casserole. Let rise in warm place for 30 to 40 minutes or until light. Bake for 40 minutes or until golden brown. Brush top with butter; sprinkle with coarse salt.

Approx Per Serving: Cal 166; Prot 6.8 g; T Fat 2.9 g; Chol 33.6 mg;
  Carbo 27.4 g; Sod 336.0 mg; Potas 74.1 mg.

Marcia A. Flax
Springfield, Ohio

REUBEN LOAF

Yields: 8 servings *Pan Size: baking sheet* *Preheat: 400 degrees*

31/4 cups flour
1 tablespoon sugar
1 teaspoon salt
1 package rapid-rise yeast
1 cup hot (130-degree) water
1 tablespoon margarine

1/2 cup Thousand Island salad
  dressing
6 ounces corned beef, sliced
4 ounces Swiss cheese, sliced
1 8-ounce can sauerkraut
1 egg white, beaten

Mix 21/4 cups flour, sugar, salt and yeast in large bowl. Stir in hot water and margarine. Add enough remaining 1 cup flour to make soft dough. Knead on floured surface for 4 minutes or until smooth and elastic. Roll into 10x14-inch rectangle on greased baking sheet. Spread salad dressing down center. Layer with corned beef, cheese and drained sauerkraut. Cut rectangle from each side toward filling into 1-inch diagonal strips. Fold strips alternately over filling. Place baking sheet, covered, over large shallow pan half-filled with boiling water. Let rise for 15 minutes. Brush loaf with egg white. Bake for 25 minutes or until loaf tests done. Serve warm.

Approx Per Serving: Cal 368; Prot 15.9 g; T Fat 13.6 g; Chol 60.2 mg;
  Carbo 44.7 g; Sod 847.0 mg; Potas 175.0 mg.

Martha Atchley
O.T. Autry Area Vocational Technical Center
Enid, Oklahoma

DAKOTA BREAD

Yields: 10 servings	Pan Size: 9 inch	Preheat: 350 degrees

1 package dry yeast	2 to 2½ cups bread flour
½ cup warm (115-degree)	½ cup whole wheat flour
water	¼ cup wheat germ
2 tablespoons sunflower oil	¼ cup rye flour
1 egg	¼ cup oats
½ cup cottage cheese	1 tablespoon cornmeal
¼ cup honey	1 egg white, beaten
1 teaspoon salt	1 tablespoon oats

Dissolve yeast in warm water. Mix oil, egg, cottage cheese, honey and salt in large bowl. Stir in yeast. Add 2 cups bread flour; mix just until moistened. Stir in mixture of whole wheat flour, wheat germ, rye flour and ¼ cup oats gradually. Mix in enough remaining ½ cup bread flour to make soft dough. Knead on floured surface for 10 minutes or until smooth and elastic. Place in greased bowl, turning to grease surface. Let rise, covered with greased plastic wrap, in warm place for 30 minutes or until doubled in bulk. Punch dough down. Shape into round loaf. Place in greased pie plate sprinkled with cornmeal. Let rise, covered with greased plastic wrap, for 1 hour or until doubled in bulk. Brush with egg white; sprinkle with oats. Bake for 35 to 40 minutes or until bread tests done. Remove to wire rack to cool. May cover with foil for the last 15 minutes of baking to avoid overbrowning.

Approx Per Serving: Cal 235; Prot 7.9 g; T Fat 4.6 g; Chol 28.9 mg;
Carbo 41.0 g; Sod 269.0 mg; Potas 123.0 mg.

The Honorable George Mickelson
Governor of South Dakota
Pierre, South Dakota

MIXED BATTER BREAD

Yields: 1 loaf	Pan Size: 4x8 inch	Preheat: 375 degrees

1 package dry yeast	2 teaspoons salt
2 cups lukewarm water	2 cups cooked grits
2 tablespoons shortening	Flour
2 tablespoons sugar	

Dissolve yeast in water in large bowl. Add shortening, sugar, salt and grits; mix well. Add enough flour to make stiff batter. Spoon into greased loaf pan. Let rise in warm place until doubled in bulk. Bake for 55 minutes or until golden brown.

Nutritional information not available.

Ellen C. Vaughan
Columbia, South Carolina

GERMAN CHRISTMAS BREAD

Yields: 84 slices	Pan Size: seven 5x9 inch	Preheat: 375 degrees

1 cup dates	2 cups water
1 cup raisins	3 cups sugar
1 cup currants	28 cups flour
1 cup water	1 cup melted butter
3 packages dry yeast	1 cup melted shortening
1 cup warm water	1 tablespoon salt
4 cups milk	1 cup maraschino cherries

Bring first 3 ingredients to a boil in 1 cup water in saucepan. Cool. Dissolve yeast in warm water. Combine milk, 2 cups water, yeast, sugar and 14 cups flour in large bowl; mix well. Add butter, shortening and salt; mix well. Stir in fruit mixture and cherries. Add remaining 14 cups flour gradually, kneading until firm. Knead on floured surface for 5 minutes or until smooth and elastic. Place in greased bowl, turning to grease surface. Let rise in warm place until doubled in bulk. Shape into 7 loaves. Place in greased loaf pans. Bake for 40 minutes or until golden.

Approx Per Slice: Cal 246; Prot 5.1 g; T Fat 5.5 g; Chol 7.5 mg; Carbo 44.1 g; Sod 101.0 mg; Potas 109.0 mg.

Muriel Copp
Red Wing, Minnesota

SWEDISH RYE BREAD

Yields: 48 slices	Pan Size: four 5x9 inch	Preheat: 375 degrees

2¹/2 packages dry yeast	1 cup milk, scalded
¹/2 cup warm water	¹/2 cup packed brown sugar
1 tablespoon sugar	1¹/2 cups boiling water
4 tablespoons molasses	2 cups rye flour
4 tablespoons shortening	6 to 7 cups all-purpose flour
2 teaspoons salt	

Dissolve yeast in warm water. Add sugar. Combine next 6 ingredients in bowl. Add rye flour gradually; mix well. Blend in yeast mixture and enough white flour to make stiff dough. Knead in remaining flour. Let rise until doubled in bulk. Punch dough down. Let rise until doubled in bulk. Divide into 4 portions; shape into loaves on lightly floured surface. Place in greased loaf pans. Let rise until doubled in bulk. Bake for 15 minutes. Reduce temperature to 350 degrees. Bake for 45 minutes or until golden brown. Brush loaves with shortening.

Approx Per Slice: Cal 109; Prot 2.8 g; T Fat 1.5 g; Chol 0.7 mg; Carbo 21.2 g; Sod 94.2 mg; Potas 101.0 mg.

Fay G. Larson
Lincoln, Nebraska

VERSATILE SWEET DOUGH

Yields: 30 rolls   *Pan Size: 7x11 inch*   *Preheat: 375 degrees*

2 teaspoons sugar	2¹/₂ cups warm water
¹/₄ cup warm water	¹/₂ cup sugar
1 package dry yeast	¹/₄ cup margarine
1 package quick-rise yeast	2 eggs, beaten
7 cups flour	1 tablespoon salt

Mix 2 teaspoons sugar and ¹/₄ cup warm water in 1 cup measure. Stir in 2 packages yeast. Let stand until cup is almost full. Place flour in large bowl. Make well in center. Add 2¹/₂ cups warm water, ¹/₂ cup sugar, margarine, eggs, salt and yeast mixture; stir until stiff. Knead in enough flour to make dough smooth and elastic. Place in greased bowl, turning to grease surface. Let rise, covered, until doubled in bulk. Punch dough down. Let rise, covered, until doubled in bulk. Punch dough down. Shape by ¹/₄ cupfuls into balls; place in well-greased baking pan. Let rise until doubled in bulk. Bake for 15 minutes or until golden brown. Brush with melted margarine. Rolls are particularly good when made with potato water.

VARIATIONS:

Loaves—Prepare dough as above through second rising. Divide into 3 portions. Shape into loaves; place in greased loaf pans. Let rise until almost doubled in bulk. Bake on middle oven rack at 325 degrees for 45 minutes or until golden brown. Remove to wire rack; brush tops with butter. Cool completely. May store unsliced loaves in plastic freezer bags in refrigerator for up to 6 months. Thaw at room temperature for several hours. Slice and wrap in foil. Heat at 250 degrees for 20 minutes. Yield: 3 loaves.

Cinnamon Pull-Aparts—Prepare dough as above through second rising. Microwave ¹/₄ cup margarine in 1¹/₂-quart glass bowl on High for 45 seconds. Stir in ¹/₂ cup packed brown sugar and 1 tablespoon light corn syrup. Microwave for 1¹/₄ minutes. Sprinkle with desired amount of pecans. Pinch off small portions of dough. Dip into melted margarine; coat with mixture of 1 cup sugar and 4 teaspoons cinnamon. Arrange over pecans until bowl is ¹/₃ filled. Let rise until bowl is almost full. Bake at 350 degrees for 45 minutes or until deep brown. Place serving plate over top; invert and remove bowl. Serve for breakfast or dessert. Yield: 6 servings.

Approx Per Roll: Cal 140; Prot 3.7 g; T Fat 2.2 g; Chol 18.3 mg;
    Carbo 26.0 g; Sod 237.0 mg; Potas 42.4 mg.
    Nutritional information is for basic recipe only.

Leslie Alexander
Towanda, Illinois

MAPLE-NUT CINNAMON ROLLS

Yields: 24 rolls   *Pan Size: 9x13 inch*   *Preheat: 350 degrees*

1/2 cup maple-flavored syrup
1/4 cup packed brown sugar
1/4 cup margarine, softened
1/4 teaspoon maple flavoring
2/3 cup chopped walnuts
1 package dry yeast
1/4 cup warm water
1 cup milk
1/2 cup melted margarine

1/3 cup packed brown sugar
1 1/2 teaspoons salt
2 eggs
1 cup quick-cooking oats
3 to 3 1/2 cups flour
2 tablespoons melted
   margarine
2/3 cup packed brown sugar
1 teaspoon cinnamon

Spread mixture of first 5 ingredients in greased baking pan. Dissolve yeast in warm water. Combine milk, 1/2 cup margarine, 1/3 cup brown sugar and salt in large saucepan. Scald; cool to lukewarm. Add eggs, yeast and oats. Add enough flour to knead easily. Knead on floured surface until smooth and elastic. Place in greased bowl, turning to grease surface. Let rise for 1 1/2 hours. Roll into 12x24-inch rectangle on floured surface. Brush with 2 tablespoons melted margarine; sprinkle with mixture of brown sugar and cinnamon. Roll as for jelly roll from wide end. Cut into 1-inch slices. Place in prepared pan. Let rise, covered, in warm place until doubled in bulk. Bake until golden. Cool for 1 minute. Invert onto serving plate.

Approx Per Roll: Cal 224; Prot 3.9 g; T Fat 8.9 g; Chol 24.2 mg;
   Carbo 32.6 g; Sod 220.0 mg; Potas 121.0 mg.

Carolyn Davis, Former President
National Assoc. of Voc. H. Economics Teachers
Covington, Indiana

CLOVER LEAF YEAST ROLLS

Yields: 30 rolls   *Pan Size: muffin cups*   *Preheat: 450 degrees*

1 cake compressed yeast
1/2 cup sugar
1/2 cup shortening
1 egg

Lukewarm water
4 cups flour
1 teaspoon salt
1/2 cup melted butter

Cream yeast, sugar and shortening in bowl. Beat egg in 2-cup measure; add enough water to measure 2 cups. Sift flour and salt together. Add to creamed mixture alternately with egg mixture, mixing well after each addition. Chill, covered, for 2 hours. Shape into small balls. Dip into melted butter; place 3 balls in each muffin cup. Let rise until doubled in bulk. Bake for 10 minutes or until brown.

Approx Per Roll: Cal 135; Prot 2.2 g; T Fat 6.8 g; Chol 17.4 mg;
   Carbo 16.2 g; Sod 99.9 mg; Potas 28.6 mg.

Martha Crisp
Owensboro, Kentucky

FOLD-OVER ROLLS

Yields: 60 rolls	Pan Size: 9x13 inch	Preheat: 450 degrees

4 cups milk
1 cup shortening
1 cup sugar
1 package dry yeast
¼ cup lukewarm water

12 cups (or more) flour
1 tablespoon salt
1 teaspoon soda
1 teaspoon baking powder

Combine milk, shortening and sugar in saucepan. Bring just to a boil; remove from heat. Cool to lukewarm. Dissolve yeast in lukewarm water. Add to milk mixture. Add enough flour to make of batter consistency. Let rise, lightly covered, for 2 hours. Add salt, soda, baking powder and enough flour to make of biscuit dough consistency. Roll into rectangle on floured surface. Cut with biscuit cutter. Fold each roll in half; place on baking sheet. Dot with butter. Let rise for 2 to 3 hours or until almost doubled in bulk. Bake until golden brown.

Approx Per Roll: Cal 144; Prot 3.2 g; T Fat 4.2 g; Chol 2.2 mg;
    Carbo 23.2 g; Sod 133.0 mg; Potas 48.1 mg.

Mary D. Long
Hernando, Mississippi

PEPPERONI BREAD

Yields: 8 servings	Pan Size: 9x13 inch	Preheat: 350 degrees

1 loaf frozen bread dough
1 egg, beaten
¼ cup grated Parmesan cheese
⅛ teaspoon oregano
5 ounces sliced pepperoni

5 ounces sliced Baby Swiss
    cheese
Cornmeal
Oil
Oregano

Thaw dough. Place in greased bowl, turning to grease surface. Let rise, covered, for 2½ hours or until doubled in bulk. Turn dough onto floured board. Roll into ¼-inch thick rectangle. Mix egg, Parmesan cheese and ⅛ teaspoon oregano. Brush half the mixture down center. Top with pepperoni and Swiss cheese. Fold sides over filling, sealing edges and folding ends under. Sprinkle greased baking pan with cornmeal. Place loaf on pan, seam side down. Brush with oil. Sprinkle with oregano. Bake for 30 minutes or until golden brown.

Nutritional information not available.

Clifford Migal
Cincinnati, Ohio

Artist: *Lisa Marie Timblin*—Lawrence County AVTS; Gerald Zona, Teacher;
    Ellwood, Pennsylvania
Artist: *Todd Arrington*—Putnam County Vo-Tech; Lynne McNiel, Teacher;
    Eleanor, West Virginia

DESSERTS

All-American Dessert Buffet for a Crowd

Texas Sheet Cake
page 176

Mississippi Mud Cake
page 176

Lane Cake
page 178

Aunt Pittypat's Pecan Pound Cake
page 181

Grandma's Fresh Apple Cake
page 174

Easy Microwave Fudge
page 184

Derby Pie
page 193

Miniature Pecan Tarts
page 197

Pumpkin Mousse in Miniature Cream Puffs
page 173

Champagne Punch
page 34

APPLE BAKE

Yields: 15 servings   *Pan Size: 9x13 inch*   *Preheat: 350 degrees*

7 cups sliced apples
2 eggs
1¹/₂ cups flour
1 cup packed brown sugar
1 cup sugar

2 teaspoons baking powder
1 teaspoon salt
¹/₂ cup melted margarine
Cinnamon to taste

Place apples in glass baking dish. Combine eggs and next 5 dry ingredients in bowl; mix with fork until crumbly. Sprinkle over apples. Pour margarine over top. Sprinkle with cinnamon. Bake for 1 hour. Serve warm with ice cream or whipped topping. *(30-40 min. long enough)*

Approx Per Serving: Cal 247; Prot 2.3 g; T Fat 7.1 g; Chol 36.5 mg;
Carbo 44.7 g; Sod 274.0 mg; Potas 133.0 mg.

Dianne Rider
Hazel, South Dakota

APPLE ROLL

Yields: 6 servings   *Pan Size: 2 quart*   *Preheat: 400 degrees*

1 frozen pie pastry, thawed
3 Granny Smith apples,
   peeled, finely chopped
¹/₂ teaspoon sugar
¹/₂ teaspoon cinnamon

1 tablespoon butter
2 cups water
1¹/₂ cups sugar
1 tablespoon butter

Flatten pie pastry on lightly floured surface. Place apples on dough, spreading to within 1¹/₂ inches of edge. Sprinkle with ¹/₂ teaspoon sugar and cinnamon. Dot with 1 tablespoon butter. Roll to enclose filling. Place in baking dish. Bring water and 1¹/₂ cups sugar to a boil in saucepan. Cook for 5 minutes or until sugar is completely dissolved. Add 1 tablespoon butter. Pour over apple roll. Bake for 40 to 45 minutes or until brown.

Approx Per Serving: Cal 418; Prot 2.0 g; T Fat 14.1 g; Chol 10.4 mg;
Carbo 73.8 g; Sod 217.0 mg; Potas 97.5 mg.

Gena Henson
Norcross, Georgia

SPUN BANANAS

Yields: 4 servings   *Pan Size: deep fryer*

1 egg, beaten
5 tablespoons flour
5 tablespoons cornstarch
5 tablespoons cold water
4 bananas
1 tablespoon flour

Oil for deep frying
1 tablespoon oil
6 tablespoons sugar
1 tablespoon water
1 teaspoon toasted sesame
    seed

Combine egg, 5 tablespoons flour, cornstarch and 5 tablespoons water in bowl; mix to form a smooth batter. Cut each banana into 5 diagonal slices. Sprinkle with 1 tablespoon flour. Dip in batter. Deep-fry in hot oil for 1 minute or until golden brown. Drain on paper towel. Combine 1 tablespoon oil, sugar and 1 tablespoon water in skillet. Cook over low heat until mixture spins a thread, stirring constantly. Add bananas. Stir gently to coat well. Sprinkle with sesame seed. Serve immediately.

Approx Per Serving: Cal 306; Prot 4.0 g; T Fat 5.5 g; Chol 68.5 mg;
    Carbo 63.2 g; Sod 19.0 mg; Potas 479.0 mg.
    Nutritional information does not include oil for deep frying.

Dale McKinnie
Greensboro, North Carolina

TOO GOOD TO BE TRUE BANANA DESSERT

Yields: 8 servings   *Pan Size: 10 inch*   *Preheat: 375 degrees*

1/3 cup melted margarine
1 cup vanilla wafer crumbs
1/2 cup chopped pecans
1 cup miniature marshmallows
1 cup semisweet chocolate
    chips
1/2 cup milk

3 bananas, sliced
1 large package vanilla instant
    pudding mix
1 1/2 cups milk
1 1/2 cups whipped topping
2 cups miniature
    marshmallows

Mix margarine, cookie crumbs and pecans in bowl. Press over bottom and side of pie plate. Bake for 5 minutes. Melt 1 cup marshmallows and chocolate chips with 1/2 cup milk in double boiler; mix well. Pour into prepared plate. Top with sliced bananas. Prepare pudding mix according to package directions using 1 1/2 cups milk. Fold in whipped topping and 2 cups marshmallows. Pour over bananas. Chill for up to 5 hours.

Approx Per Serving: Cal 825; Prot 7.3 g; T Fat 31.1 g; Chol 26.0 mg;
    Carbo 139.0 g; Sod 444.0 mg; Potas 403.0 mg.

Sara Terry
Auburn, Alabama

CARAMEL CRUNCH

Yields: 12 servings	*Pan Size: 9x13 inch*	*Preheat: 350 degrees*

1¾ cups flour
2 cups packed brown sugar
1 teaspoon soda
1 teaspoon vanilla extract

2 eggs, well beaten
2 cups chopped pecans
16 ounces whipped topping

Combine flour, brown sugar, soda, vanilla, eggs and pecans in bowl; mix well. Pat into greased baking pan. Bake for 25 to 30 minutes or until golden brown. Cool. Crumble baked mixture into large bowl. Mix in whipped topping. Spread in dish. Chill in refrigerator overnight. Freeze until firm. Garnish with whipped cream and maraschino cherries. Store in freezer for up to 1 week.

Approx Per Serving: Cal 469; Prot 4.9 g; T Fat 24.1 g; Chol 45.7 mg;
Carbo 61.6 g; Sod 106.0 mg; Potas 239.0 mg.

Carolyn Cotton
AVA Teacher of the Year 1989
Bristow, Oklahoma

BLUEBERRY CHEESECAKE

Yields: 16 servings	*Pan Size: two 8-inch springforms*	*Preheat: 275 degrees*

1 cup sugar
24 ounces cream cheese,
   softened
4 eggs
½ teaspoon lemon juice
½ teaspoon vanilla extract
2 graham cracker pie crusts

2 cups sour cream
½ cup sugar
½ teaspoon vanilla extract
1   16-ounce can blueberries
½ cup sugar
1½ tablespoons cornstarch
Juice of 1 lemon

Cream 1 cup sugar and cream cheese in mixer bowl until light and fluffy. Blend in eggs, ½ teaspoon lemon juice and ½ teaspoon vanilla. Pour into pie shells. Bake for 30 minutes. Cool for 1 hour. Combine sour cream, ½ cup sugar and ½ teaspoon vanilla in bowl; mix well. Spoon over cheesecake. Increase oven temperature to 450 degrees. Bake for 7 minutes longer. Cool. Chill in refrigerator overnight. Drain blueberries, reserving juice. Blend juice with ½ cup sugar, cornstarch and lemon juice in saucepan. Cook until thickened, stirring constantly. Stir in blueberries. Cool. Spread over cheesecake. Store in refrigerator for up to 3 days. May substitute 1 can cherry, blueberry or pineapple pie filling for topping in recipe if desired.

Approx Per Serving: Cal 550; Prot 7.5 g; T Fat 33.2 g; Chol 128.0 mg;
Carbo 57.8 g; Sod 400.0 mg; Potas 200.0 mg.

Belva R. Post
Salt Lake City, Utah

CHEESECAKE CUPCAKES

Yields: 24 servings   *Pan Size: muffin cups*   *Preheat: 350 degrees*

24 vanilla wafers	2 eggs
3/4 cup sugar	1 teaspoon vanilla extract
16 ounces cream cheese, softened	1 21-ounce can cherry pie filling
2 teaspoons lemon juice	

Place 1 vanilla wafer in bottom of each paper-lined muffin cup. Combine sugar, cream cheese, lemon juice, eggs and vanilla in bowl; mix well. Spoon into prepared muffin cups. Bake for 20 minutes. Remove to wire rack to cool. Top with pie filling.

Approx Per Serving: Cal 165; Prot 2.6 g; T Fat 9.3 g; Chol 46.0 mg; Carbo 18.9 g; Sod 134.0 mg; Potas 60.5 mg.

Mary Payne Hairald
Nettleton, Mississippi

SOUTHERN CHEESECAKE

Yields: 16 servings   *Pan Size: 9-inch springform*   *Preheat: 350 degrees*

1 cup graham cracker crumbs	4 eggs
2 tablespoons sugar	2 egg yolks
3 tablespoons melted margarine	1 1/2 teaspoons vanilla extract
32 ounces cream cheese, softened	8 ounces sour cream
3/4 cup sugar	3 tablespoons sifted confectioners' sugar
	2 teaspoons vanilla extract

Mix graham cracker crumbs, 2 tablespoons sugar and margarine in bowl. Press firmly over bottom of springform pan. Bake for 8 minutes. Cool completely. Beat cream cheese in mixer bowl until light. Add sugar gradually, beating until fluffy. Add eggs and egg yolks, mixing well after each addition. Mix in 1 1/2 teaspoons vanilla. Pour into prepared pan. Bake for 10 minutes. Reduce oven temperature to 200 degrees. Bake for 50 minutes longer. Combine sour cream, confectioners' sugar and 2 teaspoons vanilla. Spread over hot cheesecake. Increase oven temperature to 350 degrees. Bake for 15 minutes. Cool to room temperature on wire rack. Chill for 8 hours to overnight. Place on serving plate; remove side of pan. Serve garnished with sweetened strawberries. Note: This cheesecake is always served at the ballot counting meeting for the AVA Board of Directors' election.

Approx Per Serving: Cal 382; Prot 7.6 g; T Fat 28.4 g; Chol 171.0 mg; Carbo 25.3 g; Sod 306.0 mg; Potas 144.0 mg.

Ione Phillips
AVA Assistant Executive Director for Professional Development
Annandale, Virginia

MICROWAVE QUICK CHERRY CHEESECAKE

Yields: 8 servings   *Pan Size: 8 inch*   ≈M≈

1/4 cup butter	1 egg
1 1/4 cups graham cracker crumbs	1 tablespoon lemon juice
2 tablespoons sugar	1/4 teaspoon almond extract
8 ounces cream cheese	1 cup cherry pie filling
1/4 cup sugar	1 cup sour cream
	2 tablespoons sugar

Microwave butter on High in glass pie plate for 30 seconds or until melted. Mix in graham cracker crumbs and 2 tablespoons sugar. Press over bottom and side of plate. Microwave cream cheese on High in glass bowl for 30 seconds. Beat until smooth. Add 1/4 cup sugar, egg, lemon juice and flavoring; mix well. Pour into prepared plate. Spoon pie filling over top. Microwave on High for 3 minutes or until set around edges, turning plate once; center will still be soft. Spread with mixture of sour cream and 2 tablespoons sugar. Microwave for 1 minute longer. Cool to room temperature. Store in refrigerator.

Approx Per Serving: Cal 471; Prot 7.0 g; T Fat 27.8 g; Chol 93.5 mg;
    Carbo 50.4 g; Sod 440.0 mg; Potas 210.0 mg.

Shirley A. Dear
Dover, Delaware

UNBAKED CHEESECAKE

Yields: 16 servings   *Pan Size: 13x13 inch*

28 graham crackers, crushed	1 cup boiling water
1/2 cup melted margarine	1 cup sugar
1 teaspoon confectioners' sugar	8 ounces cream cheese, softened
1 3-ounce package lemon gelatin	1 cup whipping cream, whipped

Combine graham cracker crumbs, margarine and confectioners' sugar in bowl; mix well. Reserve 1/4 cup crumbs. Press remaining mixture into glass dish. Dissolve gelatin in boiling water. Cream sugar and cream cheese in mixer bowl until light and fluffy. Mix in gelatin. Fold in whipped cream. Pour into prepared dish. Sprinkle with reserved crumbs. Chill until firm.

Approx Per Serving: Cal 272; Prot 2.8 g; T Fat 17.4 g; Chol 35.8 mg;
    Carbo 27.5 g; Sod 207.0 mg; Potas 63.1 mg.

Paul O. Lentz, AVA Building Fund Chairman
AVA Cookbook Committee
Concord, North Carolina

CHOCOLATE AND RASPBERRY CHEESECAKE

Yields: 12 servings   Pan Size: 10-inch springform   Preheat: 350 degrees

2½ cups chocolate wafer
  crumbs
½ cup sugar
½ cup melted butter
24 ounces cream cheese,
  softened
1 cup ricotta cheese
1 cup sugar

2 eggs
8 ounces German's sweet
  chocolate
2 tablespoons heavy cream
1 cup sour cream
¼ cup strong coffee
¼ cup Framboise
1 teaspoon vanilla extract

Mix cookie crumbs, ½ cup sugar and butter in bowl. Sprinkle over bottom and side of lightly greased springform pan. Beat cream cheese and ricotta cheese in mixer bowl until smooth. Mix in 1 cup sugar. Add eggs; mix well. Melt chocolate with cream in double boiler. Add melted chocolate, sour cream, coffee, liqueur and vanilla to cheese mixture; mix well. Pour into prepared pan. Bake for 1 hour and 15 minutes. Cool to room temperature. Chill for 3 hours or longer. Place on serving plate; remove side of pan. Garnish with whipped cream and chocolate curls.

Approx Per Serving: Cal 779; Prot 11.3 g; T Fat 50.9 g; Chol 180.0 mg;
  Carbo 72.9 g; Sod 453.0 mg; Potas 252.0 mg.

MaryEllen Royce, Chief, Vo-Tech Unit
Department of Education
Montpelier, Vermont

MOLLY'S FROZEN OREO DELIGHT

Yields: 12 servings   Pan Size: 9x13 inch

1 8-ounce package Oreo
  cookies
¼ cup melted margarine
½ gallon vanilla ice cream,
  softened
¼ cup chocolate syrup

½ cup chopped pecans
¼ cup caramel syrup
1 21-ounce can cherry pie
  filling
9 ounces whipped topping

Process Oreo cookies and margarine in food processor container until well mixed. Press over bottom of dish. Layer half the ice cream and chocolate syrup in prepared dish. Add pecans and half the caramel syrup. Repeat layers with remaining ice cream and syrups. Freeze for 20 minutes. Add pie filling just before serving. Top individual serving with whipped topping.

Approx Per Serving: Cal 538; Prot 6.1 g; T Fat 29.0 g; Chol 39.3 mg;
  Carbo 67.0 g; Sod 353.0 mg; Potas 299.0 mg.

Marsha Pattison
Boles Acres, New Mexico

CHOCOLATE PECAN CARAMEL TORTE

Yields: 16 servings   Pan Size: 10-inch springform   Preheat: 350 degrees

8½ ounces chocolate wafers
2 tablespoons sugar
¼ cup melted unsalted butter
2 cups packed light brown
   sugar
1 cup unsalted butter
⅛ teaspoon salt
½ cup whipping cream
2 cups chopped pecans
16 ounces bittersweet or
   semisweet chocolate

4 egg yolks
6 tablespoons strong coffee
½ cup sugar
1 cup unsalted butter
6 egg whites
4 teaspoons warm water
½ cup pecan halves
2 tablespoons whipping
   cream

Line bottom of springform pan with foil; spray with nonstick cooking spray. Process cookies and 2 tablespoons sugar in food processor container until fine crumbs. Drizzle in ¼ cup butter, processing for 5 seconds or until mixed. Press over bottom of prepared pan. Bake for 5 minutes. Cool. Heat brown sugar, 1 cup butter and salt in heavy saucepan until brown sugar is dissolved. Add ½ cup cream. Simmer until mixture coats spoon. Reserve half the caramel mixture for topping. Stir chopped pecans into remaining caramel mixture. Pour into cooled crust. Chill until set. Place half the chocolate in food processor container. Add remaining chocolate through tube, processing until consistency of small beads. Add egg yolks; process for 5 seconds. Heat coffee, ½ cup sugar and 1 cup butter in saucepan. Add to food processor container, processing until smooth; scrape sides as necessary. Transfer to large bowl; wash food processor. Drizzle mixture of egg whites and water into food processor container, processing until stiff peaks form. Fold into chocolate mixture. Chill until almost set. Spoon over caramel layer in crust. Chill until set. Arrange pecan halves on top. Reheat reserved caramel mixture adding 2 tablespoons cream if necessary for desired consistency; cool slightly. Spoon or brush over top. Chill for 2 hours or longer. Place on serving plate; remove side of pan. Use the best quality chocolate available for this recipe.

Approx Per Serving: Cal 698; Prot 6.5 g; T Fat 52.6 g; Chol 152.0 mg;
   Carbo 58.4 g; Sod 115.0 mg; Potas 352.0 mg.

Marilyn Jenkins
AVA Vice President
Evergreen Park, Illinois

HORTENSE'S CHOCOLATE PUDDING CAKE

Yields: 12 servings   *Pan Size: 8x8 inch*   *Preheat: 350 degrees*

1 cup sifted flour	1 teaspoon vanilla extract
3/4 cup sugar	1/2 cup chopped walnuts
2 teaspoons baking powder	1/4 cup unsweetened baking
1/2 teaspoon salt	cocoa
2 tablespoons melted butter	1 cup sugar
3/4 cup milk	1 cup hot water

Combine first 4 ingredients in bowl. Add melted butter, milk, vanilla and walnuts; mix well. Pour into greased baking pan. Sprinkle with mixture of cocoa and 1 cup sugar. Pour hot water over top. Bake for 30 minutes.

Approx Per Serving: Cal 211; Prot 2.6 g; T Fat 6.0 g; Chol 7.2 mg;
    Carbo 39.0 g; Sod 168.0 mg; Potas 77.9 mg.

Sheri Klein
Elko, Nevada

BRENDA'S FRUIT PIZZAS

Yields: 16 servings   *Pan Size: two 12 inch*   *Preheat: 400 degrees*

1/2 cup margarine, softened	1 10-ounce package frozen
1/2 cup oil	whole strawberries,
1 1/2 cups sugar	thawed
2 eggs	8 ounces cream cheese,
2 3/4 cups flour	softened
2 teaspoons cream of tartar	1/2 cup sugar
1 teaspoon soda	2 bananas, sliced
1/4 teaspoon salt	1 tablespoon lemon juice
1 16-ounce can pineapple	2 kiwifruit, peeled, sliced
tidbits	3 tablespoons cornstarch
1 12-ounce can mandarin	
oranges	

Combine margarine, oil, 1 1/2 cups sugar and eggs in mixer bowl. Add flour, cream of tartar, soda and salt; mix well. Press into round pans. Bake for 8 minutes. Cool. Drain canned and frozen fruits, reserving all juices. Beat cream cheese, 1/2 cup sugar and 2 tablespoons reserved juice in mixer bowl until smooth. Spread over cooled crusts. Dip bananas in lemon juice. Arrange bananas and remaining fruits over creamed layer. Blend remaining reserved juice with cornstarch in saucepan. Cook until thickened, stirring constantly. Drizzle over fruit. Chill until serving time.

Approx Per Serving: Cal 339; Prot 4.6 g; T Fat 18.6 g; Chol 49.7 mg;
    Carbo 40.1 g; Sod 215.0 mg; Potas 225.0 mg.

Brenda Costin
Maryville, Missouri

FRUIT PIZZA

| Yields: 12 servings | Pan Size: 12 inch | Preheat: 375 degrees |

1½ cups flour
¾ cup margarine, softened
¾ cup chopped pecans
8 ounces cream cheese, softened
¾ cup sugar
1 12-ounce can mandarin oranges, drained

2 bananas, sliced
1 tablespoon lemon juice
1 21-ounce can cherry pie filling, drained
1 12-ounce can pineapple tidbits, drained
1 cup apricot preserves
½ cup chopped pecans

Mix flour, margarine and ¾ cup pecans in bowl. Pat into round pan. Bake for 12 to 15 minutes or until light brown. Cool. Beat cream cheese and sugar in mixer bowl until fluffy. Spread on crust. Arrange circle of oranges around edge of pizza, leaving some oranges for second circle. Dip bananas in lemon juice. Arrange circles of bananas, cherries and pineapple inside oranges, placing fruits close together. Repeat circles with remaining fruits. Heat preserves in saucepan just until of consistency of syrup. Drizzle over fruit. Sprinkle with ½ cup pecans.

Approx Per Serving: Cal 546; Prot 5.5 g; T Fat 26.9 g; Chol 20.6 mg; Carbo 75.3 g; Sod 319.0 mg; Potas 294.0 mg.

Mary Beth Stine, Former AVA Vice President
Home Economics Education Division
Flora, Illinois

FRUIT TRIFLE

| Yields: 12 servings | Pan Size: glass trifle dish |

1 16-ounce sponge cake
1 6-ounce package strawberry gelatin
2 16-ounce cans fruit cocktail, drained

1 large package vanilla pudding and pie filling mix, prepared
1 cup whipping cream, whipped

Crumble cake into trifle dish. Prepare gelatin according to package directions. Cool to room temperature. Pour over cake. Chill until set. Spoon fruit cocktail over top. Spread cooled pudding over fruit cocktail. Chill until set. Top with whipped cream. Garnish with chocolate curls. May vary fruit and gelatin or flavor with Brandy or Bourbon as desired.

Approx Per Serving: Cal 292; Prot 5.2 g; T Fat 9.5 g; Chol 107.0 mg; Carbo 48.6 g; Sod 218.0 mg; Potas 129.0 mg.

Sally Carder
Arkansas Department of Education
Little Rock, Arkansas

FROZEN ICE CREAM CAKE

Yields: 12 servings   Pan Size: 10-inch springform   Preheat: 350 degrees

1³/4 cups Oreo cookie crumbs
6 tablespoons melted
  margarine
1/2 gallon vanilla ice cream,
  softened

1/2 gallon chocolate ice cream,
  softened
12 ounces whipped topping
Food coloring

Mix cookie crumbs with margarine in bowl. Reserve 1/2 cup. Press remaining mixture over bottom of waxed paper-lined pan. Bake for 5 minutes. Chill. Spread vanilla ice cream over crust. Sprinkle with reserved crumbs. Freeze until firm. Top with chocolate ice cream. Freeze until firm. Place on serving plate. Loosen side with knife; remove side. Freeze until serving time. Frost with whipped topping tinted with food coloring as desired. Process cookies in food processor container to make crumbs easily. Substitute ice cream flavors of your choice.

Approx Per Serving: Cal 661; Prot 8.5 g; T Fat 38.6 g; Chol 78.7 mg;
    Carbo 72.8 g; Sod 385.0 mg; Potas 406.0 mg.

Betty Rinehimer
Smithville, New Jersey

FROZEN RAINBOW DELIGHT

Yields: 12 servings   Pan Size: 9x13 inch

1 pint whipping cream
3 tablespoons sugar
1 teaspoon vanilla extract
18 coconut macaroons, crushed

1 cup chopped walnuts
1 pint orange sherbet
1 pint lime sherbet
1 pint raspberry sherbet

Whip cream in mixer bowl until soft peaks form. Mix in sugar and vanilla. Fold in crushed macaroons and walnuts. Spread half the mixture evenly in dish. Spoon sherbet into prepared dish, alternating flavors. Top with remaining whipped cream mixture. Freeze, covered, until firm. Use only red and green sherbets for a Christmas dessert.

Approx Per Serving: Cal 406; Prot 4.1 g; T Fat 25.8 g; Chol 71.5 mg;
    Carbo 42.9 g; Sod 106.0 mg; Potas 193.0 mg.

Ruby Trow
Whittier, California

LEMON CREAM COOLER

Yields: 6 servings   *Pan Size: glass bowl*

1 3-ounce package lemon
    gelatin
1/2 cup sugar
1/2 teaspoon salt
1 cup boiling water

1 6-ounce can frozen
    lemonade concentrate
1 cup whipping cream,
    whipped

Dissolve gelatin, sugar and salt in boiling water in bowl. Stir in lemonade. Chill until thickened. Fold in whipped cream. Chill until firm.

Approx Per Serving: Cal 305; Prot 2.2 g; T Fat 14.7 g; Chol 54.3 mg;
    Carbo 43.5 g; Sod 239.0 mg; Potas 49.6 mg.

The Honorable Gerald L. Baliles
Governor of Virginia
Richmond, Virginia

MARINATED PEACHES

Yields: 8 servings   *Pan Size: deep dish*

16 fresh ripe peaches
1 cup light rum
1 cup Brandy

2 cups packed brown sugar
4 cups heavy cream

Combine peaches with water to cover in saucepan. Boil for 1 minute; drain. Skin peaches under cold running water. Slice peaches. Combine with remaining ingredients in dish. Marinate in refrigerator overnight.

Approx Per Serving: Cal 821; Prot 3.7 g; T Fat 44.2 g; Chol 163.0 mg;
    Carbo 86.1 g; Sod 69.7 mg; Potas 623.0 mg.

Jim Campbell
Bear, Delaware

POPCORN CAKE DESSERT

Yields: 16 servings   *Pan Size: tube pan*

1/2 cup margarine
1/2 cup oil
1 pound marshmallows

4 quarts popped popcorn
1 pound M&M's
2 cups peanuts

Melt margarine, oil and marshmallows in large saucepan, stirring constantly. Pour over popcorn, candies and peanuts in bowl; mix well. Press into oiled tube pan. Let stand for 1 hour. Unmold onto serving plate.

Nutritional information not available.

Billye Griswold
White Hall, Illinois

PRETZEL DESSERT

Yields: 18 servings   *Pan Size: 9x13 inch*   *Preheat: 400 degrees*

2 cups crushed pretzels
3/4 cup melted margarine
3 tablespoons sugar
8 ounces cream cheese, softened
1 cup sugar

12 ounces whipped topping
1 6-ounce package strawberry gelatin
2 cups boiling water
2 10-ounce packages frozen strawberries

Mix pretzels, margarine and 3 tablespoons sugar in bowl. Press into baking pan. Bake for 8 minutes. Beat cream cheese and 1 cup sugar in mixer bowl until light and fluffy. Fold in whipped topping. Spread over pretzel layer. Dissolve gelatin in boiling water in bowl. Stir in strawberries. Pour over cheese layer. Chill until serving time.

Approx Per Serving: Cal 370; Prot 4.8 g; T Fat 17.6 g; Chol 13.8 mg;
    Carbo 49.3 g; Sod 568.0 mg; Potas 95.2 mg.

Gladys M. Schoenknecht
Rochester, Michigan

BREAD PUDDING with Whiskey Sauce

Yields: 8 servings   *Pan Size: 3 quart*   *Preheat: 350 degrees*

1 16-ounce loaf French bread
4 cups milk
4 eggs, beaten
2 cups sugar
2 tablespoons vanilla extract
1 cup seedless raisins

2 apples peeled, sliced
1/4 cup butter
1 cup sugar
1/2 cup melted butter
1 egg, beaten
1 ounce whiskey

Crumble bread into milk in large bowl; mix well. Add 4 eggs, 2 cups sugar, vanilla, raisins and apples; mix well. Melt 1/4 cup butter in baking dish. Pour in pudding mixture. Bake for 50 minutes or until set. Cool. Mix 1 cup sugar and 1/2 cup butter in double boiler. Mix in 1 egg. Cook until thickened, stirring constantly. Cool. Stir in whiskey. Serve with pudding.

Approx Per Serving: Cal 868; Prot 14.1 g; T Fat 33.0 g; Chol 250.0 mg;
    Carbo 131.0 g; Sod 621.0 mg; Potas 461.0 mg.

Ellen Coody, Former Executive Director
Georgia Vocational Assn.
Stone Mountain, Georgia

PUMPKIN MOUSSE

Yields: 4 servings   *Pan Size: medium bowl*

1 small package vanilla instant pudding mix 1 cup milk 1 cup canned pumpkin	1/4 cup sugar 1 teaspoon cinnamon 1/4 teaspoon nutmeg 1 cup whipped topping

Combine pudding mix, milk, pumpkin, sugar, cinnamon and nutmeg in bowl. Beat for 2 minutes or until thickened. Fold in whipped topping gently. Chill until serving time. May be used as filling for cream puffs or spooned into graham cracker pie shell if desired.

Approx Per Serving: Cal 245; Prot 2.9 g; T Fat 7.1 g; Chol 8.3 mg;
   Carbo 44.6 g; Sod 176.0 mg; Potas 213.0 mg.

Frances G. Bliven
Oneonta, New York

VERMONT INDIAN PUDDING

Yields: 8 servings   *Pan Size: 2 quart*   *Preheat: 325 degrees*

1 quart milk 1/3 cup cornmeal 1 cup Vermont maple syrup 2 tablespoons melted butter 1 egg, well beaten	1/2 cup golden raisins 1/2 teaspoon cinnamon 1/2 teaspoon nutmeg 1/2 teaspoon salt

Scald milk in heavy saucepan. Stir in cornmeal. Cook for 15 minutes, stirring occasionally. Stir in maple syrup. Cook for 5 minutes longer; remove from heat. Add butter, egg, raisins, cinnamon, nutmeg and salt; mix well. Pour into buttered baking dish. Set in shallow pan of hot water. Bake for 1 1/2 hours. Serve warm with hard sauce, ice cream or additional maple syrup.

Approx Per Serving: Cal 262; Prot 5.6 g; T Fat 7.8 g; Chol 58.5 mg;
   Carbo 44.0 g; Sod 224.0 mg; Potas 309.0 mg.

Elizabeth Ducolon
Burlington, Vermont

GRANDMA'S FRESH APPLE CAKE

Yields: 16 servings   *Pan Size: 10 inch*   *Preheat: 350 degrees*

3 cups sifted flour	3/4 cup water
1 1/2 teaspoons nutmeg	1 1/2 cups ground unpeeled
1 1/2 teaspoons cinnamon	apples
1 1/2 teaspoons salt	3/4 cup shortening
1 1/2 cups chopped walnuts	1 1/2 cups sugar
1 1/2 cups raisins	3 eggs
1 1/2 teaspoons soda	

Combine flour, nutmeg, cinnamon, salt, walnuts and raisins in bowl. Dissolve soda in water in small bowl; stir in apples. Cream shortening, sugar and eggs in mixer bowl until light and fluffy. Add raisin mixture alternately with apple mixture, mixing well after each addition. Pour into greased tube pan. Bake for 1 hour and 15 minutes or until cake tests done.

Approx Per Serving: Cal 375; Prot 5.5 g; T Fat 17.9 g; Chol 51.4 mg;
     Carbo 51.1 g; Sod 294.0 mg; Potas 218.0 mg.

Russell L. Blackman
Former AVA Vice President, Region V
Aurora, Colorado

BETTER THAN SEX CHOCOLATE CHIP CAKE

Yields: 12 servings   *Pan Size: tube pan*   *Preheat: 350 degrees*

1 2-layer package butter recipe cake mix	1/4 cup water
1 4-ounce package instant vanilla pudding mix	1 cup sour cream
4 eggs	1 6-ounce package semisweet chocolate chips
1/2 cup oil	1/2 cup chopped pecans

Combine cake mix, pudding mix, eggs, oil, water and sour cream in bowl; mix well. Fold in chocolate chips and pecans. Pour into greased pan. Bake for 1 hour or until cake tests done.

Approx Per Serving: Cal 409; Prot 4.8 g; T Fat 25.8 g; Chol 99.8 mg;
     Carbo 42.7 g; Sod 273.0 mg; Potas 119.0 mg.

Maurine R. Humphris
Ogden, Utah

BLACK RUSSIAN CAKE

Yields: 16 servings   *Pan Size: bundt pan*   *Preheat: 350 degrees*

1 2-layer package Swiss chocolate cake mix	1 cup cool strong coffee
	¼ cup Kahlua
1 4-ounce package fudge chocolate instant pudding mix	¼ cup Crème de Cacao
	1 cup confectioners' sugar
½ cup oil	1 cup cool strong coffee
4 eggs, at room temperature	2 tablespoons Kahlua
	2 tablespoons Crème de Cacao

Combine first 7 ingredients in mixer bowl. Beat at medium speed for 3 minutes. Pour into greased and floured pan. Bake for 45 minutes or until cake tests done. Cool in pan for 20 minutes. Invert onto serving plate. Punch holes in cake. Blend confectioners' sugar and remaining ingredients in bowl. Spoon over warm cake gradually. Let stand overnight.

Nutritional information not available.

Frances Bishop
Home Economics Teacher, Sr. High School
Denton, Texas

DECADENT CHOCOLATE FUDGE CAKE with Frosting

Yields: 12 servings   *Pan Size: 10-inch springform*   *Preheat: 350 degrees*

¾ cup melted butter	3 tablespoons water
1½ cups sugar	¾ cup finely chopped pecans
1½ teaspoons vanilla extract	3 egg whites
3 egg yolks	⅛ teaspoon cream of tartar
9 tablespoons baking cocoa	⅛ teaspoon salt
½ cup flour	4 ounces bittersweet chocolate
3 tablespoons oil	¼ cup whipping cream

Line bottom of pan with foil. Butter foil and side of pan. Blend butter, sugar and vanilla in large mixer bowl. Beat in egg yolks 1 at a time. Add cocoa, flour, oil and water; beat well. Beat egg whites with cream of tartar and salt until stiff. Fold into chocolate mixture gently. Pour into prepared pan. Bake for 45 minutes. Cool for 1 hour. Chill, covered, until firm. Remove side of pan; place on serving plate. Melt bittersweet chocolate and cream in small saucepan over very low heat, stirring constantly. Cool until thickened, beating frequently. Spread over top and side of cake.

Approx Per Serving: Cal 391; Prot 4.2 g; T Fat 27.2 g; Chol 106.0 mg; Carbo 37.6 g; Sod 138.0 mg; Potas 148.0 mg.

MaryEllen Royce, Chief, Vo-Tech Unit
Department of Education
Montpelier, Vermont

MISSISSIPPI MUD CAKE with Frosting

Yields: 15 servings   *Pan Size: 9x13 inch*   *Preheat: 350 degrees*

4 eggs
2 cups sugar
1¹/₂ cups flour
¹/₄ teaspoon salt
¹/₂ cup unsweetened baking
  cocoa
1 cup melted margarine
1 teaspoon vanilla extract
1 cup chopped pecans

1 10-ounce package miniature
   marshmallows
1 pound confectioners' sugar
¹/₂ cup margarine, softened
¹/₂ cup evaporated milk
¹/₃ cup unsweetened baking
   cocoa
1 teaspoon vanilla extract

Beat eggs with sugar in large mixer bowl. Sift in flour, salt and ¹/₂ cup cocoa; beat well. Add melted margarine, 1 teaspoon vanilla and pecans; mix well. Pour into pan. Bake for 35 minutes. Top with marshmallows. Bake for 5 minutes or until marshmallows melt. Beat confectioners' sugar and remaining ingredients in bowl until smooth. Spread over hot cake.

Approx Per Serving: Cal 634; Prot 5.5 g; T Fat 26.4 g; Chol 75.5 mg;
  Carbo 99.2 g; Sod 311.0 mg; Potas 135.0 mg.

The Honorable Floyd D. Spence
U.S. House of Representatives, South Carolina
Columbia, South Carolina

TEXAS SHEET CAKE with Frosting

Yields: 36 servings   *Pan Size: 10x15 inch*   *Preheat: 375 degrees*

1 cup margarine
1 cup water
¹/₄ cup unsweetened baking
  cocoa
2 cups flour
2 cups sugar
¹/₂ teaspoon salt
2 eggs

¹/₂ teaspoon soda
¹/₂ cup sour cream
¹/₂ cup margarine
¹/₄ cup unsweetened baking
  cocoa
6 tablespoons milk
1 pound confectioners' sugar
1 teaspoon vanilla extract

Bring first 3 ingredients to a boil in saucepan; remove from heat. Add flour, sugar and salt; mix well. Mix in eggs, soda and sour cream. Pour into greased and floured pan. Bake for 20 minutes. Bring ¹/₂ cup margarine, ¹/₄ cup cocoa and milk to a boil in saucepan; remove from heat. Add confectioners' sugar and vanilla; mix well. Spread over cake.

Approx Per Serving: Cal 200; Prot 1.5 g; T Fat 8.9 g; Chol 17.0 mg;
  Carbo 29.8 g; Sod 138.0 mg; Potas 37.0 mg.

Alice Karen Hite, Executive Director
Ohio Vocational Association
Worthington, Ohio

COCONUT ICEBOX CAKE with Frosting

Yields: 12 servings   *Pan Size: two 8 inch*   *Preheat: 350 degrees*

1 cup sugar
16 ounces whipped topping
1 12-ounce package frozen
  coconut, thawed

2 cups sour cream
1 2-layer package yellow cake
  mix

Combine sugar, whipped topping, coconut and sour cream in bowl; mix well. Refrigerate, covered, overnight. Prepare and bake cake mix according to package directions. Split each layer into 2 layers. Spread coconut mixture between layers and over top and side of cake. Store in refrigerator. May be refrigerated for up to 1 week.

Approx Per Serving: Cal 489; Prot 3.9 g; T Fat 29.4 g; Chol 17.0 mg;
  Carbo 55.1 g; Sod 211.0 mg; Potas 164.0 mg.

Linda F. Widenhouse
Concord, North Carolina

COCONUT WAIT CAKE with Frosting

Yields: 12 servings   *Pan Size: two 8 inch*   *Preheat: 350 degrees*

2 cups sugar
2 cups sour cream
1 12-ounce package frozen
  coconut, thawed

1 2-layer package butter
  recipe cake mix
1½ cups whipped topping

Mix sugar, sour cream and coconut in bowl. Chill in refrigerator. Prepare and bake cake according to package directions. Split each layer into 2 layers. Reserve 1 cup coconut mixture. Spread remaining coconut mixture between layers. Mix whipped topping into reserved coconut mixture; spread over top and side of cake. Seal in airtight container. Chill in refrigerator for 3 days before serving.

Approx Per Serving: Cal 461; Prot 3.5 g; T Fat 22.1 g; Chol 16.8 mg;
  Carbo 65.1 g; Sod 204.0 mg; Potas 158.0 mg.

Martha Barnhill
Redington Beach, Florida

LANE CAKE with Frosting

Yields: 16 servings   *Pan Size: three 9 inch*   *Preheat: 350 degrees*

1 cup butter, softened
2 cups sugar
6 egg whites
3 cups flour
1 cup milk
1 teaspoon vanilla extract
2 cups sugar

3/4 cup butter
9 egg yolks
1¹/₂ cups chopped pecans
1¹/₂ cups raisins
1 cup shredded coconut
1 teaspoon vanilla extract

Cream 1 cup butter and 2 cups sugar in bowl until light and fluffy. Add egg whites; mix well. Add flour and milk alternately, beating well after each addition. Add vanilla. Pour into prepared cake pans. Bake for 30 minutes or until cake tests done. Combine remaining 2 cups sugar and 3/4 cup butter with egg yolks in double boiler. Cook until thickened, stirring constantly. Stir in pecans and remaining ingredients. Cool. Spread between layers and over top and side of cake.

Approx Per Serving: Cal 656; Prot 7.5 g; T Fat 33.7 g; Chol 209.0 mg;
    Carbo 85.6 g; Sod 218.0 mg; Potas 256.0 mg.

Sonia Parmer
President Elect, NCLA
Largo, Florida

LEMON FRUITCAKE

Yields: 16 servings   *Pan Size: tube pan*   *Preheat: 225 degrees*

1 pound butter, softened
1 pound light brown sugar
6 eggs, separated
2 cups flour
1/2 teaspoon salt
1 teaspoon baking powder

3 tablespoons lemon extract
1 pound chopped pecans
1 cup candied cherry halves
1 cup chopped candied
   pineapple
2 cups flour

Cream butter and brown sugar in large bowl until light and fluffy. Add egg yolks 1 at a time, beating well after each addition. Sift 2 cups flour, salt and baking powder into bowl. Add to creamed mixture alternately with lemon extract, mixing well after each addition. Dredge pecans and fruit with 2 cups flour; add to mixture. Beat egg whites until stiff; fold into mixture. Pour into wel-greased pan. Let stand in refrigerator overnight. Bake for 3 hours. Invert onto serving plate.

Approx Per Serving: Cal 733; Prot 8.2 g; T Fat 44.7 g; Chol 165.0 mg;
    Carbo 79.6 g; Sod 320.0 mg; Potas 270.0 mg.

The Honorable Robin M. Tallon
U.S. House of Representatives, South Carolina
Florence, South Carolina

GERMAN OAT CAKE with Topping

Yields: 16 servings   *Pan Size: 9x13 inch*   *Preheat: 350 degrees*

1 cup quick-cooking oats
1/2 cup butter
4 ounces German sweet
  chocolate, broken
1 1/4 cups milk, scalded
1 1/2 cups sifted flour
1 cup sugar
1/2 teaspoon salt

1 teaspoon soda
1 cup packed brown sugar
3 eggs
6 tablespoons butter
3/4 cup packed brown sugar
1/4 cup cream
1/2 cup chopped pecans

Combine oats, 1/2 cup butter, chocolate and hot milk in bowl. Let stand for 20 minutes. Sift flour, sugar, salt and soda into large bowl. Add 1 cup brown sugar, eggs and chocolate mixture; mix well. Pour into greased pan. Bake for 35 minutes or until cake tests done. Mix 6 tablespoons butter, 3/4 cup brown sugar and cream in saucepan. Bring to a boil, stirring constantly. Boil for 2 minutes or until slightly thickened, stirring constantly. Pour over hot cake. Top with pecans.

Approx Per Serving: Cal 387; Prot 4.4 g; T Fat 18.6 g; Chol 86.2 mg;
  Carbo 53.0 g; Sod 237.0 mg; Potas 191.0 mg.

Cecilia Wineman
Seattle, Washington

OATMEAL CAKE with Topping

Yields:16 servings   *Pan Size: 9x13 inch*   *Preheat: 350 degrees*

1 cup oats
1/2 cup margarine
1 1/4 cups boiling water
1 cup sugar
1 cup packed brown sugar
2 eggs
1 1/3 cups flour
1 teaspoon soda
1 teaspoon baking powder

1 teaspoon cinnamon
1/4 cup evaporated milk
6 tablespoons melted
  margarine
1 teaspoon vanilla extract
1 cup coconut
1/2 cup chopped pecans
1/2 cup packed brown sugar

Mix first 3 ingredients in bowl. Let stand for 20 minutes. Add 1 cup sugar, 1 cup brown sugar and eggs; mix well. Add mixture of flour, soda, baking powder and cinnamon; mix well. Pour into greased and floured pan. Bake for 35 minutes or until cake tests done. Spread mixture of evaporated milk and remaining ingredients over hot cake. Broil until brown.

Approx Per Serving: Cal 319; Prot 3.1 g; T Fat 15.4 g; Chol 35.4 mg;
  Carbo 43.8 g; Sod 236.0 mg; Potas 148.0 mg.

Martha Atchley
O.T. Autry Area Vocational Technical Center
Enid, Oklahoma

PINEAPPLE CAKE with Frosting

Yields: 15 servings   *Pan Size: 9x13 inch*   *Preheat: 350 degrees*

1   2-layer package yellow
    cake mix
4 eggs
1 cup crushed pineapple

1 cup oil
2 cups confectioners' sugar
1/4 cup margarine, softened
1/2 cup crushed pineapple

Combine cake mix, eggs, 1 cup pineapple and oil in bowl; mix well. Pour into prepared pan. Bake for 35 to 45 minutes or until cake tests done. Combine confectioners' sugar and margarine in bowl. Add enough remaining 1/2 cup pineapple to make of spreading consistency. Spread over cake. May substitute white cake mix for yellow.

Approx Per Serving: Cal 345; Prot 2.7 g; T Fat 20.9 g; Chol 73.1 mg;
    Carbo 37.6 g; Sod 194.0 mg; Potas 46.2 mg.

Rebecca Baird
Calhoun, Kentucky

CREAM CHEESE POUND CAKE

Yields: 18 servings   *Pan Size: bundt pan*   *Preheat: 325 degrees*

2 cups butter, softened
8 ounces cream cheese,
    softened
3 cups sugar
6 eggs

3 cups cake flour
2 tablespoons vanilla extract
1 1/2 cups chopped black
    walnuts

Cream butter and cream cheese in large bowl. Add sugar gradually, beating until light and fluffy. Add eggs 1 at a time, beating well after each addition. Blend in flour gradually; mix well. Stir in vanilla and walnuts. Spoon into greased and floured pan. Bake for 1 hour or until cake tests done. Cool in pan for 10 minutes. Invert onto serving plate.

Approx Per Serving: Cal 518; Prot 7.9 g; T Fat 32.8 g; Chol 160.0 mg;
    Carbo 50.8 g; Sod 234.0 mg; Potas 119.0 mg.

Alma Willis Dunn
Atlanta, Georgia

AUNT PITTYPAT'S PECAN POUND CAKE with Glaze

Yields: 18 servings   *Pan Size: 10-inch tube pan*   *Preheat: 325 degrees*

1 cup shortening	1/2 cup Tennessee whiskey
2 1/2 cups sugar	1 cup finely chopped pecans
6 eggs	2 cups confectioners' sugar
3 cups sifted cake flour	1 tablespoon Tennessee
1 teaspoon salt	whiskey
1 teaspoon nutmeg	2 tablespoons water

Cream shortening and sugar in large mixer bowl until light and fluffy. Add eggs 1 at a time, beating well after each addition. Sift flour, salt and nutmeg into bowl. Add to egg mixture alternately with sour cream and 1/2 cup whiskey; mix just until well blended. Fold in pecans. Pour into prepared tube pan. Bake for 1 hour and 15 minutes or until toothpick inserted in center comes out clean. Cool in pan for 15 minutes. Remove to wire rack to cool completely. Make Gone with the Wind Glaze by blending confectioners' sugar and whiskey with enough water to make of pouring consistency. Pour over cake. May decorate with pecans halves.

Approx Per Serving: Cal 407; Prot 4.6 g; T Fat 17.9 g; Chol 91.3 mg;
    Carbo 54.6 g; Sod 143.0 mg; Potas 67.4 mg.

Ellen Coody, Former Executive Director
Georgia Vocational Association
Stone Mountain, Georgia

BASIC POUND CAKE

Yields: 18 servings   *Pan Size: tube pan*   *Preheat: 325 degrees*

1 1/2 cups margarine, softened	3 1/2 cups flour
2 teaspoons vanilla extract	1/2 teaspoon baking powder
3 cups sugar	1 cup milk
6 eggs	

Cream margarine, vanilla and sugar in mixer bowl until light and fluffy. Add eggs 2 at a time; beat for 2 minutes after each addition. Sift flour and baking powder into bowl. Add to egg mixture alternately with milk; mix well. Pour into greased and floured pan. Bake for 1 1/2 hours or until cake tests done. May substitute flavoring of choice for vanilla or substitute 1/2 cup baking cocoa for 1/2 cup flour.

Approx Per Serving: Cal 387; Prot 5.2 g; T Fat 17.8 g; Chol 93.2 mg;
    Carbo 52.6 g; Sod 243.0 mg; Potas 71.4 mg.

Ruby Lentz
Concord, North Carolina

PRIZE POUND CAKE

Yields: 15 servings   *Pan Size: tube pan*   *Preheat: 325 degrees*

2 cups sugar	3 cups flour
1/2 cup margarine, softened	2 teaspoons baking powder
1/2 cup shortening	1/8 teaspoon salt
4 eggs	3/4 cup milk
1/4 cup (about) milk	1 teaspoon vanilla extract

Grease and flour bottom of tube pan; line with waxed paper. Cream sugar, margarine and shortening in mixer bowl until light and fluffy. Place eggs in 1 cup measure; add enough milk to measure 1 cup. Add to creamed mixture; mix well. Sift flour, baking powder and salt into bowl. Add to creamed mixture alternately with 3/4 cup milk, 1/4 at a time; mixing well after each addition. Add vanilla. Pour into prepared pan. Bake for 1 hour and 15 minutes or until cake tests done.

Approx Per Serving: Cal 340; Prot 4.8 g; T Fat 15.2 g; Chol 75.3 mg; Carbo 46.6 g; Sod 170.0 mg; Potas 67.4 mg.

Barbara Ann Reed
Hammonton, New Jersey

PRUNE CAKE

Yields: 12 servings   *Pan Size: 10-inch tube*   *Preheat: 350 degrees*

2 cups sugar	1 teaspoon nutmeg
1 cup oil	1 teaspoon allspice
3 eggs	2 4-ounce jars baby food
2 cups self-rising flour	prunes with tapioca
1 teaspoon cinnamon	1 cup chopped pecans

Cream sugar and oil in mixer bowl. Add eggs 1 at a time, beating well after each addition. Sift in flour and spices; mix well. Stir in prunes and pecans. Pour into greased and floured pan. Bake for 45 minutes or until cake tests done. Cool in pan for 10 minutes. Invert onto serving plate. May add lemon glaze if desired. This is a very moist cake which keeps and freezes well.

Approx Per Serving: Cal 468; Prot 4.5 g; T Fat 26.5 g; Chol 68.5 mg; Carbo 55.9 g; Sod 243.0 mg; Potas 139.0 mg.

Susan Imel
Columbus, Ohio

BUCKEYES

Yields: 60 pieces   *Pan Size: double boiler*

1 pound peanut butter
1 cup butter, softened
1½ pounds confectioners'
  sugar

12 ounces chocolate chips
¼ bar paraffin

Combine peanut butter, butter and confectioners' sugar in bowl; mix well. Shape into bite-sized balls. Melt chocolate chips and paraffin in double boiler. Dip peanut butter balls into chocolate mixture, leaving a small portion uncovered. Place on tray. Chill until firm.

Approx Per Piece: Cal 144; Prot 2.4 g; T Fat 9.0 g; Chol 8.3 mg;
    Carbo 15.7 g; Sod 57.4 mg; Potas 73.0 mg.

Jim Frasier
Loveland, Ohio

CHOCOLATE-COVERED PECAN CARAMELS

Yields: 100 pieces   *Pan Size: 3 quart*

1 cup margarine
1 pound dark brown sugar
1 14-ounce can sweetened
  condensed milk
1 cup light corn syrup

1 cup finely chopped pecans
1 teaspoon vanilla extract
1 11-ounce package milk
  chocolate chips
⅔ bar paraffin

Melt margarine in heavy saucepan. Add brown sugar, condensed milk and corn syrup; blend well. Cook over medium heat for 15 to 20 minutes or to 248 degrees on candy thermometer, firm-ball stage, stirring frequently with wooden spoon. Remove from heat. Stir in pecans and vanilla. Pour into buttered foil-lined 8x8-inch pan. Let stand until firm. Lift foil from pan. Cut into ¾-inch squares with buttered knife. Melt chocolate chips and paraffin in double boiler over boiling water. Dip caramel squares 1 at a time into chocolate mixture to coat; place on waxed paper. Let stand until firm. Wrap in plastic wrap. Store in refrigerator or freezer. Bring almost to room temperature before serving.

Approx Per Piece: Cal 79; Prot 0.6 g; T Fat 4.1 g; Chol 1.4 mg;
    Carbo 11.0 g; Sod 30.4 mg; Potas 47.4 mg.

Mrs. Carl E. Beeman
Gainesville, Florida

DIFFERENT VANILLA FUDGE

Yields: 96 pieces   *Pan Size: 9x12 inch*

2 cups sugar	1 cup chopped pecans
1 cup evaporated milk	1 cup flaked coconut
½ cup margarine	1 cup graham cracker crumbs
20 large marshmallows	

Combine sugar, evaporated milk and margarine in heavy saucepan. Cook over medium heat to 235 degrees on candy thermometer, soft-ball stage. Remove from heat. Add marshmallows; stir until melted. Add pecans, coconut and crumbs; mix well. Press into buttered pan. Cool completely before cutting into squares.

Approx Per Piece: Cal 54; Prot 0.5 g; T Fat 2.5 g; Chol 0.8 mg;
     Carbo 7.8 g; Sod 30.0 mg; Potas 22.6 mg.

Vicki H. O'Dell
Holly Springs, Mississippi

EASY MICROWAVE FUDGE

Yields: 24 pieces   *Pan Size: 8x8 inch*   ≈M≈

1 16-ounce package chocolate-covered old-fashioned creme drops	3 tablespoons peanut butter
	1 cup chopped pecans

Combine candy and peanut butter in glass bowl. Microwave on Medium for 2 minutes or until melted; stir until blended. Stir in pecans. Pour into greased pan or drop by spoonfuls onto waxed paper. Let stand until firm.

Nutritional information not available.

Wanda Hightower
Athens, Alabama

MICROWAVE PEANUT CLUSTERS

Yields: 10 servings   *Pan Size: 2 quart*   ≈M≈

1 cup raw peanuts	1 tablespoon butter
1 cup sugar	1 teaspoon vanilla extract
1/2 cup light corn syrup	1 teaspoon soda
1/8 teaspoon salt	

Combine peanuts, sugar, corn syrup and salt in casserole. Microwave on High for 3½ to 4 minutes; mix well. Microwave for 4 minutes longer. Stir in butter and vanilla. Microwave for 3 minutes longer. Add soda; stir gently until light and fluffy. Pour onto buttered foil; spread thin. Cool. Break into small pieces.

Approx Per Serving: Cal 215; Prot 3.8 g; T Fat 8.3 g; Chol 3.1 mg;
    Carbo 34.6 g; Sod 129.0 mg; Potas 108.0 mg.

Susan Webber
Prosser, Washington

MICROWAVE CARAMEL CORN

Yields: 24 servings   *Pan Size: 3 quart*   ≈M≈

1/2 cup butter	1/2 teaspoon salt
1/4 cup corn syrup	1/2 teaspoon soda
1 cup packed brown sugar	6 quarts popped popcorn

Combine butter, corn syrup, brown sugar and salt in glass bowl. Microwave on High until mixture comes to a boil. Microwave for 2½ minutes. Stir in soda. Pour over popcorn in large paper bag sprayed with nonstick cooking spray; stir lightly. Microwave popcorn in bag for 1 minute; stir. Microwave for 1½ minutes longer. Tear bag open; spread apart to cool. Store in airtight container. Note: Be sure that paper bag used in microwave oven is not made of recycled paper.

Approx Per Serving: Cal 108; Prot 1.0 g; T Fat 4.2 g; Chol 10.4 mg;
    Carbo 17.4 g; Sod 99.9 mg; Potas 53.3 mg.

Linda Baldock
Clovis, New Mexico

JUDY'S MICROWAVE CARAMEL CORN

Yields: 10 servings　　　　*Pan Size: glass 2 quart*　　　　≈M≈

1/2 cup melted margarine	1/2 teaspoon salt
1 cup packed brown sugar	1/2 teaspoon soda
1/4 cup white corn syrup	3 1/2 quarts popped popcorn
1 teaspoon vanilla extract	

Combine margarine, brown sugar, corn syrup, vanilla and salt in glass bowl. Microwave on High for 1 1/2 minutes or until mixture comes to a boil. Stir well. Microwave for 3 minutes longer. Stir in soda. Pour over popcorn in paper bag; stir gently with wooden spoon. Close bag. Microwave on High for 3 minutes, shaking after 1 1/2 minutes. Spread popcorn on waxed paper. Let stand until crisp. Note: Be sure that paper bag used in microwave oven is not made of recycled paper. Do not double recipe.

Approx Per Serving: Cal 228; Prot 1.5 g; T Fat 9.7 g; Chol 0.0 mg;
　　Carbo 35.9 g; Sod 228.0 mg; Potas 110.0 mg.

Judy Roush
Ag in the Classroom, Columbus, Ohio

SCRUMSHEROOS

Yields: 24 servings　　　*Pan Size: 9x13 inch*　　　*Preheat: 350 degrees*

1 cup flour	1　10-ounce package
1/2 cup packed brown sugar	marshmallows
1/2 cup margarine, softened	1/4 cup milk
1 cup chocolate chips	1　5-ounce can chow mein
1 cup peanut butter	noodles
1/2 cup packed brown sugar	

Combine flour, 1/2 cup brown sugar and margarine in bowl; mix well. Pat into greased baking pan. Bake for 15 minutes. Sprinkle with chocolate chips. Combine peanut butter, 1/2 cup brown sugar, marshmallows and milk in large saucepan. Heat over low heat until melted, stirring constantly; remove from heat. Stir in chow mein noodles. Spread over chocolate chips. Cool. Cut into squares.

Approx Per Serving: Cal 254; Prot 5.0 g; T Fat 13.4 g; Chol 1.0 mg;
　　Carbo 31.7 g; Sod 170.0 mg; Potas 145.0 mg.

Debra Evans
Fall River, Kansas

APPLE COOKIES

Yields: 36 cookies	Pan Size: cookie sheet	Preheat: 400 degrees

1¹/₃ cups brown sugar, packed
¹/₂ cup shortening
1 egg
2 cups flour
1 teaspoon soda
¹/₂ teaspoon salt
¹/₂ teaspoon nutmeg

1 teaspoon cloves
1 teaspoon cinnamon
¹/₄ cup apple juice
1 cup chopped apple
1 cup chopped walnuts
1 cup raisins

Cream brown sugar and shortening in bowl until light and fluffy. Add egg; mix well. Combine flour, soda, salt, nutmeg, cloves and cinnamon. Add dry ingredients to creamed mixture alternately with apple juice, mixing well after each addition. Stir in apple, walnuts and raisins. Drop by tablespoonfuls 2 inches apart onto greased cookie sheet. Bake for 11 to 14 minutes or until brown.

Approx Per Cookie: Cal 121; Prot 1.5 g; T Fat 5.2 g; Chol 7.6 mg;
Carbo 18.2 g; Sod 59.4 mg; Potas 96.3 mg.

Charlotte J. O'Mara
Macedon, New York

ORANGE AND CHOCOLATE OAT BRAN BROWNIES

Yields: 24 brownies	Pan Size: 9x12 inch	Preheat: 350 degrees

1 cup oat bran
1 cup orange juice
¹/₂ cup butter
²/₃ cup semisweet chocolate
  chips
1¹/₂ cups honey

4 eggs
1 teaspoon vanilla extract
¹/₄ teaspoon salt
1 cup whole wheat flour
¹/₂ cup semisweet chocolate
  chips

Combine oat bran with orange juice in bowl. Let stand for 1 to 2 hours. Melt butter with ²/₃ cup chocolate chips in saucepan over low heat; remove from heat. Fold in honey. Add eggs 1 at a time, mixing well after each addition. Stir in vanilla, salt, flour and ¹/₂ cup chocolate chips. Pour into greased baking pan. Bake for 20 to 30 minutes or until brownies test done.

Approx Per Brownie: Cal 183; Prot 2.9 g; T Fat 8.0 g; Chol 56.0 mg;
Carbo 29.5 g; Sod 69.3 mg; Potas 112.0 mg.

Ellen C. Vaughan
Columbia, South Carolina

CARAMEL CHOCOLATE SQUARES

Yields: 48 squares   *Pan Size: 9x13 inch*   *Preheat: 350 degrees*

1 14-ounce package light
   caramels
¹/₃ cup evaporated milk
1 2-layer package German
   chocolate cake mix

³/₄ cup melted butter
¹/₃ cup evaporated milk
1 cup chopped walnuts
1 cup chocolate chips

Melt caramels in ¹/₃ cup evaporated milk in double boiler. Combine cake mix, butter, ¹/₃ cup evaporated milk and walnuts in large bowl; mix well. Press half the mixture into greased and floured baking pan. Bake for 6 minutes. Sprinkle with chocolate chips. Spread with caramel mixture. Crumble remaining chocolate mixture over cake. Bake for 15 minutes longer. Cool. Refrigerate for 30 minutes; cut into small squares.

Approx Per Square: Cal 128; Prot 1.4 g; T Fat 7.4 g; Chol 9.1 mg;
    Carbo 15.2 g; Sod 90.9 mg; Potas 52.0 mg.

Judy Wagner
ERIC Clearinghouse on Adult, Career, and Vocational Education
Columbus, Ohio

CHEWY CHOCOLATE COOKIES

Yields: 48 cookies   *Pan Size: cookie sheet*   *Preheat: 350 degrees*

1¹/₄ cups butter
2 cups sugar
2 eggs
2 teaspoons vanilla extract
2 cups flour

³/₄ cup unsweetened baking
   cocoa
1 teaspoon soda
1 cup finely chopped pecans

Cream butter and sugar in bowl until light and fluffy. Add eggs and vanilla; mix well. Combine flour, cocoa and soda in bowl. Stir into creamed mixture. Mix in pecans. Drop by teaspoonfuls onto ungreased cookie sheet. Bake for 15 minutes or until edges are firm.

Approx Per Cookie: Cal 117; Prot 1.9 g; T Fat 6.8 g; Chol 24.4 mg;
    Carbo 13.4 g; Sod 61.3 mg; Potas 46.9 mg.

Rita M. Lentz
Charlotte, North Carolina

COCONUT MACAROONS

Yields: 24 cookies   *Pan Size: cookie sheet*   *Preheat: 350 degrees*

2 cups flaked coconut   1 teaspoon vanilla extract
1/2 cup sweetened condensed
  milk

Combine coconut and condensed milk in bowl. Add vanilla; mix well. Drop by teaspoonfuls 1 inch apart onto greased cookie sheet. Bake for 10 minutes or until light brown. Remove to wire rack immediately.

Approx Per Cookie: Cal 44; Prot 0.7 g; T Fat 2.8 g; Chol 2.2 mg;
  Carbo 4.5 g; Sod 9.4 mg; Potas 47.4 mg.

Constance Handy Spohn
Cobleskill, New York

COWBOY-COWGIRL COOKIES

Yields: 48 cookies   *Pan Size: cookie sheet*   *Preheat: 360 degrees*

1 cup margarine, softened   1/2 teaspoon baking powder
1 cup sugar   1 teaspoon soda
1 cup packed brown sugar   1/2 teaspoon salt
2 eggs   2 cups oats
1 teaspoon vanilla extract   1 cup chocolate chips
2 cups flour

Cream margarine and sugars in bowl until light and fluffy. Add eggs and vanilla; mix well. Sift flour, baking powder, soda and salt into bowl. Stir sifted dry ingredients, oats and chocolate chips into creamed mixture. Drop by teaspoonfuls onto cookie sheet. Bake for 6 to 10 minutes or until brown.

Approx Per Cookie: Cal 120; Prot 1.5 g; T Fat 5.6 g; Chol 11.4 mg;
  Carbo 16.9 g; Sod 99.4 mg; Potas 49.6 mg.

Char Madsen
Sturgis, South Dakota

FORGOTTEN COOKIES

Yields: 36 cookies   *Pan Size: cookie sheet*   *Preheat: 350 degrees*

2 egg whites
1/4 teaspoon salt
2/3 cup sugar

4 drops of vanilla extract
1 cup chopped pecans
1 cup chocolate chips

Combine egg whites and salt in mixer bowl; beat until stiff. Mix in sugar gradually. Stir in vanilla and pecans. Fold in chocolate chips gently. Drop by heaping teaspoonfuls onto foil-lined cookie sheet. Place cookies in preheated oven; turn off oven. Let stand for 2 hours to overnight.

Approx Per Cookie: Cal 61; Prot 0.6 g; T Fat 3.9 g; Chol 0.0 mg;
    Carbo 7.0 g; Sod 18.4 mg; Potas 32.0 mg.

Joan Parker
Washington, Oklahoma

WANDERING JEWS

Yields: 48 cookies   *Pan Size: cookie sheet*   *Preheat: 350 degrees*

1 cup butter, softened
1 1/2 cups sugar
3 eggs
3 cups (about) flour
1 teaspoon soda
1 teaspoon cinnamon
1 teaspoon cloves
1 teaspoon nutmeg

1 teaspoon salt
2 cups chopped dates
3/4 cup chopped pecans
1/4 cup packed brown sugar
1/4 cup butter
6 tablespoons milk
1 1/2 cups (about)
    confectioners' sugar

Cream 1 cup butter and sugar in bowl until light and fluffy. Add eggs; mix well. Stir in mixture of flour, soda, cinnamon, cloves, nutmeg, salt, dates and pecans. Drop by teaspoonfuls onto greased cookie sheet. Dough should hold well-rounded shape. Bake for 12 to 15 minutes or until brown. Melt brown sugar with 1/4 cup butter in small saucepan. Stir in milk gradually. Cook for 3 minutes. Blend in enough confectioners' sugar to make of spreading consistency. Spread on cooled cookies.

Approx Per Cookie: Cal 138; Prot 1.6 g; T Fat 6.6 g; Chol 30.3 mg;
    Carbo 19.2 g; Sod 108.0 mg; Potas 75.4 mg.

Byrl R. Shoemaker, Ph.D.
AVA President, 1964-1965
Building Fund Chairman, 1986-1987
Columbus, Ohio

BUCKEYE PIE

Yields: 6 servings	Pan Size: 9 inch	Preheat: 350 degrees

1½ cups chocolate cookie
  crumbs
6 tablespoons melted
  margarine
2 tablespoons sugar
4 ounces cream cheese,
  softened

⅓ cup peanut butter
1 cup confectioners' sugar
2 cups whipped topping
1 4-ounce box chocolate
  instant pudding mix
1 cup milk
2 cups whipped topping

Combine cookie crumbs, margarine and sugar in bowl; mix well. Press mixture into 9-inch pie plate. Bake for 5 to 7 minutes or until firm. Cool. Beat cream cheese, peanut butter and confectioners' sugar in mixer bowl until light and fluffy. Blend in 2 cups whipped topping. Pour into cooled pie shell. Combine pudding mix with milk in bowl; mix until thickened. Fold in 2 cups whipped topping. Layer chocolate mixture over peanut butter mixture in pie shell. Chill for 6 hours or more. Garnish with additional whipped topping. Note: This recipe was developed by vocational student Margaret Brumbaugh, who was a state FHA/HERO Contest winner from Penta County Vocational School.

Approx Per Serving: Cal 841; Prot 9.6 g; T Fat 65.3 g; Chol 136 mg;
  Carbo 60.6 g; Sod 474.0 mg; Potas 265.0 mg.

Gail F. Lindsay, President
National Association of Vocational Home Economics Teachers
Maumee, Ohio

CARAMEL PIE

Yields: 6 servings	Pan Size: 9 inch	Preheat: 400 degrees

1 14-ounce can sweetened
  condensed milk
1 cup coconut
½ cup pecans

1 9-inch graham cracker pie
  shell
2 bananas, sliced
3 tablespoons lemon juice

Pour sweetened condensed milk into buttered pie plate. Cover with foil; place in large pan of hot water. Bake for 1 hour or until thick and caramel-colored. Cool. Combine with coconut and pecans in bowl; mix well. Pour into pie shell. Brush bananas with lemon juice; arrange on pie. Garnish with whipped topping. Serve immediately. May substitute strawberries, melted chocolate chips or crushed pineapple for bananas. Note: Do not cook condensed milk in can.

Approx Per Serving: Cal 635; Prot 9.2 g; T Fat 31.6 g; Chol 22.5 mg;
  Carbo 83.5 g; Sod 406.0 mg; Potas 575.0 mg.

Pat Wenger
Little Rock, Arkansas

CARAMEL PECAN PIE

Yields: 6 servings　　　*Pan Size: 10 inch*　　　*Preheat: 400 degrees*

1 unbaked 10-inch deep-dish
　pie shell
3 eggs
3/4 cup sugar
1 tablespoon flour

1 cup dark corn syrup
1/2 cup margarine, melted
1/2 cup milk
1 teaspoon vanilla extract
1 cup chopped pecans

Bake pie crust for 10 minutes. Remove from oven. Reduce temperature to 250 degrees. Beat eggs in mixer bowl. Add mixture of sugar and flour; mix well. Blend in corn syrup, margarine, milk and vanilla, mixing well after each addition. Stir in pecans. Pour into pie shell. Bake for 1 hour or until set. Cool on wire rack. May serve warm with ice cream or whipped cream.

Approx Per Serving: Cal 728; Prot 7.4 g; T Fat 42.1 g; Chol 140.0 mg;
　Carbo 85.1 g; Sod 443.0 mg; Potas 165.0 mg.

Frances C. Melton
Florida Department of Education
Tallahassee, Florida

CHRISTMAS PIE

Yields: 6 servings　　　*Pan Size: 9 inch*

1/2 cup sugar
1/4 cup flour
1 envelope unflavored gelatin
1/2 teaspoon salt
13/4 cups milk
3/4 teaspoon vanilla extract
1/4 teaspoon almond extract

3 egg whites
1/2 cup sugar
1/4 teaspoon cream of tartar
1 cup flaked coconut
2 cups whipped topping
1 baked 9-inch pie shell

Blend 1/2 cup sugar, flour, gelatin and salt in medium saucepan. Stir in milk gradually. Bring to a boil over medium heat, stirring constantly. Cook for 1 minute. Place saucepan in cold water; cool until mixture mounds when dropped from spoon. Add flavorings. Beat egg whites, 1/2 cup sugar and cream of tartar in mixer bowl until stiff peaks form. Fold into cooled mixture. Stir in coconut and whipped topping. Pour into pie shell. Chill until set. Garnish with maraschino cherries or gumdrops.

Approx Per Serving: Cal 480; Prot 8.2 g; T Fat 23.2 g; Chol 9.6 mg;
　Carbo 61.7 g; Sod 427.0 mg; Potas 197.0 mg.

Cindy Muir
Topeka, Kansas

CRANBERRY VELVET PIE

Yields: 6 servings　　　　　*Pan Size: 9 inch*

1½ cups graham cracker
　crumbs
6 tablespoons butter, softened
8 ounces cream cheese,
　softened

1 cup whipping cream
¼ cup sugar
½ teaspoon vanilla extract
1　16-ounce can whole
　cranberry sauce

Combine graham cracker crumbs and butter in bowl; mix well. Press over bottom and side of pie plate. Chill until firm. Beat cream cheese in mixer bowl until light and fluffy. Blend whipping cream, sugar and vanilla in mixer bowl; whip just until thick. Stir into cream cheese mixture gradually. Fold in cranberry sauce. Spoon into pie shell. Freeze until firm. Thaw for 10 minutes before serving.

Approx Per Serving: Cal 674; Prot 4.9 g; T Fat 40.9 g; Chol 127.0 mg;
　Carbo 75.7 g; Sod 333.0 mg; Potas 136.0 mg.

Susan Westrom
Starkville, Mississippi

DERBY PIE

Yields: 6 servings　　　*Pan Size: 10 inch*　　　*Preheat: 350 degrees*

½ cup melted margarine
1 cup sugar
4 eggs, beaten
1 cup light corn syrup

1 tablespoon Bourbon
1 cup chopped pecans
½ cup chocolate chips
1 unbaked 10-inch pie shell

Combine margarine, sugar, eggs, corn syrup and Bourbon in bowl; mix until smooth. Stir in pecans and chocolate chips. Pour into pie shell. Bake for 45 minutes or until toothpick inserted in center comes out clean.

Approx Per Serving: Cal 781; Prot 8.2 g; T Fat 47.4 g; Chol 183.0 mg;
　Carbo 87.0 g; Sod 428.0 mg; Potas 201.0 mg.

Linda Cinnamon
St. Petersburg, Florida

KENTUCKY HIGH DAY PIE

Yields: 6 servings   *Pan Size: 9 inch*   *Preheat: 350 degrees*

1 cup sugar
2 eggs, slightly beaten
1/2 cup melted margarine
1 teaspoon vanilla extract
1/4 cup cornstarch
1 cup semisweet chocolate
  chips

1 cup chopped pecans
1   9-inch unbaked pie shell
1/2 cup heavy cream
2 tablespoons confectioners'
  sugar
1/2 teaspoon vanilla extract

Mix sugar and eggs in bowl. Add margarine and vanilla; mix well. Add cornstarch; blend well. Stir in chocolate chips and pecans. Pour into pie shell. Bake for 40 to 50 minutes or until toothpick inserted in center comes out clean. Cool. Whip cream in bowl until soft peaks form. Add confectioners' sugar and vanilla gradually, beating constantly. Spread over pie. May substitute Bourbon for vanilla.

Approx Per Serving: Cal 812; Prot 7.2 g; T Fat 58.0 g; Chol 118.0 mg;
    Carbo 73.8 g; Sod 397.0 mg; Potas 237.0 mg.

Kathy Jo Somers
Julian, North Carolina

LEMON ANGEL PIE

Yields: 6 servings   *Pan Size: 9 inch*   *Preheat: 250 degrees*

4 egg whites
1/2 teaspoon cream of tartar
1 cup sugar
4 egg yolks

1/2 cup sugar
3 tablespoons lemon juice
3 teaspoons grated lemon rind
1 cup whipped cream

Beat egg whites and cream of tartar in mixer bowl until soft peaks form. Add 1 cup sugar gradually, beating until stiff peaks form. Pour into greased and floured pie plate. Bake for 1 hour. Cool. Combine egg yolks, 1/2 cup sugar, lemon juice and rind in double boiler. Cook over hot water until thick, stirring constantly. Cool. Layer 1/2 cup whipped cream and cooled lemon custard over meringue. Top with remaining 1/2 cup whipped cream. Chill for 24 hours.

Approx Per Serving: Cal 252; Prot 4.5 g; T Fat 11.1 g; Chol 208.0 mg;
    Carbo 34.9 g; Sod 47.0 mg; Potas 77.2 mg.

Helen C. Hall
Athens, Georgia

SUMMER PEAR PIE

Yields: 6 servings   *Pan Size: 9 inch*   *Preheat: 425 degrees*

1 recipe 2-crust pie pastry
¼ cup packed brown sugar
½ cup sugar
3 tablespoons flour
½ teaspoon nutmeg
½ teaspoon cinnamon

⅛ teaspoon salt
6 cups sliced peeled pears
2 teaspoons lemon juice
2 teaspoons grated lemon rind
1 tablespoon butter, softened

Line pie plate with half the pie pastry. Sprinkle mixture of sugars, flour, nutmeg, cinnamon and salt over pears in bowl; toss lightly to coat. Spoon into pastry-lined pie plate. Sprinkle with lemon juice and rind. Dot with butter. Top with remaining pastry. Trim and seal edges; cut vents. Bake for 40 to 45 minutes or until pastry is golden brown. May omit lemon juice and rind for a sweeter pie.

Approx Per Serving: Cal 601; Prot 4.7 g; T Fat 20.6 g; Chol 5.2 mg; Carbo 85.9 g; Sod 432.0 mg; Potas 357.0 mg.

Sandra J. Durbin
Kittanning, Pennsylvania

SOUTH CAROLINA PECAN PIE

Yields: 6 servings   *Pan Size: 9 inch*   *Preheat: 360 degrees*

3 eggs
1 cup packed dark brown
  sugar
1 cup light corn syrup
1 tablespoon melted butter

⅛ teaspoon salt
1 teaspoon vanilla extract
1 cup chopped pecans
1 unbaked 9-inch pie shell

Beat eggs in mixer bowl. Add brown sugar gradually, beating constantly. Blend in corn syrup, butter, salt and vanilla. Stir in pecans. Pour into pastry shell. Bake for 1 hour or until set.

Approx Per Serving: Cal 648; Prot 6.4 g; T Fat 28.1 g; Chol 142.0 mg; Carbo 99.1 g; Sod 340.0 mg; Potas 137.0 mg.

The Honorable Strom Thurmond
U.S. Senator, South Carolina
Washington, District of Columbia

PINEAPPLE FREEZER PIE

Yields: 10 servings   *Pan Size: 9x9 inch*

1/2 cup sugar
1 tablespoon flour
1 cup pineapple juice
1 teaspoon soda
2 teaspoons margarine
2 eggs, beaten

1 tablespoon lemon juice
1 cup crushed pineapple
8 ounces vanilla wafers,
  crushed
1 pint whipping cream,
  whipped

Combine sugar and flour in small saucepan. Add pineapple juice and soda. Cook over low heat until thickened, stirring constantly. Stir in margarine. Remove from heat. Add eggs, lemon juice and pineapple, mixing well after each addition. Line pan with vanilla wafers. Layer pineapple mixture and whipped cream 1/2 at a time in pan, ending with whipped cream. Freeze for 8 hours.

Approx Per Serving: Cal 418; Prot 3.9 g; T Fat 25.0 g; Chol 134.0 mg;
    Carbo 46.5 g; Sod 227.0 mg; Potas 244.0 mg.

Garland J. Kidd
Buchanan, Virginia

PUMPKIN PIE

Yields: 6 servings   *Pan Size: 9 inch*   *Preheat: 400 degrees*

6 tablespoons packed brown
  sugar
1 1/2 teaspoons salt
1 teaspoon cinnamon
1/2 teaspoon ginger
1/8 teaspoon cloves

3 eggs, slightly beaten
1 1/2 cups low-fat milk
1/2 cup corn syrup
1 1/2 cups canned pumpkin
1 unbaked 9-inch pie shell

Combine brown sugar, salt, cinnamon, ginger and cloves in bowl. Stir in eggs. Add milk, syrup and pumpkin; mix well. Pour into pie shell. Bake for 1 hour or until set. May substitute puréed winter squash for pumpkin.

Approx Per Serving: Cal 368; Prot 7.6 g; T Fat 14.2 g; Chol 142.0 mg;
    Carbo 55.1 g; Sod 803.0 mg; Potas 320.0 mg.

Teresa M. Stone
Tacoma, Washington

GRANDMA PENNEKAMP'S SUGAR PIE

Yields: 6 servings	Pan Size: 9 inch	Preheat: 375 degrees

2¹/2 cups packed brown sugar
1 unbaked 9-inch pie shell

¹/4 cup whipping cream
2 tablespoons butter, softened

Sprinkle enough brown sugar in bottom of pie shell to measure ¹/2 inch. Pour cream gradually over brown sugar. Dot with butter. Bake for 15 to 20 minutes or until bubbly.

Approx Per Serving: Cal 560; Prot 2.1 g; T Fat 17.5 g; Chol 23.9 mg;
 Carbo 102.0 g; Sod 260.0 mg; Potas 339.0 mg.

Wendy Smythe
Palm Beach Gardens, Florida

MINIATURE PECAN TARTS

Yields: 24 tarts	Pan Size: miniature muffin cups	Preheat: 350 degrees

¹/2 cup margarine, softened
3 ounces cream cheese,
 softened
1 cup flour
1 egg, slightly beaten

²/3 cup packed brown sugar
1 tablespoon melted margarine
¹/2 teaspoon vanilla extract
¹/8 teaspoon salt
1 cup chopped pecans

Cut margarine and cream cheese into flour in bowl. Shape into ball or long roll. Divide into 24 small balls. Press over bottom and side of muffin cups to form tart shells. Combine egg, brown sugar, margarine, vanilla, salt and pecans in bowl. Pour into muffin cups. Bake for 20 to 25 minutes or until set.

Approx Per Tart: Cal 128; Prot 1.5 g; T Fat 9.2 g; Chol 15.3 mg;
 Carbo 10.8 g; Sod 83.8 mg; Potas 54.2 mg.

Dewey and Mary Jewel Adams
Delaware, Ohio

Nutritional Guidelines

The editors have attempted to present these family recipes in a form that allows approximate nutritional values to be computed. Persons with dietary or health problems or whose diets require close monitoring should not rely solely on the nutritional information provided. They should consult their physicians or a registered dietitian for specific information.

Abbreviations for Nutritional Analysis

Cal—Calories	Chol—Cholesterol	Potas—Potassium
Prot—Protein	Carbo—Carbohydrates	g—gram
T Fat—Total Fat	Sod—Sodium	mg—milligram

Nutritional information for these recipes is computed from information derived from many sources, including materials supplied by the United States Department of Agriculture, computer databanks and journals in which the information is assumed to be in the public domain. Many specialty items, new products, and processed foods may not be available from these sources or may vary from average values used in these analyses. More information on new and/or specific products may be obtained by reading the nutrient labels. Unless otherwise specified, the nutritional analysis of these recipes is based on the following guidelines.

- All measurements are level.
- Artificial sweeteners vary in use and strength so should be used "to taste," using the recipe ingredients as a guideline.
- Alcoholic ingredients have been analyzed as used, although cooking causes the evaporation of alcohol thus decreasing caloric content.
- Buttermilk, sour cream, and yogurt are commercial-type.
- Canned soup is 10 ounce condensed.
- Chicken, cooked for boning and chopping, has been skinned and stewed; this method yields the lowest caloric values.
- Cottage cheese is cream-style with 4.2% creaming mixture. Dry-curd cottage cheese has no creaming mixture.
- Eggs are all large.
- Flour is unsifted all-purpose flour.
- Garnishes, serving suggestions and other optional additions and variations are not included in the analysis.
- Margarine and butter are regular, not whipped or presoftened.
- Milk is whole milk, 3.5% butterfat. Lowfat milk is 1% butterfat. Evaporated milk is canned milk, not sweetened condensed.
- Oil is any cooking oil. Shortening is vegetable shortening.
- Salt to taste as noted in the method has not been included in the nutritional analysis.

Substitution Chart

	Instead of:	Use:
Baking	1 teaspoon baking powder	¼ teaspoon soda plus ½ teaspoon cream of tartar
	1 tablespoon cornstarch (for thickening)	2 tablespoons flour or 1 tablespoon tapioca
	1 cup sifted all-purpose flour	1 cup plus 2 tablespoons sifted cake flour
	1 cup sifted cake flour	1 cup minus 2 tablespoons sifted all-purpose flour
	1 cup dry bread crumbs	¾ cup cracker crumbs
Dairy	1 cup buttermilk	1 cup sour milk or 1 cup yogurt
	1 cup heavy cream	¾ cup skim milk plus ⅓ cup butter
	1 cup light cream	⅞ cup skim milk plus 3 tablespoons butter
	1 cup sour cream	⅞ cup sour milk plus 3 tablespoons butter
	1 cup sour milk	1 cup milk plus 1 tablespoon vinegar or lemon juice or 1 cup buttermilk
Seasoning	1 teaspoon allspice	½ teaspoon cinnamon plus ⅛ teaspoon cloves
	1 cup catsup	1 cup tomato sauce plus ½ cup sugar plus 2 tablespoons vinegar
	1 clove of garlic	⅛ teaspoon garlic powder or ⅛ teaspoon instant minced garlic or ¾ teaspoon garlic salt or 5 drops of liquid garlic
	1 teaspoon Italian spice	¼ teaspoon each oregano, basil, thyme, rosemary plus dash of cayenne
	1 teaspoon lemon juice	½ teaspoon vinegar
	1 tablespoon mustard	1 teaspoon dry mustard
	1 medium onion	1 tablespoon dried minced onion or 1 teaspoon onion powder
Sweet	1-ounce square chocolate	¼ cup cocoa plus 1 teaspoon shortening
	1⅔ ounces semisweet chocolate	1 ounce unsweetened chocolate plus 4 teaspoons granulated sugar
	1 cup honey	1 to 1¼ cups sugar plus ¼ cup liquid or 1 cup corn syrup or molasses
	1 cup granulated sugar	1 cup packed brown sugar or 1 cup corn syrup, molasses or honey minus ¼ cup liquid

Equivalent Chart

	When the recipe calls for:	Use:
Baking Essentials	½ cup butter 2 cups butter 4 cups all-purpose flour 4½ to 5 cups sifted cake flour 1 square chocolate 1 cup semisweet chocolate pieces 4 cups marshmallows 2¼ cups packed brown sugar 4 cups confectioners' sugar 2 cups granulated sugar	1 stick 1 pound 1 pound 1 pound 1 ounce 1 6-ounce package 1 pound 1 pound 1 pound 1 pound
Cereal & Bread	1 cup fine dry bread crumbs 1 cup soft bread crumbs 1 cup small bread cubes 1 cup fine cracker crumbs 1 cup fine graham cracker crumbs 1 cup vanilla wafer crumbs 1 cup crushed cornflakes 4 cups cooked macaroni 3½ cups cooked rice	4 to 5 slices 2 slices 2 slices 28 saltines 15 crackers 22 wafers 3 cups uncrushed 1 8-ounce package 1 cup uncooked
Dairy	1 cup freshly grated cheese 1 cup cottage cheese 1 cup sour cream 1 cup whipped cream ⅔ cup evaporated milk 1⅔ cups evaporated milk	¼ pound 1 8-ounce carton 1 8 -ounce carton ½ cup heavy cream 1 small can 1 13-ounce can
Fruit	4 cups sliced or chopped apples 1 cup mashed banana 2 cups pitted cherries 3 cups shredded coconut 4 cups cranberries 1 cup pitted dates 1 cup candied fruit 3 to 4 tablespoons lemon juice plus 　1 teaspoon grated rind ⅓ cup orange juice plus 2 teaspoons 　grated rind 4 cups sliced peaches 2 cups pitted prunes 3 cups raisins	4 medium 3 medium 4 cups unpitted ½ pound 1 pound 1 8-ounce package 1 8-ounce package 1 lemon 1 orange 8 medium 1 12-ounce package 1 15-ounce package

	When the recipe calls for:	Use:
Meats	4 cups chopped cooked chicken 3 cups chopped cooked meat 2 cups cooked ground meat	1 5-pound chicken 1 pound, cooked 1 pound, cooked
Nuts	1 cup chopped nuts	4 ounces, shelled 1 pound, unshelled

Vegetables	2 cups cooked green beans
	
	2¹/₂ cups lima beans or red beans
	4 cups shredded cabbage
	1 cup grated carrots
	1 4-ounce can mushrooms
	1 cup chopped onion
	4 cups sliced or chopped raw
	    potatoes
	2 cups canned tomatoes
		¹/₂ pound fresh
		    or 1 16-ounce can
		1 cup dried, cooked
		1 pound
		1 large
		¹/₂ pound, fresh
		1 large
		4 medium
		
		1 16-ounce can

Measurement Equivalents

1 tablespoon = 3 teaspoons
2 tablespoons = 1 ounce
4 tablespoons = ¹/₄ cup
5 tablespoons + 1 teaspoon
  = ¹/₃ cup
8 tablespoons = ¹/₂ cup
12 tablespoons = ³/₄ cup
16 tablespoons = 1 cup
1 cup = 8 ounces per ¹/₂ pint
4 cups = 1 quart
4 quarts = 1 gallon
6¹/₂ to 8-ounce can = 1 cup
	10¹/₂ to 12-ounce can = 1¹/₄ cups
	14 to 16-ounce can (No.300) =
	  1³/₄ cups
	16 to 17-ounce can (No. 303) = 2 cups
	1-pound 4-ounce can or 1-pint
	  2-ounce can (No. 2) = 2¹/₂ cups
	1-pound 13-ounce can (No. 2¹/₂) =
	  3¹/₂ cups
	3-pound 3-ounce can or 46-ounce can
	  = 5³/₄ cups
	6¹/₂-pound or 7-pound 5-ounce can
	  (No. 10) = 12 to 13 cups

Metric Equivalents

Liquid	Dry
1 teaspoon = 5 milliliters 1 tablespoon = 15 milliliters 1 fluid ounce = 30 milliliters 1 cup = 250 milliliters 1 pint = 500 milliliters	1 quart = 1 liter 1 ounce = 30 grams 1 pound = 450 grams 2.2 pounds = 1 kilogram

NOTE: The metric measures are approximate benchmarks for purposes of home food preparation.

Quantities to Serve 100

Baked beans . . . . 5 gallons
Beef . . . . 40 pounds
Beets . . . . 30 pounds
Bread . . . . 10 loaves
Butter . . . . 3 pounds
Cabbage for slaw . . . . 20 pounds
Cakes . . . . 8 cakes
Carrots . . . . 33 pounds
Cauliflower . . . . 18 pounds
Cheese . . . . 18 pounds
Chicken for chicken pie . . . . 40 pounds
Coffee . . . . 3 pounds
Cream . . . . 3 quarts
Fruit cocktail . . . . 1 gallon
Fruit juice . . . . 4 (No. 10) cans
Fruit salad . . . . 20 quarts
Ground beef . . . . 30 to 36 pounds
Ham . . . . 40 pounds
Ice Cream . . . . 4 gallons
Lettuce . . . . 20 heads
Meat loaf . . . . 24 pounds
Milk . . . . 6 gallons
Nuts . . . . 3 pounds
Olives . . . . 1¾ pounds
Oysters . . . . 18 quarts
Pickles . . . . 2 quarts
Pies . . . . 18 pies
Potatoes . . . . 35 pounds
Roast pork . . . . 40 pounds
Rolls . . . . 200 rolls
Salad dressing . . . . 3 quarts
Scalloped potatoes . . . . 5 gallons
Soup . . . . 5 gallons
Sugar cubes . . . . 3 pounds
Tomato juice . . . . 4 (No. 10) cans
Vegetables . . . . 4 (No. 20) cans
Vegetable salad . . . . 20 quarts
Whipping cream . . . . 4 pints
Wieners . . . . 25 pounds

Index

Page numbers of Recipes yielding 10 servings
or more are preceded by a Q for Quantity.

APPETIZERS
Beef Steak Tartar, 14
Beer Balls, Q14
Cheese
    Cheddar Crackers, Q15
    Dips. *See* Dips
    Parmesan Cheese Cubes, Q15
    Super Cheese Twists, Q16
    Surprise Cheese Puffs, Q16
Clams
    Clams Casino, Q17
    Microwave Stuffed Clams, Q17
Dips/Spreads
    Caramel Apple Dip, Q23
    Cheese
        Brie en Croute au Poire, Q23
        Brie in Phyllo, Q24
        Cheese Ball, Q24
        Cheese Fondue, Q25
        Hot Cheese Dip, Q25
        Oregon Cheese Ball, Q26
        Pineapple Cheese
            Sculpture, Q26
    Crab and Artichoke Dip, Q27
    Fruit Dip, Q27
    Guacamole Dip, 28
    Guatamalan Guacamole Dip, 28
    Holiday Pâté, 29
    Microwave Party Appetizer
        Pie, 29
    Nobody Knows Relish Dip, Q30
    Salmon Ball, Q32
    Shrimp
        Molded Shrimp Spread, Q33
        Shrimp Dip, Q32
    Taco Dip, Q30
    Tuna
        Tuna Dip, 31
        Zesty Tuna Dip, 31
Ham
    Country Ham Balls, Q19
    Ham Appetizers, Q18
    Ham Rolls, Q18
    Ham and Sauerkraut Balls, Q19
Oyster Cracker Snack Mix, Q20
Pepper Jelly, Q20
Pizza
    Party Pizza, Q21

    Polish Pizza, Q21
Sausage Balls, Q22
Sherried Walnuts, Q22
Water Chestnuts
    Bacon Water Chestnuts, Q13
    Barbecued Water
        Chestnuts, Q13
BEEF
Barbecued
    Barbecued Brisket, Q57
    Barbecued Steak, 57
Beef and Barley Soup, 40
Beef Filets Wellington with
        Golden Tarragon Sauce, 58
Beef Stroganoff, 60
Corned Beef Casserole, 62
Fajitas con Avocado, 59
Roasts
    Barbecued Brisket, 57
    Italian Beef, Q60
Steak
    Barbecued Steak, 57
    Sour Cream Steak, 59
Stew
    Cowboy Stew, 61
    January Stew, 61
    Minnesota Stew with Biscuit
        Topping, 62
BEVERAGES
Cold
    Punches
        Celebration Punch, Q33
        Champagne Punch, Q34
        Holiday Punch, Q35
        Mint Sparkle, Q34
    Sangria, Q35
Hot
    Mexican Chocolate, 36
    Percolator Brew, Q36
BREADS
Biscuits
    Angel Biscuits, Q152
    Southern Biscuits, Q130
Chocolate Doughnuts, Q133
Coconut-Orange Toast, Q131
Coffee Cakes
    Cinnamon
        Pull-Aparts, Q134, Q156

Monkey Bread, Q134
Sour Cream Coffee Cake, Q132
Sour Cream and Pecan Coffee
      Cake, Q132
Coffee Can English Muffin
      Bread, Q135
Corn Bread
    Corn Bread You Eat with a
      Fork, Q150
    Mexican Corn Bread, Q150
Hush Puppies
    Florida's Best Hush
      Puppies, Q151
    Spicy Hush Puppies, Q151
Loaves, Quick
    Banana Bread, 144
        Buttermilk Banana
          Bread, 145
    Brown Bread, 145
    Butter Brickle Bread, Q133
    Cheese-Onion Bread, 146
    Choose-a-Flavor Bread, 146
    Fresh Apple Loaf, Q144
    Date Bread, 147
    Pear-Pecan Bread, 147
    Pumpkin Bread, Q148
    Strawberry Nut Bread, Q148
    Walnut-Cranberry Bread, Q149
    Zucchini Bread, 149
Loaves, Yeast
    Cracked Wheat Bread, Q152
    Dakota Bread, 154
    Dilly Casserole Bread, 153
    German Christmas Bread, Q155
    Mixed Batter Bread, 154
    Reuben Loaf, 153
    Southwest Virginia Brown
      Bread, Q135
    Swedish Rye Bread, Q155
    Versatile Sweet Dough, Q156
Pepperoni Bread, 158
Pull-Aparts
    Buttered Pull-Aparts, Q134
    Cheese Pull-Aparts, Q134
    Cinnamon
        Pull-Aparts, Q134, Q156
    Mexican Pull-Aparts, Q134
    Monkey Bread, Q134
    Onion Pull-Aparts, Q134
Muffins
    Apple Oat Bran Muffins, Q136
    Blueberry Muffins, Q136
    Bran Muffins, Q137
    Peabody Hotel Muffins, Q137
    Zucchini Muffins, 138
Pancakes

Baked Strawberry Pancakes, 138
Swedish Oatmeal
      Pancakes, Q139
Rolls
    Clover Leaf Yeast Rolls, Q157
    Fold-Over Rolls, Q158
    Versatile Sweet Dough, Q156
Sweet Rolls. See also Coffee Cakes
    Cinnamon
        Pull-Aparts, Q134, Q156
    Cinnamon Rolls, Q140
    Maple-Nut Cinnamon
        Rolls, Q157
Waffles
    Easy Club Soda Waffles, 140
    Gingerbread Waffles, 139
CAKES
Apple
    Grandma's Fresh Apple
      Cake, Q174
Chocolate
    Better Than Sex Chocolate
      Chip Cake, Q174
    Black Russian Cake, Q175
    Decadent Chocolate Fudge
      Cake, Q175
    Mississippi Mud Cake, Q176
    Texas Sheet Cake, Q176
Coconut
    Coconut Icebox Cake, Q177
    Coconut Wait Cake, Q177
Lane Cake, Q178
Lemon Fruitcake, Q178
Oatmeal
    German Oat Cake, Q179
    Oatmeal Cake, Q179
Pineapple Cake, Q180
Pound Cakes
    Aunt Pittypat's Pecan Pound
      Cake, Q181
    Basic Pound Cake, Q181
    Cream Cheese Pound
      Cake, Q180
    Prize Pound Cake, Q182
Prune Cake, Q182
CANDIES
Buckeyes, Q183
Chocolate-Covered Pecan
      Caramels, Q183
Fudge
    Different Vanilla Fudge, Q184
    Easy Microwave Fudge, Q184
Microwave Caramel Corn, Q185
    Judy's Microwave Caramel
      Corn, Q186
Microwave Peanut Clusters, Q185

Scrumsheroos, Q186
CHICKEN
Barbecue Sauce for Chicken, 79
Brunswick Stew, Q86
Casseroles
    Chicken and Broccoli
        Casserole, 85
    Chicken Casserole, 86
    Chicken Tortilla Casserole, 81
    Hot Chicken Salad, Q88
Chicken à la Berry, 81
Chicken Amaretto, 80
Chicken Breasts Piquant, 84
Chicken Parmesan, 83
Chinese Chicken with Walnuts, 82
Creamy Chicken, 82
Microwave Golden Chicken
    Imperial, 79
Microwave Herb and Cheese
    Chicken Breasts, 83
Oven-Fried Chicken, 80
Pies
    Easy Chicken Pie, 87
    Florida Chicken Pie, 87
Poppy Seed Chicken, 84
Sautéed Chicken Raspberry, 85
COOKIES
Apple Cookies, Q187
Caramel Chocolate
    Squares, Q188
Chewy Chocolate
    Cookies, Q188
Coconut Macaroons, Q189
Cowboy-Cowgirl Cookies, Q189
Forgotten Cookies, Q190
Orange and Chocolate Oat Bran
    Brownies, Q187
Wandering Jews, Q190
**Cornish Hens with Pineapple-
Wild Rice Stuffing**, 90
DESSERTS
Apple
    Apple Bake, Q161
    Apple Roll, 161
Banana
    Spun Bananas, 162
    Too Good to be True Banana
        Dessert, 162
Caramel Crunch, Q163
Cheesecakes
    Blueberry Cheesecake, Q163
    Cheesecake Cupcakes, Q164
    Chocolate and Raspberry
        Cheesecake, Q166
    Microwave Quick Cherry
        Cheesecake, 165

    Southern Cheesecake, Q164
    Unbaked Cheesecake, Q165
Chocolate
    Chocolate and Raspberry
        Cheesecake, Q166
    Chocolate Pecan Caramel
        Torte, Q167
    Hortense's Chocolate Pudding
        Cake, Q168
    Molly's Frozen Oreo
        Delight, Q166
Frozen
    Frozen Ice Cream Cake, Q170
    Frozen Rainbow Delight, Q170
    Judy's Frozen Fruit Cups, Q125
    Molly's Frozen Oreo
        Delight, Q166
Fruit
    Brenda's Fruit Pizza, Q168
    Fruit Pizza, Q169
    Fruit Trifle, Q169
    Judy's Frozen Fruit Cups, Q125
Lemon Cream Cooler, 171
Marinated Peaches, 171
Popcorn Cake Dessert, Q171
Pretzel Dessert, Q172
Puddings
    Bread Pudding, 172
    Pumpkin Mousse, 173
    Vermont Indian Pudding, 173
EGG DISHES
Breakfast Eggs, Q126
Breakfast Pizza, 127
Brunch Strata, 127
Chili Cheese Casserole, Q128
Green Chili Breakfast Eggs, 128
Judy's Oven Omelet, 129
Posner's Famous Spinach
    Quiche, 129
Quick Quiche, 130
FISH. *See also* Shellfish
Baked Fish in Vinegar Sauce, 92
Jasper's Bag-Shook Catfish, 93
Oven-Fried Orange Roughy, 93
Salmon
    Italian Salmon, 94
    Pacific Baked Salmon
        Supreme, 94
    Poached Salmon, 95
    Poached Salmon with
        Raspberry Beurre Blanc, 95
Seafood Newburg, Q97
Tuna
    Hot Tuna Melts, Q96
    Microwave Tuna and Rice
        Casserole, 96

GAME
Alaskan Curried Moose and
    Lentil Stew, 77
Pheasant
    Cheese Baked Pheasant, 91
    Crock•Pot Creamed
        Pheasant, 91
Venison
    Venison Special, Q78
    Venison Stew, 78
    Vermont Venison Marinade, 77
GROUND BEEF
Barbecued
    Barbecued Meatballs and
        Sauce, Q63
    Barbecued Sauerkraut, Q63
Beef Steak Tartar, 14
Chili
    Cincinnati Chili, 65
    Gordo's Industrial Strength
        Voc Ed Chili, 66
Ground Beef Soup, Q43
Meat Loaf, Q67
    Carla's Meat Loaf, 66
Pasta
    Baked Lasagna Supreme, 67
    Spaghetti Pie, Q68
Pita Burgers, 65
Pies
    Meatsee Pie, 68
    Spaghetti Pie, Q68
Sopa de Fideo, 70
Tacos by Rodger, 69
Very Easy Stuffed Cabbage, 70
Wyoming Fifty-Dollar
    Hamburger, 64
HAM
Appetizers. *See* Appetizers
Casseroles
    Donna's Ham Casserole, Q73
    Ham Casserole, 73
Loaves
    Ham Loaf with Mustard
        Sauce, Q74
    Ham Loaves, Q74
PIES
Buckeye Pie, 191
Caramel Pie, 191
    Caramel Pecan Pie, 192
Christmas Pie, 192
Cranberry Velvet Pie, 193
Derby Pie, 193
Grandma Pennekamp's Sugar
    Pie, 197
Kentucky High Day Pie, 194
Lemon Angel Pie, 194

Miniature Pecan Tarts, Q197
Pineapple Freezer Pie, Q196
Pumpkin Pie, 196
South Carolina Pecan Pie, 195
Summer Pear Pie, 195
PORK
Chops
    Baked Pork Chops and Rice, 71
    French Onion Pork Chops and
        Rice, 71
    Pork Chop Marinade, 72
Green Chili for Smothered
        Burritos, Q72
Ham. *See* Ham
SALADS
Dressings
    Julia's Asparagus Dressing, Q54
    VIP Dressing, Q54
Fruit Salads
    Apple Salad, Q46
    Apricot Salad, Q47
    Frozen Cranberry Salad, Q47
    Jiffy Lime Salad, 48
    Judy's Frozen Fruit Cups, Q125
    Pineapple and Cream Cheese
        Salad, 48
    White Fruit Salad, Q49
Main Dish Salads
    Chicken Salad, 49
    Crab Meat Salad, 50
    Shrimp Salad, 51
Vegetable Salads
    Broccoli and Cauliflower
        Salad, 51
    Cabbage Slaw, Q51
    Fresh Vegetable Salad, 52
    Jalapeño Frito Salad, Q52
    Marinated Vegetable Salad, Q53
    Spinach and Bacon Salad, Q53
    VIP Tossed Salad, 54
SAUSAGE
Apple and Sausage Ring, 126
Breakfast Eggs, Q126
Breakfast Pizza, 127
Brunch Strata, 127
Frogmore Stew, Q76
Kielbasa Boiled Dinner, Q75
Microwave Lasagna, Q75
Sausage and Bean Polenta, 76
SHELLFISH
Coquilles Saint Jacques, Q103
Crab
    Cakes
        Harry Beck's Crab Cakes, 97
        Mary's-Land Crab Cakes, 98
        Norfolk Crab Cakes, 98

Casseroles
  Crab Casserole, 99
  Jean's Crab Casserole, Q99
  Seafood Mornay, 100
Easy Seafood Pasta, 104
Oysters
  Fried Oysters, 101
  Oyster Casserole, 101
Seafood Casserole, 104
Seafood Newburg, Q97
Shrimp
  Ann McDermott's Shrimp with
    Black-Eyed Peas, 103
  Coquilles Saint Jacques, Q103
  Lime and Ginger Shrimp, 102
  Shrimp Etouffée, 102
Stuffed Lobster à la Ralph, 100
SIDE DISHES
Arroz con Jocoqui, 119
Golden Tarragon Sauce, 58
Hominy
  Green Chili Hominy
    Casserole, 118
  Hominy Casserole, 118
Hot Curried Fruit, Q125
Linguini with Lemon Sauce, 119
Rice
  Arroz con Jocoqui, 119
  Curried Rice with Raisins, 120
  Dutch Rice, 120
  Elizabeth Rice, Q121
  Fried Rice, 121
  Green and Gold Pilaf, 122
Shoe Peg Corn Relish, Q122
SOUPS
A. J.'s Catfish Chowder, 42
Bavarian Spinach Soup, Q45
Beef and Barley Soup, Q40
Broccoli
  Elegant Swiss Broccoli Soup, 41
  Microwave Cream of Broccoli
    Soup, 40
  Picante Cheese and Broccoli
    Soup, 41
Charleston She-Crab Soup, 43
Cold
  Gazpacho, Q39
  Lisa's Favorite Fruit Soup, 39

Cream Cheese and Leek Soup, 42
Ground Beef Soup, Q43
Lobster Soup, 44
Potato Soup, 44
Vegetable
  Microwave Vegetable
    Chowder, 45
  Zesty Vegetable and Rice
    Soup, 46
TURKEY
Ground Turkey
  Ground Turkey Lasagna, 89
  Ground Turkey Spaghetti
    Sauce, 89
Stir-Fry Turkey Dinner, 90
Turkey Casserole, 88
VEGETABLES
Asparagus Casserole, 107
Broccoli
  Broccoli and Onion
    Deluxe, Q108
  Broccoli and Rice Casserole, 108
  Broccoli Casserole, 107
  Broccoli 'N Rice 'R Nice, 109
Cabbage
  Barbecued Cabbage, 109
Carrots
  Copper Pennies, 110
Cheesy Vegetable Casserole, 118
Corn
  Corn and Bean Delight, 112
  Corn Custard, Q110
  Corn Pudding, 111
  Scalloped Corn, 111
  Shoe Peg Corn and Green
    Bean Casserole, Q112
  Shoe Peg Corn Relish, Q122
Pea and Broccoli Casserole, 113
Potatoes
  Baked Potato Fans, 113
  Judy's Potato Casserole, 114
  Potato Casserole, Q114
  Potatoes for a Crowd, Q115
  Potato Holiday, 115
  Scalloped Potatoes, Q116
Spinach
  Swiss Spinach, 116
Sweet Potato Casserole, 117

THE WORKING COOK   The American Vocational Association
1410 King Street
Alexandria, Virginia 22314

Please send _____ copies of **The Working Cook**, at $10.00 per copy plus $2.00 shipping and handling per book.

☐ I am enclosing a check made out to The AVA Building Fund.

☐ I would like to charge my order to my VISA_____ MasterCard_____.
   Card # _____   Expiration date_____

☐ I am enclosing an additional donation to the Building Fund
   of $_____.

Name _____   AVA Member ? _____
Address _____   AVA Division _____
Address _____   Phone (___)_____
City_____ State_____ Zip _____

THE WORKING COOK   The American Vocational Association
1410 King Street
Alexandria, Virginia 22314

Please send _____ copies of **The Working Cook**, at $10.00 per copy plus $2.00 shipping and handling per book.

☐ I am enclosing a check made out to The AVA Building Fund.

☐ I would like to charge my order to my VISA_____ MasterCard_____.
   Card # _____   Expiration date_____

☐ I am enclosing an additional donation to the Building Fund
   of $_____.

Name _____   AVA Member ? _____
Address _____   AVA Division _____
Address _____   Phone (___)_____
City_____ State_____ Zip _____